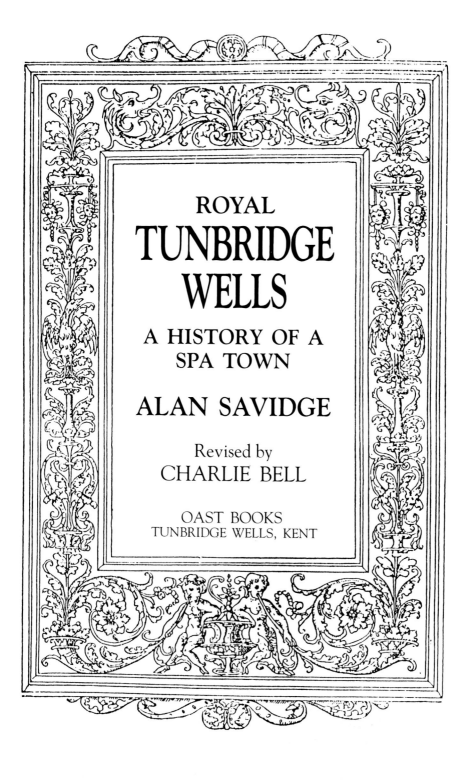

ROYAL
TUNBRIDGE WELLS

A HISTORY OF A SPA TOWN

ALAN SAVIDGE

Revised by
CHARLIE BELL

OAST BOOKS
TUNBRIDGE WELLS, KENT

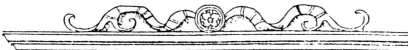

ROYAL
TUNBRIDGE
WELLS

In the same series:
Memories of a Village Rectory (Revised Edition) 1993
Royal Visitors to Tunbridge Wells

First published in the UK in 1995 by
Oast Books
12 Dene Way, Speldhurst
Tunbridge Wells, Kent TN3 0NX

ISBN 1-898594-10-4

© Alan Savidge 1975 by Midas Books
Revised edition Charlie Bell 1995

Frontispiece illustration:
A Georgian view of the Chapel and Baths seen from the Common.
(Tunbridge Wells Museum and Art Gallery)

Following page:
Taking the waters in the early twentieth century.

British Library Cataloguing in Publication Data:
A catalogue record for this book is available from the British Library

Design by Words & Images, Burwash, East Sussex
Typeset by Vitaset, Paddock Wood, Kent
Printed in Great Britain by
Biddles Ltd, Guildford and King's Lynn

CONTENTS

Foreword		7
Author's Preface and note on 1994 revision		8
Chapter 1	– Setting the Scene	13
Chapter 2	– In the Wings	20
Chapter 3	– Lord North's Discovery: Les Eaux de Scandale	27
Chapter 4	– Something Like a Town	43
Chapter 5	– Georgian Noon: Beau Nash	62
Chapter 6	– Georgian Afternoon	79
Chapter 7	– Winds of Change	95
Chapter 8	– New Town	108
Chapter 9	– Railways and Builders	130
Chapter 10	– The Modern Jerusalem	151
Chapter 11	– Royal Tunbridge Wells	172
Chapter 12	– The Twentieth Century	191
A Short Bibliography		214
Appendix I	– A short list of Dates	216
Appendix II	– Analysis of Chalybeate Spring Water	216
Appendix III	– Rules and Regulations for the Company resorting to the Wells	217
Index		218

ABBREVIATIONS

Arch. Cant.	– Archaeologia Cantiana
BM	– British Museum
CSP	– Calendar of State Papers
HMC	– Historic Manuscripts Commission
KAO	– Kent Archives Office
KCM	– King Charles the Martyr
LM	– Lewis Melville
MB	– Margaret Barton
M/C	– Master of Ceremonies
T-W	– Tunbridge Wells

"Taking the Waters" The Famous Chalybeate Spring, Tunbridge Wells

FOREWORD

It is twenty years since Alan Savidge's excellent history of Royal Tunbridge Wells was published and – reading it today – if it lacks anything, it is a final chapter to bring it up to date. This has now been elegantly and expertly done by Charlie Bell, who lives in Burwash and so must be considered to be impartial.

In his Foreword to the original edition, Lord Abergavenny says he often spent hours trying to park his car while shopping in the Wells, which he considered his 'home town'. I am under the impression that this modern curse is less of an affliction now than in his day – but that may be only because my wife, who is a Catholic, is entitled to park in the grounds of St Augustine's, free of charge. This has obvious advantages, but above all it allows me to view *en passant* the handsome facade of the Calverley Hotel and the ornate entrance to Calverley Park Crescent, two of the architectural glories of Tunbridge Wells.

For this is what I love about Tunbridge Wells: a feeling of history and a sense of style. From King James to Gospel John; from Lord North [who founded the place] to William Makepeace Thackeray; from Lord Dowding, of Battle of Britain fame, to HW Fowler, the great grammarian; from Beau Nash to . . . our town still has great charm. We must preserve it. As Charlie Bell concludes: 'Tunbridge Wells is still a suitable place to spend a day, a week, a month, a year or even a lifetime.' I may not live in Tunbridge Wells, but I have lived in Penshurst for half a lifetime, which I feel is almost as good.

Sandy Gall
Penshurst, 1995

AUTHOR'S PREFACE

Since 1766, when Thomas Benge Burr wrote his excellent *History of Tunbridge Wells* – the source of all subsequent accounts – there has been a steady stream of '*Descriptive Guides*' and journalistic essays on the town. Most of them have sketched or summarised its earlier history; but few have surveyed it at any length, and still fewer have brought it near to modern times. Thus Lewis Melville's *Society at Tunbridge Wells in the Eighteenth Century and After* (1912) and Miss Margaret Barton's *Tunbridge Wells* (1937) offer fascinating reading of the halcyon days of the fashionable spa, but have less to say of the town that succeeded it. The last survey in any detail, edited by Dr JCM Given (then honorary curator of the museum) in 1946, included the local history but was more concerned with the *natural* history of the neighbourhood.

I have therefore thought fit to produce at full length – if not at very great length – an historical study of Tunbridge Wells, reaching from ancient times, before, indeed, the place existed under that name, to our own. I cannot claim this as in any sense a definitive history. As it is, I have been reluctantly compelled at some points, in the words of Lord North, discoverer of the Wells, 'rather (to) open the door on a large prospect than (to) give it'. It is my hope that such prospects may attract later students of the local history to venture farther.

Any student or writer upon the golden age of the Wells and Walks will owe much to the pioneer work of Lewis Melville and the careful researches of Miss Barton into contemporary sources of information. These, based largely upon travellers' tales, passages or remarks in letters and memoirs, a good deal of versifying and tittle-tattle, are apt to be defective, confusing and at times misleading. If here and there I have drawn conclusions differing from these authors – and others – this has been after taking pains to check references, or in the light of other information or my own judgement. I have also been able to find some new sources here and there, to add to the collection.

ACKNOWLEDGEMENTS

I have troubled a number of persons and institutions for information and help, and have everywhere met with their patience and courtesy. To Mr Julian Fall of Messrs Goulden and Curry, the Tunbridge Wells booksellers, I owe a special debt for his encouragement from the outset and crucial support in getting the book published. I must also mention especially Mr CW Chalklin of Reading University, local historian of the parish of Tonbridge, who kindly allowed me to read and quote from the MS of his unfinished study of *The Rise of an English Town: Tunbridge Wells, 1680-1840*, and for expert introduction to a field of history new to me; Dr HCF Lansberry, a tutor in the Oxford University External Studies Department, who gave me the report of his study group in the town on the 1851 census; Miss Jean Mauldon of the town's reference library and Mr RGE Sandbach, curator of the Museum, for their interest and ready help over six years of my importuning them; Mrs Florence Clemetson, OBE, lately Editor-in-Chief, and Mr FA Chapman, and Mr G Macledon and the staff of the Courier Newspaper Group for their kind interest and for their hospitality during my reading of back-numbers, Mr John Booth and Mrs Vivienne Couldrey for their careful help in reducing the original text when economy became necessary; Miss Kathleen Strange and Mr Kenneth Pengelly for their scrutiny of the very difficult proofs.

I remember also with gratitude the help of Mr J Adamson, Mr G Bass and Mr Hill of the Town Hall; Mr Guy Acloque of the Grosvenor Estates; Mr R Armstrong, Records Officer of the Church Commissioners; Mr EC Baker, MBE; Mr RGW Bill, Lambeth Palace Librarian; Miss M Blair-Black, Economic Survey Officer, British Rail, Southern Region; Mr JM Bridgeman; the County Archivists of Kent and Suffolk; Mr GD Copus; Messrs Cripps, Harries and Hall, solicitors; Mr David Erskine; Mr Arthur Friend; Mr Barry Funnell; Mr MJH Girling, lately Town Clerk of Tunbridge Wells; Mr John Goulden; Mr MDH Larsen; Miss

Monson Road and Monson Colonnade c1900.

SJ Hardy and the staff of Tonbridge Library; Sister Mary Gregory Lewthwaite of the Convent of the Holy Child, Mayfield; the Librarians of Bromley and Hereford County; Professor Peter Murray; the reading-room staff of the British Museum, of the newspaper room, Colindale, and of British Transport Historical Records Office; Mr Hugh Reynolds; Mr GN Stone and Mr C Vinn of Messrs. Buss, Stone and Company, solicitors; Councillor Mrs Myrtle Streeten and Mr Anthony Streeten; Mr JH Thomas, Lecturer in History, Portsmouth Polytechnic; Dr Philip Whitbourn; Mr H Hunter; Mr S Whittaker; Dr Malcolm Williamson and Mr Geoffrey Dunn.

Alan Savidge
October 1975

Note on the 1994 revision

Royal Tunbridge Wells has always been a popular book but has unfortunately been out of print for many years. As Alan Savidge died before he had the opportunity of writing a new version himself, I felt honoured to be given the task of producing a revised and updated edition.

Most of the text is as Mr Savidge wrote it apart from some minor revisions. I have taken the opportunity to use corrections noted by both the author himself, and by others who have been kind enough to point out obvious errors, but I have not sought to change radically the content of the first eleven chapters. Undoubtedly, more recent researches have thrown new light upon some of the subjects Savidge chose to tackle, but I did not seek to alter his words to take account of them. It seemed better to let Savidge alone in this respect, and leave others to write an entirely new history of the town. However, Chapter 12 has been completely revised in order to bring the story up to date. A lot has happened to the town since 1974.

I owe gratitude to the following for their help in various ways and, in some cases, for permission to publish extracts and pictures. They are, in random order: James Akehurst; Dr Michael Rowlands of the Tunbridge Wells Museum and Art Gallery; Bob Hardcastle; the Borough Council and in particular Tourism and Marketing; Mr Geoff Murgatroyd, Centre Manager, Royal Victoria Place; High Weald Housing Association; Norman Collins of Trinity Arts Centre; The Courier Printing and Publishing Company Ltd; The Freight Transport Association; SEEBOARD plc; The Swan Hotel, The Pantiles; J Rawson & Sons Ltd; South East Water; and British Gas.

Charlie Bell
August 1994

CHAPTER ONE

SETTING THE SCENE

The rallying-point, when the time comes to take the waters,
of all that is fairest and most gallant in both sexes.
Anthony Hamilton, Memoirs of the Court of Charles II,
by the Count de Grammont, 1714.

Algernon: Your aunt!
Jack: Yes. Charming old lady. Lives at Tunbridge Wells.
Oscar Wilde, The Importance of being Earnest, 1895.

Tunbridge Wells has been said, fancifully, to lie like ancient Rome, about seven hills. The Wells and Walks, the original settlement, lie at the bottom of a valley. Undulating hills, rising to about 400ft, nearly surround it on the north, east, and south, with Mount Sion and Grove Hill standing forward; leaving a larger opening in the west. Through this a stream flows westward to join the headwaters of the Medway. Two main axes run through the town; north-south, from Southborough and London, dividing at the Pantiles, into Frant-Eastbourne, and Eridge-Brighton branches; and the east-west, from Pembury and Hastings, dividing into two or three routes through the town, and continuing along the ridge of Mount Ephraim to Langton and East Grinstead. Roughly speaking, this ridge and road divide the lower and older town from the higher, northern development. In the valley, in which was then a desolate spot in the Weald, Lord North at the beginning of the 17th century discovered the chalybeate springs on which the town's fortunes were built. How they came to be there has given rise to an intriguing story.

One day at Mayfield in Sussex, St Dunstan, Archbishop of Canterbury 960-988AD, and patron saint of goldsmiths, was at work on a chalice (or perhaps a horseshoe) in his forge when the devil appeared to him. Some say that he made offensive remarks, others that he played the tempter, in the guise of a young woman. All agree that, on recognising his visitor, Dunstan seized the tongs, red hot from the furnace, and clapped them to the devil's nose. Howling with rage and pain, the devil landed in a great leap at a spring by the later Pantiles, where he cooled his nose in the water, imparting to it that metallic tang which the doctors later attributed to chalybeate and hailed for its curative qualities.

The essential elements in this legend, the devil and the tongs, are attested by three of Dunstan's mediaeval biographers; Osbern, Eadmer, and William of Malmesbury. He seems to have been peculiarly subject to visitations of the devil, in a variety of guises; and the story of this one became very well known. A and C Blacks' *Guide to Kent* (1886 edition) quotes 'the ancient Poem' –

> St Dunstan, as the story goes,
> Once pulled the devil by the nose
> With red hot tongs, which made him roar
> That he was heard three miles or more.

Bishop Stubbs the historian says in his introduction to the *Memorials of St Dunstan* (Rolls Series, 1874) that the story is so famous that one can hardly doubt that it had some foundations. 'It seems not unlikely that Dunstan may have taken someone by the nose and that the identification (with the devil or a woman) was an afterthought.' So, clearly, was the chalybeate touch. The biographers say nothing about this cooling-off business, and they all put the incident, not at Mayfield but at Glastonbury in Somerset, where Dunstan spent his early days as a hermit. At the former archbishops' palace at Mayfield, now the Convent of the Holy Child, you can indeed see the tongs preserved; but there is another pair, it seems, at Glastonbury. In 1972 an opera on the incident, by Malcom Williamson, with libretto by Geoffrey Dunn, was performed at the Mayfield Festival; but placed at Glastonbury.

Who gave the story the Tunbridge Wells turn remains a mystery. It is possible that when the Weald, and the taste of some of the springs there, were becoming known, local folk-lore added this explanation. There is indeed a version that the tang was caused by Dunstan cooling the tongs afterwards in a local stream. It was common to endow mineral or pure water springs with divine or saintly provenance; many holy wells come to mind, St Anne's wells at Malvern and Buxton, the famous spring of Our Lady at Walsingham, and in modern times that of Our Lady of Lourdes. As near as Rusthall, Adam's Well (not mineral), and

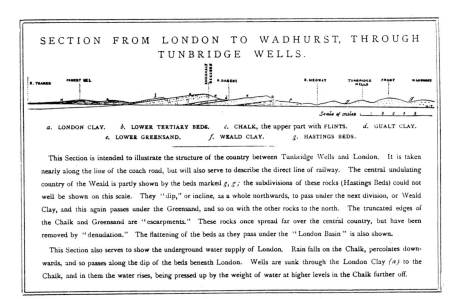

The geology of Tunbridge Wells. Taken from Pelton's Guide of 1879.

St Mary's Well at Tonbridge (chalybeate), are said to have enjoyed a local repute in olden times. Tunbridge Wells, however, did not, as such, exist then. It seems that someone must have embroidered the familiar story after the Wells had become famous.

The true origin of Tunbridge Wells is less dramatic: a matter of geology rather than hagiology, and a much longer story. It has to do with the process whereby, during thousands, millions of years, the land here was laid down, shaped and reshaped, and the waters given their mineral qualities.

The Weald, near the centre of which the town stands, is to the geologist one of the most interesting regions of Europe. The Romans called it Silva Anderida, the Anglo-Saxons Andredsweald, the wald or forest behind Anderida, the modern Pevensey. Views differ about its extent, but we may take it as lying between the North and South Downs and the Butser Hills in the west, forming a rough oval, the south-eastern end broken over by the English Channel, but in fact reappearing in the Boulogne district of France.

The spine of the anticline appears to run roughly from the Turner's Hill-Balcombe area, across Ashdown Forest to Crowborough Beacon – at 792ft the highest point in the central or High Weald, and along beyond Wadhurst towards Hawkhurst. Parallel ridges run north and south of it; and partly upon and partly enfolded within the most northerly series of these lies the town of Tunbridge Wells. From Langton along Mount Ephraim and across the steep incline of London and Grosvenor

Roads runs the massive ridge of Tunbridge Wells sand, 250ft thick in places, to the quarry whence Decimus Burton in the 19th century obtained his sandstone blocks, joining the Wadhurst clay in the former brick works at High Brooms. Quarry Road, Sandrock and Sandhurst Roads bear witness to this. From this brick and tile works and the Wadhurst clay used for them, were dug, in 1933, two sacral bones of an iguanodon, a dinosaur of the early days of the shallow Wealden lake: surely the oldest inhabitant of the future town. They are in the Natural History Museum at South Kensington; the local museum has casts.

Thrown out from the fault-line of the sandstone ridge are the Toad Rock at Rusthall and the Wellington and other rocks on the Common. In the river valley to the west rise the High Rocks, and to the south, Penn's, Harrison's, and Bowles' rocks. There are many more such outcrops in the neighbourhood: the chiding stone at Chiddingstone is one, and they stand out of the Chiddingly valley near West Hoathly. They show what denudation, by frost, by water seepage, by wind-blown sand, have done to exposed Tunbridge Wells sand-rock.

The local rocks have become showpieces of the town. The Toad Rock has been celebrated in picture postcard and geological textbook. EV Lucas declared in 1904 in the *Highways and Byways in Sussex*, that Rusthall had almost as many pilgrims as Stonehenge. The sombre woodland scenery of the High Rocks appealed to James II when he used to stay at the Wells in the 1670s as Duke of York, and the 'company'

Toad Rock Rusthall, the 'seaside' of Tunbridge Wells, seen here in a view of about 1910.

followed him there, not only to be impressed but to be amused. A maze and a bowling-green, which then meant gambling facilities, were added to nature's attractions. Romantic legends grew up, fostered no doubt by the proprietors, one of whom, CG Cowan, wrote a *Descriptive Guide* in 1964. Inevitably verses were written and inscribed upon the rocks. There were a wishing well and a Devil's Oak. After the decline of the spa, and the Gaming Act of 1845, the place remained one of the tourist attractions of the town; a jaunt from the Pantiles by brake, or, from 1907 till 1952, by train to High Rocks Halt; entered by turnstile, with teas on the former bowling-green. There was a lake for fishing and boating, and all the fun of the fair. Today, the halt, the brakes, the fun, have gone; but the 'stupendous ruins of nature' as Sprange called them in his 1786 Guide, remain, and attract enough visitors to keep the turnstile going in the summer. On the Common, the children's pattering feet gently wear down the Wellington Rocks. Harrison's Rocks, projecting from a long wooden scarp north-east of Eridge, and Bowles' not far away, are each in the hands of trusts for rock climbing and mountaineering exercises. Penn's Rocks, almost hidden in a secluded woodland valley in the same area, were once part of an estate of William Penn the Quaker.

Four streams drain the higher ground on which the town stands, running off in different directions, but all finding their way, sooner or later, into the Medway. The westward stream, closest to the town, must surely be the brook shown in Kip's engraving of 1719 as running down the Vales to join the one which cut its course down the valley below Cumberland Walk and then behind the Lower Walk of the Pantiles, forming here, until recent times, the county and parish boundary. It must have been beside its waters (lost, today, in sewers), that Lord North detected the brown scum from the nearby chalybeate springs which were to make the town's history. The geologist deduces that this mineral content (Appendix II) came from salts which were brought down with the deposits from the north of the island by the big rivers which drained into the Weald, there to be dissolved and imprisoned until, by way of springs, they reached the surface. There appear to be far more springs which become popular for their mineral properties to the north of the line of the Thames than to the south of it; but the sometimes ferruginous Tunbridge Wells sands, and the Ashdown sand too, have also delivered mineral springs in other parts of the Weald.

Upon the undulating geological structure, nature planted a rich clothing. In the gradual warming-up after the latest retreat of the ice of the glacial period, perhaps less than 50,000 years ago, the Hastings beds in their variety grew the first of the trees and undergrowth that gave the

Engraving of about 1810 entitled 'Tunbridge Wells from the race-course', showing the limited extent of the town compared with today.

(Tunbridge Wells Museum and Art Gallery)

Weald its name. Here, perhaps more than anywhere in early Britain, 'the untamed forest', as GM Trevelyan puts it in his *History of England,* 'was king. Its moist and mossy floor was hidden from heaven's eye by a close-drawn curtain woven of innumerable tree-tops, which shivered in the breezes of summer dawn and broke into wild music of millions upon millions of waking birds.' The forest has been vigorously tamed since then. In Tunbridge Wells several traces, and a splendid collection of trees – part of the town's heritage – still survive. Of the forest or chase of Southfrith, which once extended from Tonbridge as far as Mount Sion, little remains near the town except, presumably, in the north and north-east; except its name in a road or two;[1] but south of the town, a wooded belt still runs from Broadwater Forest and the Warren to Hargate Forest and across to Bell's Yew Green and Bayham. The Common, it is said (and old prints corroborate), had hardly a tree upon it at the close of the nineteenth century, but in 1975 the western part is well wooded. In the open, the gorse, bramble and bracken are rife, as indeed are ferns in great variety, including a local one, the Tonbridge filmy fern, *hymenophyllum tunbridgensis.* Many of the older flowers have gone, but over 700 varieties were said to have been collected by the Natural History Society.

As to the birds, more than half the 200 varieties breeding in Great

Britain could be found in the area in 1946.[2] The lush vegetation of woods and parks, and streams and ornamental lakes, and not least the feeding trays and other encouragements of their owners have made the place, it has been said, virtually a bird-sanctuary. Mankind's chief contribution must surely be the dog, to be seen in great numbers and variety. The open spaces are one of the town's major attributions and offer full scope for exercise.

Our other dealings with nature need no stressing: arriving effectively on the scene less than four centuries ago, we have changed it from country to town; striking however, the balance involved in *rus in urbe*, or *urbs in rure*. Rustically, the wilderness of 1606 has given way to parkland, to cultivated trees, shrubs, flowers, pets. The Romans, it is said, brought the sweet chestnut: the Wellingtonia, the massed rhododendrons, the magnolias, the tulip trees in many gardens, and other exotic plants have been introduced in more modern times. From the town-planners, public and private, have come the trees along the Pantiles, the avenue of Broadwater Down, the planting at eye-catching points, the Queen's Grove on the Common and the Grove itself: part of the leafy heritage of the town.

FOOTNOTES

1. Royal Chase and Liptraps Lane are suggestive. The first is modern, but the second much older. Southfrith was a royal chase more than once, during reversions to the Crown. Liptraps Farm was called Leaptraps Farm by Colbran 1853-60. Deer forests were surrounded by earth banks surmounted by pales to stop deer leaping over and away.

2. On flora and fauna, see chapters in JCM Given (ed), *Tunbridge Wells Past and Present*, Courier, 1946, by GE Shaw, and HWG Betteridge and PA Adolph; and of course the local museum.

The Grove c1500.

CHAPTER TWO

IN THE
WINGS

The appearance of any countryside is determined in two ways: by what man has inherited from the chaos of its first created form and what he has done with that inheritance.

Thomas Sharp, *Northumberland*, Shell Guides, Faber, 1952

From the earliest human times, before and even more after Britain was severed from the continent of Europe, Kent has had a special position on the highway of history. Trackways east and west across it go back to the Stone Age. The inhospitable Weald had little attraction for early man; but it does appear, from the small collection in the local museum of knives, arrowheads, and other Stone Age implements, and from excavations by the local archaeologist JH Money at the High Rocks in the 1950s, that men of that day found their way there, no doubt as hunters, and sheltered under the rocks for the night. In the Iron Age, in the first century BC, the people of the south-east threw up a number of fortified camps against new Celtic invaders, including the great fort of Oldbury near Ightham, Castle Hill at Tonbridge,[1] one at High Rocks, and Saxonbury,[2] south of Frant. Investigators into trackways, notably E Straker and ID Margary,[3] claim to have established a number of track-ways of this period in the Weald, including one running north and south from Oldbury through Ivy Hatch, fording or ferrying the Medway at Tonbridge, up Quarry Hill, through Southborough and Tunbridge Wells to Frant, Mark Cross and Cross-in-Hand, where it met another one running east and west along the ridge from Uckfield to a harbour at Rye. Much of these lines is now covered, significantly perhaps, by main roads: too deeply for any hard evidence to be yielded. If the case is estab-lished, our north-south axis through Tunbridge Wells was trodden by

Celtic tribesmen who had discovered how to smelt the iron ore in the Hastings Beds, and peddled it among the villages outside the Weald.

The Romans, renowned roadmakers and interested in the Wealden iron business, laid roads connecting the London area and the south-east ports, and a grid of inter-connections. The centre of the iron working was in Sussex; but some evidence of it, and Roman coins, have been discovered as near as Frant, at Harrison's Rocks, and elsewhere in our area. No civilised person, however, lived there. The nearest villas were in the river valleys and on the north Downs; and if any Roman legionary or other passer-by ever tasted the waters of the future spa, it was not as an alternative to those at Aquae (Buxton) or Aquae Sulis (Bath).

Knowing nothing of Romano-British civilisation, the Angles, Saxons, and the Jutes who landed in Kent in the fifth century AD, destroyed it wholesale. When they settled down after two centuries of fighting and confusion, from which the kingdoms of Sussex and Kent emerged for a time, we find them occupying much the same areas as their predecessors. It is not certain whether they worked any of the iron deposits. The High Weald probably remained a wilderness – 'thick and inaccessible,' wrote Bede, 'a place of retreat for large herds of deer and swine – but on the evidence of place-names, settlements must have been gradually planted on the fringe of the forest. Rotherfield (Redrefelle) was quite an important one; Mayfield we may add, on the strength of St Dunstan; and nearer home, the deceptive Saxonbury. Groombridge is a similar case; not the bridge over the Groom, but Gromenebregge; Gromen being either the name of a Saxon, or, as the Swedish scholar JK Wallenburg affirms in his *Place Names of Kent*, the Old English for a guard: the guarded bridge on the Kent-Sussex frontier. Rusthall and Speldhurst appear in a grant of lands by Egeberth King of Kent to Diora, Bishop of Rochester, in the late 8th century. Here, Professor Wallenburg considers that the Rust did relate, 'in a neighbourhood abounding in mineral springs', to taste or colour of the water. In later days, Rusthall was to set up in competition with Tunbridge Wells.

None of these names appears in the *Domesday Book* of 1086. The only names mentioned within five miles of Tunbridge Wells are Tudeley (Tuidele) and Tonbridge (Tonebrige), both held, with much besides, by Richard Fitzguislebert or Fitzgilbert, a blood relation of the Conqueror, in his strategically important castle by the Medway. The *Textus Roffensis* however, of sometime between 1100 and 1150, listing churches in the diocese of Rochester, includes, in our area, Barden (Barinden), Bidborough (Bitteberga, Bitte's Hill), Pembury (Peppingeberia), Rusthall, and Speldhurst (Speldeherste). These had probably been there before the Conquest. No doubt they were mostly small timber affairs, though the surviving parish churches at Bidborough and

Tonbridge have some Norman work in stone. Some other Old English names may be noted as appearing in early written records, and no doubt known locally before they did so: Smockham (Smocham, 1191), Hawkenbury (Hokynbury, 1258), Ramslye (Remesel, 1262), High Brooms or Broomhill (Bromgebrug, Assize Rolls, 1270). Clearly there were several settlements in the High Weald: the slow process of colonisation was under way. The most numerous, if seasonal, inhabitants must however have been the herds of cattle and especially the hogs which Bede had noted back in the eighth century, feeding on the mast of the forest trees, in denes or dens (vales) or hursts (woods) which form part of so many Wealden place names in Kent. Some of the herds travelled a long distance to pasture, by way of drovers' tracks. *Domesday Book* does record a number of manors and vills outside the Weald as having rights of pannage or pasture there. About 1100 then, we have a general picture of many miles of woodland and heath; the sound of cattle lowing and of thousands of hogs steadily munching; the smoke rising, here and there, from wood and turf shacks in settlements amid their patches of cultivation; beginning to spread inwards along trackways from the more fertile greensand and Weald clay belts and the river valleys.

In the four centuries between then and Lord North's arrival, three kinds of activity were at work in the forest screen of the Weald. One was the colonisers, slowly and steadily penetrating it: cleaning and squatting, forming manors, villages, townships, sowing and reaping, starting up industries; cloth at Cranbrook from the 14th century, hop growing from the 15th. Frant was a manor from the 11th-12th century. Groombridge had a weekly market, and fairs on three days a year, granted by Edward I in 1286: a fair survived into recent times. By 1291-2, as the *Taxatio Ecclesiastica* of Pope Nicholas IV reveals, the Weald was included in the parochial organisation of the country, though the Weald parishes were very large and sparse: Tonbridge covered 10,000 acres. Another process was more conservative: the noblemen and gentry moving into the Weald and enclosing their castles and halls in great parks for hunting. Speldhurst and Tonbridge were surrounded by them. At Penshurst, Sir John de Pulteneye, wool merchant of London, built, about 1341, the great barons' hall with stone quarried, says FW Jessup,[4] from the future Tunbridge Wells – at Quarry Hill or High Brooms, presumably: the first local industry. Southfrith, one of the forests or chases of the Lowy of Tonbridge, ran to 4,000 acres. To the south-east stretched the farms and woodlands of Bayham Abbey, granted by King John to the Premonstratensians in 1207-10. To the south, along the ridge of the anticline ran Ashdown Forest, a great royal chase, exchanged by Edward III for Richmond Park with his son John of

Rusthall Common c1910. The lack of grazing animals over the latter part of the twentieth century has changed the open character of the commons.

Gaunt. It was enclosed like the rest with fence and leap-trap ditch; and was roamed, according to an Inquisition of 1310, by 'beasts of the forest, of the chase, and of the warren', from the red deer to the coney and pheasant, for the sport of kings and their winter meat: above, protected by law, hovered birds of prey. Squatters, commoners, were not wanted here; but by quiet encroachment over long years, they established themselves and acquired rights.

Then, in the latter half of the 15th century, came iron smelting, in a big way. It is not clear whether the Saxons took it on; but the industry was certainly active about the 13th/14th century: we have some 14th century accounts, the oldest surviving, of a bloomery and forge at Tudeley in Southfrith. A century later, a new process came in from France of smelting in a blast furnace. The power for working the bellows and trip-hammers was supplied by damming streams to form ponds, and letting out the head of water down a spillway to turn water-wheels. The fuel, as before, came from the burning of wood for charcoal. The Weald, and especially the High Weald, had the ore, unlimited wood, and could provide water power: the streams might run low in dry weather, but a descending row of pen ponds would conserve the water. By Tudor and Stuart times, the Wealden industry was booming, with the noise of its forges and the turnover of profits in the coffers of the big landowners who had the sites, and a new class of ironmasters and gunfounders, who bought or leased them. The Nevills, now become Lords Bergavenny, had works at Eridge. A mortar, cast and wrought probably at Buxted and perhaps the first to be made in England, used to stand on Eridge Green, and was fired for amusement on fair days and holidays. The inn is called today the Nevill Crest and Gun. The lake in the park was their furnace pond, very large, with pen ponds to feed it. Lamberhurst and Cowden were among the leading works. Near Tunbridge Wells, Barden, between Southborough and Tonbridge; Vauxhall and 'Old Forge Farm',[5] as now known, by the brook running north to the Medway; two forges near Benhall in the south-east; and two more at Breechers and Dundale, were presumably supplied with iron from the smelting works at Furnace Wood, Tollslye, in the Bayham estate. CG Cowan adds to the numerous claims of the High Rocks 'some evidence' that the lake there, now drained away, was dammed by the Roundheads for a hammer pond.

At the height of its prosperity, in late Elizabethan times, the Weald must have been the Black Country of England; the smoke from the charcoal and the flames of some fifty furnaces visible, it is said, for miles, and some 7,000 men employed in it. The industry was, however, essentially rural, and left behind it, when iron smelting by coke in the Midlands superseded it in the 18th century, little more than the furnace and hammer ponds, a crop of suggestive place-names on the map, heaps of slag and cinder for the archaeologist, firebacks for the dealer in antiques, and the celebrated railings round St Paul's Cathedral, traditionally credited to the works at Lamberhurst and Ashburnham. How

The Picture House, Poundsbridge, near Speldhurst, previously known as Durtnoll's. One of the oldest buildings in the area, built in 1593 by the still surviving firm of Durtnell. The picture shows the building when it was a public house, c1900.

The George and Dragon, Speldhurst in a view c1910. Built about 1212, it probably became an inn in the seventeenth century.

much permanent damage the industry did to the timber of the Weald is disputable. Certainly it was serious enough at the time. By 1571, South-frith's timber had been practically exhausted, the place had become 'a heath and barren land', and the lease, which had several years to run, was surrendered by Willard the ironmaster. But nature seems quickly to have recovered. In 1697, Celia Fiennes, on tour in West Kent, found that 'most of the country is woody', though guns were being cast at Eridge; and went to Somerhill 'through much woods and lanes, and some very pleasant shades of lofty trees'. Replanting and new planting have restored the balance in spite of much devastation during the world wars.

By the time Lord North made his historic journey in 1606 from Lord Bergavenny's at Eridge, Lambarde had made his *Perambulation of Kent*, and the first county maps had appeared. Symonson's of 1596 shows Ereage in the large Waterdown Forest, stretching southward from Hares Gate,[6] which must have been near the scene of his discovery, to 'Rotherfidde'. Frant and Speldhurst are indicated by church signs, and Hungershall and Groombridge appear as small parks. The Tonbridge-Hastings road is the only one shown; but Lord North must surely have come along the Eridge road and continued up our north-south axis to gain the main road to London at Tonbridge, by now a market town. The scenery was not, it seems, very kindly. Queen Elizabeth on her way to stay with a previous Lord Bergavenny for six days in 1573 had, wrote Lord Burleigh to the Earl of Shrewsbury, 'a hard beginning of her progress in the Wilds of Kent and some parts of Sussex, where surely were more dangerous rocks and much worse ground than was in the

Peak.' The Weald, or at any rate the High Weald, had quite clearly not yet been tamed. The state of its roads seems to have become proverbial: it drove the Sackvilles to abandon Buckhurst in 1630 and the Nevills to leave Eridge for Kidbrook near East Grinstead by the middle of the century. King James, no doubt accompanied by these peers and Lord North, hunted Ashdown Forest. The Sidneys were at Penshurst; Lord Hunsdon had the Lowy; Lord Montague held the lands of Bayham Abbey, which Wolsey had suppressed in 1525-6, along with other small religious houses, including Tonbridge Priory; the Packers were shortly to acquire Groombridge Place and build the chapel there. The Barden and Bayham ironworks were probably blowing, but not, presumably, the Vauxhall furnace in Southfrith. Nearer Tonbridge the Earl of Clan-ricarde, who had just come into the estate by marrying the widow of Elizabeth's Earl of Essex, built the mansion which he cheerfully called Somerhill, in 1611. No doubt the smaller homes of the yeomen of Rusthall, Speldhurst and Pembury were undergoing the great rebuilding of the period: among them the house at Poundsbridge dated 1593, the present George and Dragon inn at Speldhurst, and the Weavers at Southborough; and a farmhouse or two since demolished or rebuilt again. There should have been something at Ramslye, perhaps at Culverden, and evidently a cottage near the future wells. For the rest, no sign yet of the town which was to prove so strange a newcomer to the Wealden scene.

FOOTNOTES

1. To avoid any confusion, we have called the old town of Tunbridge by its modern name of Tonbridge. Where Tunbridge Wells is meant, the spelling is left as Tunbridge.
2. The name is misleading. Socce, a Saxon, may have owned it; 16-17c, Sockburie, Socksbury, etc; 1809, Sacksbury; 1842 Soxenbury: A Mawer and FM Stenton. *Place Names of Sussex*, CUP 1950.
3. *A Wealden Ridgeway*, Sussex Notes & Queries 6, III; and *Roman Ways in the Weald* Phoenix House, 1948.
4. *Kent History*, Illustrated.
5. This became in the eighteenth century a powder mill, approached by Powder Mill Lane (Hasted, *History of Kent*).
6. Compare Hargate Forest on a modern map; but this is south of Broadwater Down.

CHAPTER THREE

LORD NORTH'S DISCOVERY: LES EAUX DE SCANDALE

It was this little stain which was the builder of Tunbridge Wells.
John Ruskin, Lecture 1856, *The Work of Iron in Art and Policy*;
reprinted in *The Two Paths*, 1859.

Well may they be called "les eaux de scandale", for they have nearly ruined the good name of the maids and the ladies (those who are there without their husbands) . . .
The Duc de Comminges, French Ambassador, 1663. (JJ Jusserand, 1892).

'The use of Tunbridge and Epsom waters for health and cure, I first made known to London and the King's people; the Spaw (in Germany) is a chargeable and inconvenient journey to sick bodies, besides the money it carries out of the kingdom, and inconvenient to religion.' The claim thus made, at least for Tunbridge, has never been seriously disputed, though there is more than one version of it. The author himself makes little of it; it appears as a mere marginal note in Lord North's *Forest of Varieties* of 1645, with the cryptic further remark, in the later edition, 'A Forest promiscuous of Several Seasons' Production' (1659). 'Much more I could say, but I rather hint than handle – rather open a door to a large prospect than give it.' One of his grandsons, Roger North, in his biographical writings, has much to say of him, but nothing of his discovery. We owe the first account of it to Thomas Benge Burr, member of a local family, and the first historian of Tunbridge Wells, in 1766. According to this, Dudley, third baron North, a nobleman of the court of King James I, particularly attached to the young Henry, Prince of Wales, found himself, in the spring of 1606 at the age of 25, to be suffering from 'a lingering consumptive disorder', brought on by the

Lord North, the discoverer of the Springs.   (Tunbridge Wells Museum and Art Gallery)

excesses of court life. On his physician's advice, he sought a change of air and scene, at his friend Lord Bergavenny's hunting seat at Eridge. This did him no good, and he was on his way to London and the prospect of an early grave when he happened to see the strange scum in the stream by the wayside, which reminded him of the waters of Spa, where he had been on military service. Borrowing a bowl from a neighbouring hovel, he tasted the water, had bottles fetched from Eridge, and took samples for analysis in London. This, and tests on the spot, were encouraging enough for him to return in the following year for a longer course of the water; whereafter, according to Burr, he never had the least return of his disorder. His enthusiastic recommendations in London started the long stream of pilgrims to the wells on the Kent-Sussex borders.

In this account, Benge Burr was treading 'unbeaten ground, with no other guides but some MSS collected in his own family, and the traditional reports of the most aged people who have lived in the place.' These included 'the grandchildren of Mrs Humphreys, who was the first water-dipper at Tunbridge Wells, and the very person that lent Lord

North the wooden bowl out of which he tasted the water'. This lady, he found, 'was married in the thirtieth year of her age, and soon afterwards began to dip water from the spring for the company attending the place. This trade she continued till her death, which happened in the year 1678, when she was 102 years old'. She must therefore have been born in 1576, and began dipping water soon after her marriage in 1606. This corroborates the fixing of the date by Burr for the discovery, on the strength of two other MSS, which set the 'manifestation' in the fourth year of the reign of James I. He disposes summarily of various miraculous stories, superstitions, and fabulous incidents, without mentioning St Dunstan, and examines some other traditions: that the discovery was due to a cow, which was sinking in the surrounding swamp at the time the discoverer came along; or to a sick cow which was cured and brought to give good milk after drinking the water; or that an invalid gentleman from Somerhill was the discoverer; or that the discovery was made in the reign of Mary Tudor, or even long before that. There is no real evidence, he says, to support such stories. Even if any of them had some foundation in fact, this would not invalidate Lord North's claim – which, we note, was not to have discovered the Springs, but to have made their virtues generally known. Evidently there was quite a collection of folk lore about the place.

Burr's account has been generally accepted as authoritative, and repeated, sometimes with embellishments, by later writers of histories and guides to the town. *The Camden Miscellany*,[1] however, yields another, little known version, from the handwriting of a grandson of Richard Weller, son of Alexander Weller, and steward to Lord Bergavenny's estate. 'One day when he was at Eridge Place, my Lord Abergavenny (sic) being there, they expected Lord North to come thither' from London, presumably, 'but not coming so soon as he was expected, Lord North made this excuse (when my grandfather was by and heard him) that he had stopp'd at a place about two miles distant out of curiosity, he having observed a spring by the road, the water of which had made such a tincture in the channel that he suspected it to be a mineral water, and had stayed to taste it and found by the taste that it was very much like the Spa water, and therefore advised him to send his mason or bricklayer with a few bricks to open the Spring, which he believed might be taken notice of; and this very likely is the first notice that was taken of Tunbridge Wells. My uncle told me that his father said he was then about 13 or 14 years old, which will make the time to be in 1615 or 1616.' This was nine or ten years later than that of Burr's account. Richard Weller might have been younger than he recalled: to square with Burr's version, he would have had to be a child of 4 or 5; rather young to retain such a conversation. The account is based entirely on recollection; but so is the other: we are left, in effect, with the choice between an old woman's and an old man's memory. There is no mention here of Lord North's illness and his almost miraculous cure; but as Miss Barton points out, his writings during his retirement at Kirtling in Cambridgeshire, and those of his grandson, do not support Burr in this. They reveal him as not only highly accomplished, as a young man, in the courtly pursuits of masques and tilting, poetry and music – 'full of spirit and flame', says his grandson – but also, though he lived to be 85, dying in 1666, as a lifelong hypochondriac.

However it was, Burr may fairly wonder how 'so trifling an incident as the colour of the ground about the water of a wild unused wood has filled the desert with inhabitants and made plenty smile over the barren heath.' He might have commented further on the chance that of all the chalybeate or other locally reputed healing springs in the Weald, some quite near, it was this one that caught the eye of destiny: a clear case of a friend at court. Chance, naturally, played its part in the discovery of most of the popular watering places. Bath is supposed to owe its fame to the observations of Bladud, son of King Hudibras, exiled from court as a leper and living as a swineherd, that the pigs with skin trouble were cured by wallowing in the swamps by the River Avon. He tried it, was

Eridge Castle c1910. The caption to this view reads 'The castle is situated near the picturesque village of Eridge, entered through a splendid avenue of pines. Indeed, bowery woods, belts of pine and copious running water are characteristic of this district. The first castle was allowed to run to ruin. The present one was built in the nineteenth century.'

healed, became king in due course, and moved his court to Bath. Skilli-
corne's Spring at Cheltenham dates from his observing in 1716 the
pigeons flocking to eat the salt crystals deposited by the water . . . The
anciently established habit to which we have already alluded, of drinking, or bathing in local waters reputed to cure disease or to 'do one
good', generally frowned upon as superstition at the Reformation, was
again becoming fashionable by the later 16th century. 'Spaws' were
springing up everywhere. In 1577 William Turner wrote his *Book of the
Nature and Properties as well of the Baths in England as of other Baths in
Germany and Italy*, in which he listed curable ailments from miscarriage,
barrenness, palsy, gout, to constipation, puffing up the legs with wind,
and melancholy madness. Bath, of which he took a poor view, was busy
enough for Dr J Jones to publish in 1572 *The Bathes of Bathes Ayde*, on
how to obtain the best benefit therefrom.

Lord Bergavenny, after consulting 'an eminent naturalist' who
picked the two best springs out of seven in the vicinity, obtained the
consent of the Lord of the Manor of Rusthall, whose land marched with
his at this point, and just included the site itself; and, no doubt
encouraged by Lord North, had the area cleared of scrub, the wells dug,
a stone pavement laid, and wooden railings set up to form a triangular
enclosure. But apart from Mrs Humphrey's hypothetical cottage, no
building or shelter was available; the visitors had to lodge at Tonbridge,
which became crowded during the summer by 'many great persons', as
Sir John Chamberlain wrote in 1619,[2] with their equipage and
servants, and to make the journey along the only road – which Lord
Bergavenny did proceed to improve – to the wells. There they drank
but did not stay or mingle with others: their nobility, says Burr, was too
great for them to unbend. According to Chamberlain, however, they
found the place 'not inferior to the Spa for good company, numbers,
and other appurtenancies'. The Spa itself, in 1577, was reported to
have 'only a few nasty cottages': a gravel walk between hedges or under
trees and some 'musick' seems to have sufficed for most of the new watering places. Lord North himself, though spreading the good tidings in
the capital, does not reappear on the local scene; Prince Henry had died
young in 1612; but Lord North remained at court till the 1620s and the
accession of Charles I. Then, losing hope of further advancement and
growing disillusioned, it seems, with life there, he withdrew more and
more to his country seat at Kirtling, where he occupied himself with his
family, his music, his French scholarship, and his somewhat intro-
spective writings. The former courtier did not draw sword for the King;
and indeed, served on an Admiralty commission for the Parliament,
and later become Lord Lieutenant of his county.

In 1630, however, the Kentish spa was patronised by royalty.

Charles I's queen, Henrietta Maria, came down in June and spent six weeks there, recuperating. She stayed, not at Penshurst or Eridge as royalty had done in the past, nor at Somerhill, but on Bishop's Down itself, which was cleared for a camp to be set up, with masques laid on for the young queen's amusement. What she thought of the waters does not seem to be recorded; but the story goes that she enjoyed a walk along the Frant road, where one day she rested and was refreshed under a birch tree; she had a stone erected and inscribed there to commemorate her sojourn. This was obliterated by the Roundheads, says Burr, but the Queen's Stone became the sign of an alehouse.

The royal visit was followed up by Dr Lodwick Rowzee of Ashford, who brought out a book in 1632: *The Queen's Wells, that is, a Treatise of the Nature and Vertues of Tunbridge Water*. Like Jones at Bath, he advised how this should be taken, and how important it was to follow medical guidance in taking it: he would be there each season as a consultant. In general, the water should be drunk early, on the spot, and in large quantities. 'When the Sunne beginneth to be of force, it doth attract some of the mineral spirits, and the water loses some of its strength: and betimes in the morning it is best walking . . . Those that lye not too far from the Springs, and are able to use their legges, shall doe better to come thither afoote than to ride, because so they shall heate their bodies more', though they should not sweat. Bottling for sale elsewhere would not do at all: the special qualities would rapidly deteriorate on exposure. The rule for 'a body of competent yeares and strength', scorning the pint or so recommended by 'some ignorant physicians', could be to start at 30-50 ounces (1½ to 2½ pints), and to work up to 'an hundreth, an hundreth and fiftie or two hundred ounces, more or lesse as they shall be able' – some, it is affirmed, even reached 300, or 15 pints – and down by degrees to where they began, by the time they were leaving the wells. The book was widely read, and reissued in 1671. Rowzee and Jones were pioneers of a long line of physicians, here and abroad, writing to extol the merits of newly discovered waters, or new ways of using them; imposing impressively severe disciplines, emphasising always the supreme importance of taking the cure under medical direction, preferably their own, on the spot, and deprecating the bottling of the precious fluid for drinking elsewhere. Rowzee did not however succeed in annexing the Queen's name to the wells. Of the three very large parishes whose boundaries met close by, Speldhurst may have had the best territorial claim, but it went almost unheard; Frant or Fant Wells, Lord Bergavenny's seat being in the parish, had a brief look-in; but Tonbridge, four miles off but the nearest place of any size, and patronised by the best people, was to prevail.

Not until 1636 were any buildings or shelter provided on the spot.

Then two little houses were put up for the ladies and gentlemen respectively. At the latter, called the Pipe House, a pipe could be hired and smoked for the season, for half-a-crown: Rowzee favoured pipe smoking, and, it appears, inhaling the smoke, as an accompaniment to water-drinking. Later, both places became coffee houses, with pens, ink and paper, and the pamphlets and journals of the day in place of pipes. In 1638 a walk, the popular adjunct of fashionable springs, was formed by raising and levelling a green bank, and planting two rows of trees along it; and some enterprising tradesmen had the idea of displaying their wares under the trees to the visitors as they passed up and down between their morning libations. Lodging houses began to appear at South-borough and Rusthall, both a good deal nearer than Tonbridge, but still not very convenient. So great, however, was the reputation of the water, according to Burr, that 'people gladly put up with any inconveniences on its account; and therefore when these houses were full, would pay an extravagant price for cottages, huts, or any place to screen them from the weather, rather than return home without partaking of the benefits thereof.'

The Civil War divided the local nobility and gentry. The Berga-vennys, at that time papists (their real home was then at Birling, not Eridge), the Clanricardes of Somerhill (who lost their estates), the Streatfeilds of Chiddingstone, were royalist; the Sidneys at Penshurst, Sir John Rivers at Chafford by Fordcombe, Thomas Weller in Tunbridge Castle were for the Parliament. Kent as a whole inclined rather to the King, but fortunately for Parliament, in view of its strategic importance, not wholeheartedly. 'The wild heathland south of Tonbridge,' says AM Everitt, 'where the wells discovered in James I's reign were already becoming well-known as a rustic rendezvous for jaded gentry, gamblers, and spendthrifts,' became a centre for royalist plotting, under cover of taking the waters, and for Cavalier refugees after the military collapse at Naseby in 1645. They took part in the serious rising in the south-east in 1648, coinciding with the Scottish invasion for the King. The government instructed the sheriffs and justices to 'watch and dissolve dangerous meetings' at the wells; and, according to strong local tradition, stationed Roundhead troops in the Rusthall area to keep watch and to guard the local gun foundries. There are said to have been a number of Puritan families in that area, and we have Burr's statement that the Royalists who visited the wells chose to stay at Southborough and those who favoured the Parliament, at Rusthall. The Speldhurst parson, like the rest of the local clergy, was for the King, and had given his church plate to the cause; but his successor appears to have been a Presbyterian. In 1653 Cromwell wrote to thank the patron, H Weston, for presenting Mr Draper, 'well approved by most of the good ministers hereabout,

and much desired by the honest people who are in a Religious Association hereabouts.'[3] He was expelled at the Restoration. To this Puritan
presence, tradition has credited the naming of Mounts Sion and
Ephraim. There are records of Anabaptist meetings in private houses
in the Speldhurst-Pembury area at this time but they were evidently
regarded as extremists, and the lord of the manor refused them a site for
a conventicle.

Troops and Puritans were unable to prevent continued royalist plotting. In 1659 a group of local Cavalier gentry, the Courthopes of
Wadhurst among them, were joined by royalists from London and elsewhere. Under pretence of taking the cure, and in touch with royalist
commissioners from the continent, they planned the seizure of the
Channel ports for the arrival of a royalist fleet. They managed to collect
and hide a large stock of arms and many horses, and numbers of appren-
tices left London for Tunbridge. Almost at the last minute the plot was
revealed, and the government, quickly recovering its grip, dispersed
the meeting at the wells, seized arms, horses, and many Cavaliers, and
imposed strict control over movement in the whole country. But
within a year, Kent was tumultuously welcoming King Charles II.

Although the Puritans frowned upon resorts like the wells, water
drinking went on there, and not only as cover for plotting. After the
fighting was over, Cromwell and the Council of State, with noteworthy
magnanimity and perhaps some risk, allowed more than one of their
former opponents, in prison or exile, to visit the wells for health
reasons. Among others, Lord Clanricarde appears to have been twice
permitted to visit England and take the waters near his forfeited estates.
Cromwell himself, according to Antonia Fraser,[4] tried the waters,
though not apparently, on the spot. The Countess of Devonshire
recommended them when he and his favourite daughter, both very ill,
were at Hampton Court in 1658; but 'the administering of the waters, if
they were beneficial to the Protector, only caused poor Bettie additional
agonies.' She died in August, aged only 29; and her father followed her
on 3 September. A royalist who was allowed to return from abroad, in
1651, was John Evelyn the diarist. In the next year, he was escorting his
wife and her mother on their arrival from France when, 'hearing that
the smallpox was rife in and about London, and Lady Brown having a
desire to drink Tunbridge waters, (he) carried them thither, and stayed
in a very sweet place, private and refreshing in a little cottage by the
wells.' The lady, alas, caught the scarlet fever instead, at the wells or
elsewhere, and died a month later. In 1664 he was to come again,
enjoying the solitudes and the 'extravagant turnings and insinuations'
of the beech trees, evidently at the High Rocks.

One of the first petitions received by the restored House of Lords in

1660 shows the concern of common people of the neighbourhood in the prosperity of the Wells. It came from 'inhabitants of Bidborough, Southborne (sic) and Rusthall in Kent, and other places thereabouts'. 'The wells called Tunbridge Wells,' it stated, 'have been much frequented for fifty years and upwards by many of the nobility, gentry, and others who have found much benefit by drinking the waters, and the petitioners, and many hundreds of poor people have gained a livelihood thereby, and it hath been always free for the poor women to dip and give the waters without restraint, and great charge was bestowed by noble persons to set a marble cistern in the well, and to pave it and rail it round'; but John Wybarne, a saddler, 'hath lately digged up the cistern and paving stones and carried them away, and hath cut down some of the birches set in a walk there for shadow by those who frequented the wells, and doth threaten to cut down the rest and to dig the rails about the wells, and fill them up unless he may have the ordering and disposing of the water, though the same stand in the highway at the end of a common.' Their Lordships referred the case to the justices to sort out the facts, but ordered that 'the Wells be put into the same order as they were formerly, for a public good.'[5]

So far the wells near Tonbridge had become a place visited primarily by the sick, or those who felt themselves to be so, prepared to put up with the lack of amenities at hand for the sake of the cure they sought; indeed to welcome such conditions as part of the cure. The Merrie England of the Restoration period, and its Merry Monarch, looked for and set about establishing a resort for enjoyment.

Certainly the cure continued, and many took it seriously enough. Dr Rowzee's second edition of 1671 was followed in 1687 by Dr Patrick Madan's *Philosophical and Medicinal Essay of the Waters of Tunbridge*. This expatiated at large upon the subject, and went further towards establishing the principles which the physicians were to adopt for all fashionable forms of water-cure: they must be unpleasant, they must be rigorously taken under strict medical regimen, and in return they must offer a panacea. *Per ardua ad astra*, or, as ES Turner says of the Grafenburg cold bath cure, introduced at Malvern from the continent in the nineteenth century, for heroes only. How many heroes put down Rowzee's 15 pints and more we do not know. They might well blench before Madan's prognosis. The water, he said, contained 'a calcauteous or vitriolic juice' which moved the belly to blackish secretion, and provoked plentiful urine, at the same time volatilising the effete and 'depauperated' blood, blackening the drinker's tongue with its 'sooty sulphureous minims' and producing nidorolent belches and eructations as if he had eaten hard fried eggs. It is not perhaps surprising to hear that unless the drinker followed the doctor's advice in this adventure, the steel content, even in solution, might prove a sword in a madman's hand. As with Rowzee, the water must be drunk at the very fountain head, at dawn, and with a 'facetious, merry, cheerful, gay and jovial' disposition. Thus taken, and with the physician's aid, it would dispel giddiness, passions of the heart, fainting of spirits, hypochondriac and hysteric fits, and cure obstructions of the liver and spleen, scurvy, and mad-dog bites. Much more, it would make the drinkers fruitful and prolific, enlivening and actuating the nobler parts of the body, and producing a 'sweet Balsamic, spirituous and Sanguineous Temperament, which naturally incites and inspires men and women to Amorous Emotions and Titillations, being previous dispositions enabling them to procreating.' To this end, explained the doctor, had Venus come foaming from the waters to meet her beloved Mars in the Bowels of the Earth; and from the ensuing embrace and Bed of Honour she would 'rise Tryumphing in our hemisphere, at Tunbridge, generously imparting and distributing this impregnative Faculty to her Votaries, in order to preserve and perpetuate mankind.' There is surely no more to be said.

It was in the search of fruitfulness that the Queen, Katharine of Braganza, first came to take the waters in July 1663. Charles II's mother had started a fashion by coming to recover from bearing him: his queen came in the hope of bearing a son to him. The King, his court, and his lady friends, came too. These included the beautiful Frances Stuart (Britannia on the new coinage), to whom the King had lost his heart, but she appears to have kept hers, until she married the Duke of Richmond. London, wrote the French ambassador, de Comminges, was deserted; lords, ladies, and courtesans, with no regard for those who remained had fled to Tunbridge. The royal company appears to have camped on Bishop's Down as Henrietta Maria had done; but Mount Ephraim House, which presumably was not there in 1630, is given as the lodging of the King and Queen. Nell Gwynne and Peg Hughes the player, who captivated Prince Rupert while he was there, came on a later occasion, according to Margaret Barton, and had lodgings nearby. The retinue probably stayed at Somerhill, now restored to its royalist owners; as did Anthony Hamilton and his sister Elizabeth, another famous beauty. She married the Comte de Grammont, whose celebrated memoirs, written by Anthony for him years later in France, illuminated the court life of the period. Charles himself, it appears, had been there already, when 'Minette', his sister Henrietta, Duchess of Orleans, very much his favourite, had come to stay soon after his restoration. 'I would willingly make a visit to my sister,' he scribbled across the council table one day to Hyde (Clarendon);

'When do you think I can best spare time?'

'I suppose you will go with a light train?'

'I intend to take nothing but my night-bag.'

'You will not go without forty or fifty horse?'

'I count that part of my night-bag.'

Everyone, it seems, had a good time in 1663, the Queen herself being in high spirits; but 'Les eaux,' wrote M de Comminges, 'n'ont rien produit ce que l'on avait espéré.' Rather, he reflected, 'On peut les nommer les eaux de scandale, puis qu'elles . . . ruinent les femmes et les filles de reputation (J'entends celles qui n'avaient pas leurs maris).' It is clear that most of the ladies who did go with their husbands, led by the royal Stuarts themselves, were attracted, in Margaret Barton's phrase, by the gynaecology of the place, and particularly by the hopes raised by the physicians of greater fecundity and of relief in the dreads and dangers of child-bearing or from miscarriage – grim scourges of those days, not least to royal houses. Had Katharine borne a son and heir to Charles, the waters of Tunbridge could surely have claimed a part in changing the course of history; but it was not to be. She fared no better at Bath, to which she moved and was indeed very ill by the end of the year; but she and the court came again three times between 1663 and 1670.[6] In that year James, Duke of York, the King's brother and heir brought his first wife Anne Hyde, in her tenth pregnancy and also hoping for a son, but also in vain: she died in 1671. Like Evelyn, he went for walks and admired, as mentioned earlier, the solitudes of the High Rocks – and inevitably made them popular. Their daughters Mary and Anne, the future queens, came also; the latter on the first of many visits. James was there again in 1674, looking for a son and heir by his new wife, Mary of Modena, who had also been very ill after a miscarriage; in 1684, when his two daughters came again, Anne with her new husband Prince George of Denmark; and again in 1687. In the following year Anne returned; writing to her sister, now Princess of Orange, 'the doctors tell me (this) is the best thing I can do to hinder me from miscarrying, when I am with child again.' None was to suffer more than she the miseries and uncertainties of bearing and raising children. In that year, and without benefit of Tunbridge waters, the son and heir presented to James II helped to precipitate the revolution which cost him his throne: for a time Anne, at the Wells, allowed herself to aid the doubters of the child's true parentage.

It cannot be said that the English Spaw rewarded the Stuart house for their gynaecologically assiduous attention; but we may gather that its other attractions amused them. Such repeated patronage by royal and distinguished company made the Wells, in the words of Hamilton-de-Grammont already quoted, the rallying point of all the fair and gallant of both sexes. Like Fontainebleau, it was a convenient distance from the capital; 'the place of all Europe the most rural and Simple and yet, at the same time, the most entertaining and agreeable.' As for *scandale*, 'the company, though always numerous, is always select: since those who repair thither for diversions ever exceed the number of those who go thither for health, everything there breathes with pleasure: constraint is banished, familiarity established upon the first acquaintance, and joy and pleasure are the sole sovereigns of the place.' Clearly de Grammont, and no doubt Hamilton his scribe, liked the place. The Restoration poet and rake Wilmot, Earl of Rochester, was less complimentary. He had a flair for cynical, witty satire which spared neither the King, who was most indulgent to him, nor the Company at the Wells – the 'rendevouze' in his Tunbridge Wells of 1675, not of all that was gallant, but

'---- of fools, Buffoons and Praters
Cuckolds, Whores, Citizens, their Wives and Daughters.'

Mingling with the crowd after their morning potation – which made him spew – he describes them as they come along the Walk, warts and all. In the same supercilious style which he helped to make fashionable, Thomas Rawlins, in *Tunbridge Wells, or a Day's Courtship; by a Person of Quality*, which played briefly at the Duke of York's Theatre in Dorset Square in 1678, addresses –

You ladies, who in loose body'd gown
Forsake the sneaking city,
And in whole shoals come trundling down,
Fair, foolish, foul, or witty,
Some for the scurvy, some the gout,
And some for love's disease,
Know that these Wells drive all ills out
And cure whate'er you please.

A character in Thomas Baker's more successful comedy *Tunbridge Walks, or The Yeoman of Kent*, first played in London and Bath in 1703, is amazed 'that people should come here for air . . . a damn'd hole, amidst a Parcel of confounded Hills, more stifling than a Bagnio and stinks worse than the Upper Gallery in hot weather.'

The company, we hear, 'like most public assemblies a Medley of all sorts' diverted themselves 'each to his own inclination – Beaux raffle and Dance – Cits play at Ninepins, Bowls, and Backgammon – Rakes scour the Walks, bully the Shopkeepers and beat the Fiddlers – Men of Wit rally over Claret and Fools get to the Royal Oak Lottery, where you may lose Fifty guineas in a moment, have a crown return'd you for Coach-hire, a Glass of wine and a hearty welcome. In short, 'tis a Place

Opposite: The Springs in 1664. (Tunbridge Wells Museum and Art Gallery)

wholly dedicated to Freedom, no Distinction, either of Quality or Estate, but ev'ry man that appears well, converses with the best.'

That courtship could be pretty quick and ardent on the Walks appears from a letter from William Carslake to Sir John Moore on 17th August 1678. 'We have had nothing so considerable here as the sudden marriage on Friday of last weeke of Sir William Buck, a young Bart of Lincolnshire to one Mrs Skinner, a merchant's daughter in London. She was woman or companion to the Countess of Arundell (ye lady to the eldest son of the Duke of Norfolk) whome he never sawe until he danced with her on the Thursday night but it seems he thought on her yt night and intimated something of it on the morrow on the walks on which Lord Davenport eldest son of the Earl of Scarsdale and the Lord Greye of Werke and some other young gent pressed him on to marry presently and after the morning prayers here in the new chappell they would willingly have finished the business but none of the ministers were so hardy as to adventure without a license but they at length got one from the Surrogate at Tunbridge and were married at Bidborough a little church by Southborough and on the Lord's Daye morning he came with his Lady on the walks.'[7]

How well, if at all, John Wybarne restored the cistern and paving stones he had 'digged up' we do not know; but in honour, it is said, of Queen Katharine's first visit, Lord Muskerry, who had married Margaret, heiress of the Clanricardes of Somerhill, and apparently at this time held the manor of Rusthall as well, had the railings round the springs replaced by a stone wall, renewed the paving, and put 'a handsome bason' over the main spring, and his armorial bearings on a gateway leading to it. He also replanted the avenue of trees, and provided shelter from the weather by building a hall close to the wells. His untimely death in action at sea against the Dutch put an end to his promising activities, and for some time, Rusthall and Southborough continued to cater for the main 'company resorting to the wells', laying out bowling-greens for their amusement. On the walks, as Macaulay has described it in the third chapter of his *History*, 'a kind of fair was held daily . . . The wives and daughters of the Kentish farmers came from the neighbouring villages with cream, cherries, wheatears and quails. To chaffer with them, to flirt with them, to praise their straw hats and tight heels, was a refreshing pastime of voluptuaries sick of the airs of actresses and maids of honour' – and of the air of the capital in a hot summer. On the green bank dividing the upper and lower walks, musicians entertained the company.

The wheatears were a delicacy hailed by Defoe, among others, as 'the English Ortolans, the most delicious taste for a Creature of one Mouthful (for 'tis little more) that can be imagined.' This little song bird of the same family as the thrush was (and still is) a late summer visitor from eastern Europe, trapped by the South Downs shepherds and rushed to the market. Besides this tasty and unfortunate little bird, Defoe found in the market 'an abundance of Wild Fowl, of the best sorts.' Appetites were hearty. 'You would not think how people eat here,' wrote William Congreve the dramatist in 1695 to Dennis the bookseller:[8] 'everybody has the appetite of an ostrich and as they drink steel in the morning so I believe at noon they could digest Iron.' No doubt the country air gave an edge to the appetite. For Thomas Baker, this was one of the attractions of the place: 'excellent good' he wrote to Defoe, and Mrs Montagu was to declare it incomparable. Burr devoted a whole chapter to it. It is no doubt true that the popularity of the mineral water cure at this time and during the next two centuries was directly related to the general over-eating, especially of meat, by the classes who patronised them: the paunchy portraits of the 18th century tell their own tale. Slimming, even as part of the cure, was evidently less attractive, although some followed it. Dr Cheyne, Nash's physician at Bath, reducing his own apparently colossal weight by a diet of milk and vegetables, preached it successfully to others, including, it seems, John Wesley and Nash himself, who, however, was much too fond of potatoes.

It is probable that some more buildings were put up in the 1660s, near the wells, without manorial approval; but it was not until about 1680 that a building boom got underway. We shall look more closely at this in the next chapter.

In the gossip and scandal retailed by Hamilton-de Grammont, Lady Muskerry cuts a figure of fun which appears rather pathetic today; but she has claims on our attention. Her career was certainly remarkable. She had shared exile with Henrietta Maria in France, where she met Lord Muskerry, son of the fourth earl of Clancarty. After his death in battle, she married the self-styled Viscount Purbeck, a rake and a gambler, it seems, and bore him a son, John, styled in turn Earl of Buckingham – a title borne by George Villiers, Duke of Buckingham and one of Charles II's Cabal. Both these styles and claims were shaky, for the fount of each, Purbeck's father, had been born a bastard, though his parents later married. The Buckingham claim was eventually dismissed by the House of Lords in 1709, on that ground. Purbeck was killed abroad in a duel in 1684, and the lady married this time Robert, 'Beau' Feilding, a notorious gambler at the wells and elsewhere, far worse than Purbeck. He appears twice to have tried his hand at bigamy, the second time with Charles II's former mistress Lady Castlemaine, Duchess of Cleveland, and was convicted for it at the Old Bailey. Lady Muskerry, says de Grammont, 'whose husband most assuredly never married her for beauty, was much like the generality of rich heiresses, to whom nature seems sparing of her gifts, in proportion as they are loaded with those of fortune; she had the shape of a woman big with child, without being so . . . With two legs uncommonly short, one was much shorter than the other.' She was evidently also fond of company and of dressing-up for masques and balls, and an easy victim at court to practical jokes, two of which de Grammont (whose wife, Hamilton's sister played a leading part in them) retails. On one occasion, at the wells, she had stuffed a cushion under her fancy dress to balance her figure, being in fact pregnant. During the dance, the cushion fell out, and was seized up by Buckingham (the duke) and paraded before the royal party as her newly-born child. A silly vapid woman, says Richard Church, the most fantastic of those who gave *les eaux de scandale* their reputation; whose follies, and husbands, ruined the family fortunes. Some went into hospitality, for which the Purbecks were renowned; but like the gallant Lord Muskerry her first husband, she and her son, at any rate, appear to have had a patron's concern for the welfare of the place. As we shall see, they made their contributions not only to the folly and the fun fair but also to the development, secular and religious, of the wells and the future town.

FOOTNOTES
1. See R Almack, 1855 edn. preface. p5; from Weller-Poley MSS.
2. Letters, ed E McClure, Philadelphia 1939.
3. MacKinnon, quoting letter in Augmentation books of the Commonwealth.
4. *Cromwell, Our Chief of Men*, 1973, p662.
5. HMC Reports 7, p84; House of Lords Calendar 1660; Lords Journal X129.
6. MB, 143, from study of MSS in CSP Domestic, BM, establishes 1663 and 1666. It seems clear from Bryant's record of the royal movements that the court did NOT come in 1665 to escape the Plague of London. No doubt many did escape from London then to the Wells. Pepys in his diary for 9 July 1665 saw Lady Carteret, wife of Sir G Carteret, in her chamber, 'not very well, but looks the worst I ever did see in my life. It seems that her drinking of the water at Tunbridge did almost kill her before she could with most violent physique get it out of her body again.' Clearly the water did not suit everybody.
7. HMC Reports 10 Vol IV, 129–30.
8. John Dennis, *Works*, 1721.

CHAPTER FOUR

SOMETHING LIKE A TOWN

The pretty Walk, the Crowd, the splendid Street,
Of Shops above the Market Folks that meet,
The frequent People, Gentry mix'd with Clown,
Makes up a something, something like a Town.

> *Metellus, His Dialogues, the First Part containing a Relation of a Journey*
> *to Tunbridge Wells. Also a Description of the Wells and Place. Written under*
> *that Name by a Gentleman of this Nation, sometime Gentleman-Commoner*
> *of Christ Church in Oxford. London, Thos Warren 1693.*

By the turn of the 17th century the 'spaw' habit had caught on among all classes. The patronage of the Stuarts and their queens encouraged the discovery or re-discovery of healing springs up and down the country. The intrepid horsewoman Celia Fiennes, daughter of a Cromwellian colonel, a determined and inquiring hypochondriac, toured England on a side-saddle in the reigns of William III and Anne, tried all the springs comprehensively, and wrote about them and her adventures: the first woman journalist. She collected a very mixed bag. Her favourite was St Mungo's well at Copgrove in Yorkshire – plain water. Her main tour of Kent, with Tunbridge Wells one of the centres, took place in 1697. There can be no better description of the place at the end of the century than her breathless prose, spelling and punctuation all her own; written almost, it sounds, from the saddle.

'The waters I have dranke many years with great advantage, they are from the Steele and Iron mines, very quick springs especially one well, there are two with large basons of stone fixt in the earth with several holes in the bottom by which the springs bubble up and fill it, so as it always runs over notwithstanding the quantity dipped up in a morning – which is the usual tyme the company comes – and the nearer they drink it the spring the better, it being a spiriteous water that is ready to evaporate if carry'd any way.

'They have made the Wells very comodious by the many good buildings all about it and 2 or 3 mile round, which are lodgings for the company that drinke the waters, and they have encreased their buildings so much that makes them very cheape; all people buy their own provision at the Market which is just by the Wells and furnished with great plenty of all sorts flesh fowle and fish, . . .

'The Gentry takes as a diversion while drinking the waters to go and buy their dinners it being every day's market and runs the whole length of the Walke, which is between high trees on the market side for shade and secured in a row of buildings on the right side which are shopps full of all sorts of toys, silver, china, milliners, and all sorts of curious wooden ware, which this place is noted for the delicate neate and thin ware of wood both white and Lignum vitae wood; besides which there are two large Coffee houses for Tea Chocolate etc, and two roomes for the Lottery and Hazard board; these are all built with an arch or pent-house beyond the shops some of which are supported by pillars like a peasa (piazza) . . .

'There is at the lower end of the Walke, which is a broad space before you come to the walls of the Wells, where is a large sun dial set up on severall steps of stone; thence you go straight along to a Chapple which has been built by the severall contributions of the Company every year: it's a pretty place and cost a great deal of money and every year there is a contribution for the maintenance of a minister . . .

'There are severall bowling-greens about the Wells one just at it on Mt Sion, and another up the hill called Mt Ephraim, where is also a large Chapple, where the Presbyterians have preaching, they have a minister which by the collections of the Company is also maintained all the winter to preach, as is the publick Chapple at the Walks, there is severall other bowling greens at a distance of a mile or two fitted for the Company's lodging there, as Rust Hall and Southborough; they have all houses to the greens so the Gentlemen bowle the Ladies dance or walke in the green in the afternoones, and if wet dance in the houses there being Musick maintained by the Company to play in the morning so long while they drinke the waters and in the afternoone for dancing; there are severall good taverns at the Walks and all about to supply good wine, and Brew houses for beer and Bakers for bread, but some of them come from London and spoyle the market by raiseing the price, so the higlers and hucksters in a great measure; this whole Country is full of stone and iron the earth is clay and sand.'

We see here how the place had changed in recent years. The country

Built in 1200, Bayham Abbey was a building of considerable importance. It survived the Reformation but eventually was abandoned, the roof being removed for use in the repair of farm buildings.

fair and camping ground, a sort of aristocratic Butlin's, had been, in modern jargon, developed: a holiday town was growing up. The building boom which set in from 1680 to 1700 produced, in the estimation of CW Chalklin, a settlement of about a hundred houses to serve the summer visitors. It began on the Walks. About 1676, Thomas Neale, master of the royal mint, groom-porter to Charles II, and a man of some distinction, bought the manor of Rusthall from the Purbecks. He persuaded the freehold tenants to hire to him their grazing rights on the common at 10s a year, and then in 1682 join with him in a lease for fifty years to Thomas, (later Sir Thomas) Janson, also of London, for the development of 'the ground and land now used for walkes and the Kettle Pinns or ninepinns place adjoining them'.[1] There were strict covenants, requiring that the walks and bowling green should be open to all, protecting the freeholders' grazing rights, reserving to them the appointment of dippers of the water, and providing for an appeal to a tribunal against excessive rents. The buildings to be erected could be shops, booths, rooms for coffee, drink, or games, but not dwellings or lodgings, nor any for the dressing of meat – a process likely to be offensive to the company – and part of the (lower) walks was to be reserved for coaches. According to Burr, Mount Ephraim, or Culverden, where the King and Queen stayed in 1663, was first favoured for lodging houses, and had its assembly room – brought from Rusthall, he says – and bowling green by 1670. There was also a pleasure garden, the Fishponds, laid out on Mount Ephraim 'in pretty rural taste' and very genteel (a hard-worked word in the earlier guides) until under lax management it fell upon evil days and into low company. In 1684 Lady Purbeck and her steward Thomas Weller divided up the Mount Sion area of the old manor of Southfrith into building plots, nearer the wells and before long to supplant Mount Ephraim and all others 'in the full bloom of prosperity'. Many houses, says Burr, 'some whole and entire as they were, were wheeled on sledges from Southborough, Rusthall, and Mount Ephraim, to be first in this new seat of favour;' one 'with the band of music playing in it, and the jovial company drinking success to the purchaser'. Such moving of timber-framed houses was a not uncommon practice, it appears. This one sounds like a race-meeting.

In these developments, the landowners, London speculators and shopkeepers, and local men, had their shares, large or small. In 1687 there was a disastrous fire on the Walks, from which however the place 'rose more glorious' (Burr). The opportunity was taken to build the continuous colonnade with the shops under cover in a row behind it, as they appear in Kip's engraving of 1718/9; and Celia's 'peasa'. Four of the original columns survive, at No 48, The Pantiles. A rental survey of 1700 indicates some 20 to 25 shops along here, as well as public rooms, a Great Room of 82ft frontage and a Long Room of 54ft. There were three alleys running through to the common, as there are still. On the Lower Walk, below the tree-lined bank where the musicians played, were the provision market and, at the end nearest the wells, some 20 more shops, a tavern, a coffee house, and a 'pissing house' – presumably the original adjunct to the Pipe House, or its successor. Between the two walks, a row of three or four small booths: Kip's engraving suggests that they had become substantial houses since then. No 41 was once the Gloucester Tavern, named after Queen Anne's son, and open in 1706.

The shops were mostly those of the luxury tradesmen of a holiday resort. They included, besides the essential apothecary, barbers, a shoemaker, upholsterer, watchmaker, confectioners, chandler, an 'Indian gown man' (probably a mercer and milliner), and sellers of the 'curious wooden ware', for which Celia Fiennes says the shops on the Walks were already noted. This is not be confused (though it often is) with the more prolific block or end-grain mosaic or marquetry Tunbridge Ware, developed in the late 18th and 19th centuries, of which more later. It was apparenty an inlaid wood, painted and decorated by pen and ink, and lacquered, or sold, as Celia says, in white wood for the buyer to finish. Tunbridge Wells specialised in souvenirs such as yew-wood tea sets, on sale by Restoration times, and drinking bowls and cups, to

King Charles the Martyr. A photograph of 1908 displaying one of the splendid street lights of the time.

which the *lignum vitae*, the wood of life, imported from abroad, was said to impart curative qualities. The industry, it seems, moved in from Tonbridge, where George Wise was flourishing in the 1680s. Who started it in the new town cannot now be said with certainty. According to EH and ER Pinto, The Chalet on Mount Ephraim, an old tower in the garden nearby, Gibraltar Cottage, and Jordans Place or Cottage appear as early manufactories, and Jordan, Burrows, Fenner and Nye as pioneers.

Celia's 'chapple by the walks', the present church of King Charles the Martyr, was opened for worship in 1678. Until then, there was no place of authorised public worship nearer than Frant, Speldhurst, or Tonbridge. After some years, 'the piety of our ancestors', says Burr, was at length aroused 'to build a house to the glory of God, lest the distance from every church, together with the various amusements and continued dissipations of a public place, should entirely suspend the attention due to religious duties.' Subscriptions were raised among the company from 1676 to 1684, and again, for enlarging the building, from 1688 to 1696. The subscription lists were written out alphabetically and displayed, with a full account of how the money was spent. They were in recent times salvaged from lumber, and now hang in the north and south galleries of the church. They are something of a roll-call of the top people and the gentry of the day, and give the best record available of those who resorted to the wells. Nearly 2,400 persons subscribed, some of them to both appeals, but most only one, a total of £2,177 12s 10d.

Amounts range, probably according to a pecking order, from 5s to Princess Anne's total of 60 guineas (a guinea being then £1 1s 6d). We note the Dukes of Monmouth (the rebel of 1685, 5 guineas) and Norfolk (a Catholic, as several notable subscribers were); the statesmen the Earls of Clarendon and Rochester, Lords Arundel, Effingham and Clifford, and Sydney Godolphin, John Evelyn, Esquire (twice) and Samuel Pepys, Esquire (a guinea each). Pepys' diary mentions Tunbridge more than once but does not record a visit. The gentry of Kent are well represented: Culpeper, Fane, Hussey, Packer, Twisden, but Lord Bergavenny does not appear: he was a minor in 1678. Altogether, nearly half (1,157) of the subscribers can be identified as from the noble and landed classes.

The lists record that 'the soile of the ground on which this Chapel stands, was given by Robert, Lord Purbecke, and his Lady.' There was some legal difficulty about title; but in 1703 their son John, 'Earl of Buckingham' conveyed the building and site to a body of trustees, comprising the Bishop of Rochester, the Attorney General, Lord Abergavenny, three distinguished London clergymen and seven local gentry, but no local clergy. The site on the borders of three parishes (Tonbridge, Speldhurst and Frant), and Kent and Sussex, was to be the cause of some dispute over jurisdiction in later years. The first building was put up in 1678: it must have been here that the couple engaged in the lightning courtship described in the previous chapter applied first to be married; and it is pleasing to note that Sir William Buck and his Lady appear in the lists with a guinea each. This building was extended at one end in 1682 and practically doubled in size in 1696. A plain building resulted, gabled, red-brick with a pattern of blue headers, and capped by a turret with cupola. A gallery ran round three sides of the interior, reached by two external staircases, as shown by Kip and in Josiah Dodd's 19th century sketch. These have been removed and the turret elaborated; but in the main the building, surely the oldest substantially intact building in the town, looks much the same as when it was finished. For some reason, it was set back on the site so that the north-east gallery, known while it existed as the ante-gallery, was built out over a single-storey structure which the Purbecks had let. The whole structure and site works cost £2,278 1s 7d. Some £1,400 went to Mr Green, John Waghorne, and Edward Martin for bricklayer's, mason's, carpenter's and joiner's work on the 'skelliton' of the chapel.

The glory of the building is the ceiling, the work of two men, one unknown, the other famous. For 'the fretwork and plain ceiling and other plasterer's work' on the first stage, and for his draft of the additional ceiling for stage two, John Wetherell received £62 and 10s respectively. Henry Doogood, Sir Christopher Wren's chief plasterer in his St Paul's and City church work, who was happy to carry out the draft, 'with greater bravura' says John Newman, received £128 for this. Wetherell, who must clearly have had a local reputation, may have been called away by another engagement, and left his sketch for Doogood. Between them they produced the best piece of workmanship in Tunbridge Wells; a series of shallow domes, outlined by wreaths or chains of fruit and husks, and surrounded by acanthus mouldings; the spaces between the domes filled with palms and winged heads, in much variety, of *putti* who looked down upon the congregation. The design is in the style of the later 17th century, when elaborate ceilings and decoration inside plain church exteriors were not uncommon, as in some of Wren's churches; but the contrast here is remarkable.

Offsetting the Puritan Mounts Ephraim and Sion, 'the courtiers' Chapel' was dedicated in 1684, it appears, to King Charles the Martyr; but the diocesan archives are silent on this point. Two sermons, preached that season by Dr Anthony Walker, from Revelation 1.7 – 'and worship him who made heaven and earth, the sea and the fountains of water' – were published under the title '*Fax Fonte Accensa: Fire out of Water* ' . . . Walker expressed the hope 'that in due time (the chapel) may be as conveniently endowed as it is commodiously built, that there may be Wells of Salvation for the poor Neighbourhood all the Year; and . . . the Word may be preached in Season and out of (Water) Season.' Pious hopes, at the time. The first minister appointed appears to have been Mr Raisbury in 1709, and it was late in the 18th century before a minister resided out of season as well as in it; for endowment, two centuries had to pass. At first, it appears, the pulpit was supplied from clergymen coming to the Wells in the season. In that golden age of the Ministry of the Word well known preachers gave the chapel a reputation for good sermons, delivered from its three-decker pulpit. There, in the tense atmosphere of 1688, Princess Anne heard Tillotson, soon to be Archbishop of Canterbury, deliver a strong attack on the Roman Catholics.

In the Revolution to follow, the Dissenters at least, received the toleration which Charles and James themselves appear to have wanted for them. In 1689 the local Presbyterians lost no time in forming a church, and obtained a licence to meet on Sundays in the ballroom of Mount Ephraim House, using, it is said, a portable pulpit, fixed to the wainscot. The first minister, D Stott, came from Norwich, followed in 1700 by the mathematician and theologian Humphrey Ditton. No local landowner would let Dissenters have a site for a chapel until the Baptist Jordan (apparently the Tunbridge Ware maker, who gave his name, it appears, to Jordan's Cottage and Jordan's Lane, now Church Road), bought in his own name a cottage and garden on Mount Sion from Thomas Seal, a Quaker. A chapel was opened on the site in August 1720: John Archer's sermon survives in print. A manuscript record also survives of the early activities of the Baptists in their private meetings in the Pembury-Speldhurst area, which appear to go back as far as 1642. It contains a number of disciplinary entries, e.g. a resolution condemning members who sat by the fire and went off to sleep, and the case of John Mercer, 1698–9, in trouble for 'getting drunk and swearing when a Trooper in the Militia band.'[2]

The Wells had become a summer town, alive from May to October. In the winter the Walks were deserted, the shops shut and the lodging houses empty, many of the lessees hibernating in London, Bath or elsewhere. But Walker's reference to the 'poor neighbourhood' suggests that there was by now a permanent settlement of working-people who got a living from the summer visitors and found some stand-by agricultural work in the off-season. They became numerous enough, before the end of the 17th century, to arouse the company, influenced no doubt by the concern which produced the Charity Schools movement of the period, to set up a school to provide for fifty or more poor boys and girls, who were to be instructed in the three Rs by the King Charles chapel clerk, and later by the minister. Their schoolroom was the ante-gallery of the chapel, except in winter, when they adjourned to a warmer coffee-house.

For managing the school, and for taking care of 'the greater comfort of the Walks', the company resorting to the Wells set up their own representative institution and elected officers: the beginnings of local government, based on the chapel as elsewhere it was based on the parish church and vestry. From 1713, this was put on the regular basis of a monthly general meeting, on the first Wednesday in the summer months, after Morning Prayer, with the minister present. This would choose each month, from the contributors, a treasurer and three or four trustees: for the winter, local gentry were elected. They met in the chapel vestry, quite frequently in the summer months, and kept an eye on the comfort of the Walks. The minute-books tell of benches, fencing, lighting, attending to the trees; an annual contract for watering to lay the dust; a greatcoat for the sweeper; gates to keep stray horses out of the Lower Walk. Finance, including the minister's stipend, came from collections on the Walks: a regular if informal system grew up of subscriptions and contributions, exacted for this or that or the other amenity or social obligation. Two, later three, charity sermons were also preached during the season. The embryo town or village was thus something of a self-governing community; though subject, for the general purposes of local government, such as it then was, to the vestries of the parishes – mostly Tonbridge, it seems – in which it had grown up; and of course to the justices, the real rulers of the country-side, until the 19th century.

To the amenities, as well as to the chapel building, Princess Anne as a frequent visitor made her own contributions, including in 1696 a stone basin for the second spring, 'on the left as you enter,' says Burr, 'and distinguished from the other by its iron bars.' In 1698, her son the Duke of Gloucester, then a boy of five years with a large head, due to water on the brain and made still heavier by a wig, stumbled and fell over while playing soldiers on the walks. She gave £100 with instructions to have some paving done. The local management proved dilatory, and on her next visit the work had not been done. With the usual profuse apologies it was at once executed – under a supervisor left in charge by her – and for good measure the promenade and entrance square paved with the pantiles from which they later took their name. The offended princess, however, vowed never to set foot in the place again; and, characteristically she kept her word, unmoved by the planting of the Queen's Grove on the Common in honour of her accession to the throne

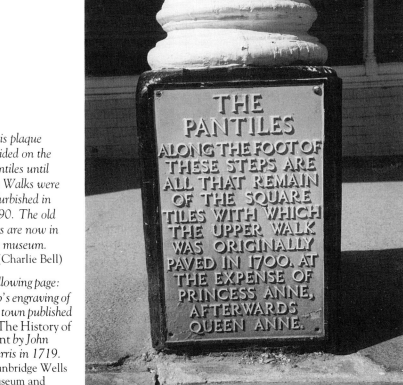

This plaque resided on the Pantiles until the Walks were refurbished in 1990. The old tiles are now in the museum.
(Charlie Bell)

Following page: Kip's engraving of the town published in The History of Kent *by John Harris in 1719.*
(Tunbridge Wells Museum and Art Gallery)

Mount Ephraim

Thompsons

High House

Mortons

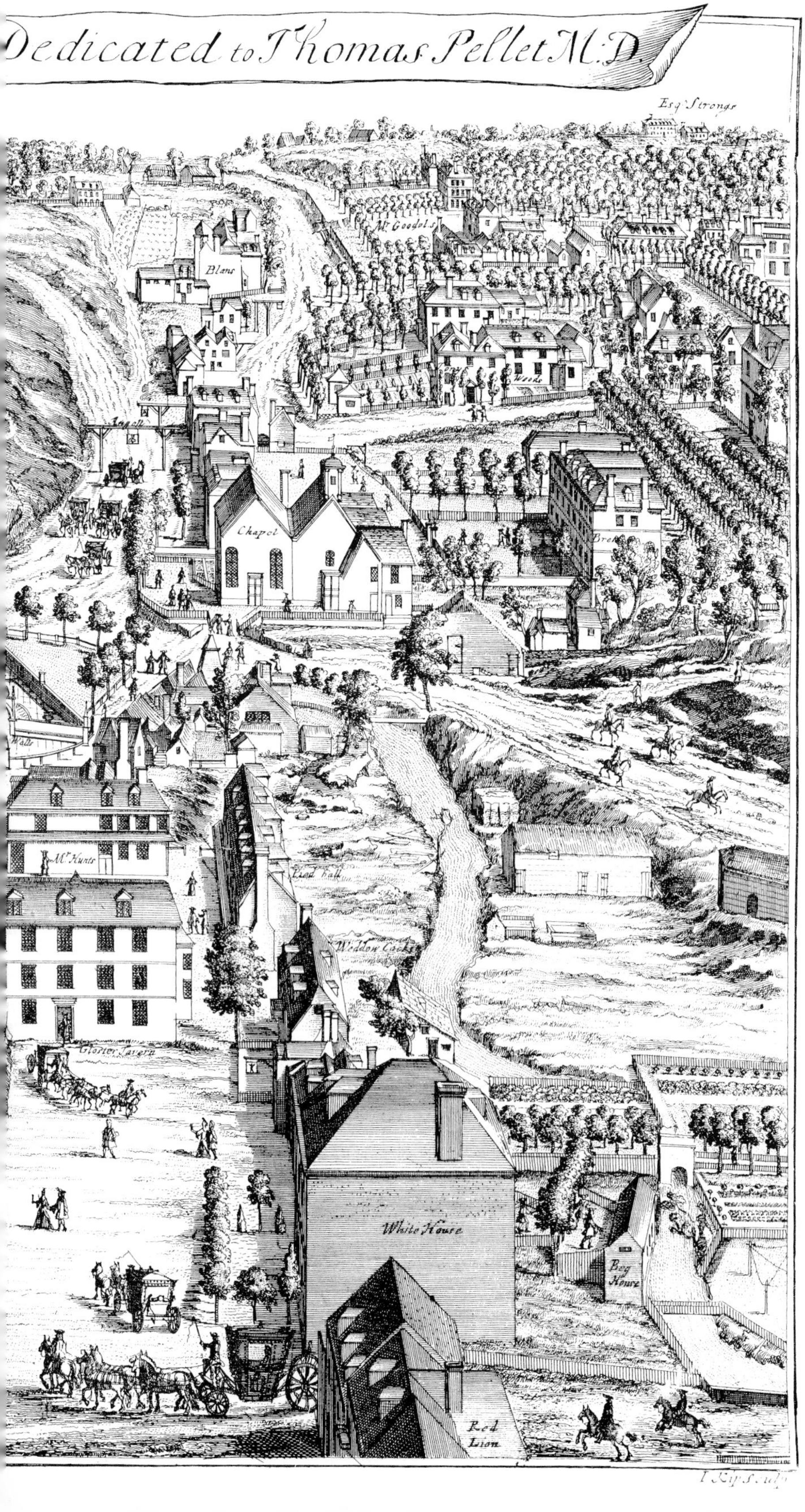

Esq Strongs

Mr Goodes

Blant

Angell

Chapel

Brew

Mr Hunts

Red Hall

Wedden Cooks

Gloster Tavern

White House

Bog House

Red Lion

J. Kip Sculp

in 1702: she went to Bath instead. In the following year however, through the last act of patronage on the part of the Muskerry-Purbeck family, the new town gained another Grove, on Mt Sion. Evidently in need of money after the ravages of the family fortunes, John, the heir and 'Earl of Buckingham', sold off, between 1702 and 1710, much of the old manor of Southfrith, including land for building on Mt Sion; mostly to the lessees, some of whom had been enjoying the Grove as an open space. To secure this amenity, a deed of endowment of 20 April, 1703 declared that it should be preserved 'as a grove, shade or walk' for the benefit, in effect, of all the local inhabitants, 'with the trees growing or to grow hereafter', which were not to be cut down or destroyed. The trust remained in operation until 1890 when the corporation took over responsibility.

Bathing in the mineral waters had its advocates who preferred this therapy to drinking them. Bath's fame lay in its hot springs; but in 1707 Dr Browne of Bath and London drew attention to the long-established popularity of cold baths in the North, in his *Account of the Wonderful Cures Perform'd by the Cold Baths, with Advice to the Water Drinkers at Tunbridge, Hampstead, Astrope, Nasborough, and all the other Chalibeate Spaws: Wherein the Usefulness of Cold Bathing is further recommended to the Lovers of Coffee, Tea, Chocolate, Brandy, &c. Preferring the Use of Bathing in Those Springs before the Drinking of their Waters*. The potency of the latter was apt, he said, to vary considerably: some ladies at Tunbridge had complained that it gave them 'great oppressions' the morning after. Taking the hint, James Long next year built a cold bath at Rusthall, 'esteemed equal' says Burr, 'to any in the kingdom, being most plentifully supplied with the finest rock water from the neighbouring hills.' It was all very elegant and entertaining, with fountains, 'amusing waterworks' and a handsome bath house, its rooms containing diverting curiosities to 'surprise the company.' Thus was Rusthall brought into the swim; but like the Fishponds, the place before long fell into decay, as Burr reports, though the bath was still there in 1766, and is today. Tunbridge Wells, it seems, had recently recovered the initiative with another cold bath, a furlong from the Walks. This may have been the enterprise of Todd of the Sussex Tavern, about 1750, mentioned in later guide-histories. A bowling-green was added; but the whole affair was later written-off as 'the Folly'. It had long disappeared when in 1971-72, some workmen revealed and reported, and the archaeological efforts of the Streeten family established, the remains of a cold bath and a spring for drinking. This is now preserved under covers, at the foot of the Common and the edge of the main road, opposite the later Bath House in the Pantiles itself. As for Adam's Well at Rusthall, Burr says it was very good for mangy dogs, and 'might be found of no small service to those who are afflicted with scorbutic cutaneous complaints.' Sprange's *Guide* of 1786 says that a bath was also put up here, for the public benefit, by Mr Pinchbeck, former master of one of the Tunbridge Wells assembly rooms.

The first building boom must have produced most of the town that appears in Kip's engraving of 1719 and John Bowra's *Survey* of 1738, and was to remain substantially unchanged for the rest of the 18th century. Apart from the Walks and the public buildings, most of the larger houses appear to have been lodgings and residences, as they still were in Barrow's map of 1808. How much of this first enterprise remains today? Certainly nothing so recognisably authentic as King Charles' church, but the layout of the old town has not, in general, been greatly changed, and it is likely that some of the present buildings incorporate, behind later façades and beneath taller structures, parts of the first ones. No 16, The Pantiles indeed carries a plaque dating it back to 1664; on what evidence is not clear, unless the original building was reckoned to be the dippers' hall or shelter put up by Lord Muskerry in that year. This, and the tall tile-hung building attached, now No 14, appear in Kip's engraving to be the last in the row. No 7, opposite, claims to have been originally built as a private house in 1660, the very year of the Restoration and Wybarne's case. If so, it would pretty certainly have been a timber structure, put up perhaps illicitly on the common of the manor.[3]

In 1732, the lease of the Upper Walks for building development expired; and a dispute broke out between the new lord of the manor (Conyers) and the freeholders over the division of the spoils – the buildings erected under the lease, and the greatly improved rental these would command. The lord expected the lion's share: the freeholders demanded full compensation for their contribution – the loss of herbage – and were opposed to any further erosion of this for building. They were led by the Earl of Abergavenny (as by now known), who besides being by far the largest freeholder tenant, with 226 acres of the manor including the Lower Walk and some land south of the stream, had his own interest as the great landowner to the south of that. He had himself built the houses on the Lower Walk, and was accused by the lord of seeking to enclose them. After a lengthy lawsuit, a compromise was reached, and embodied in a statute later designated The Rusthall Manor Act, 1739.[4] This divided the Upper Walks into three lots to be drawn; two to the lord of the manor and one to a trust on behalf of the freeholders. They drew lot B, now Nos 18-44 the Pantiles, known as the Walks Estate. The freeholders, some fifty, it appears in the Act, had shares in the trust estate according to the rental value of their respective holdings; a total of 391, of which Lord Abergavenny had 100, and some

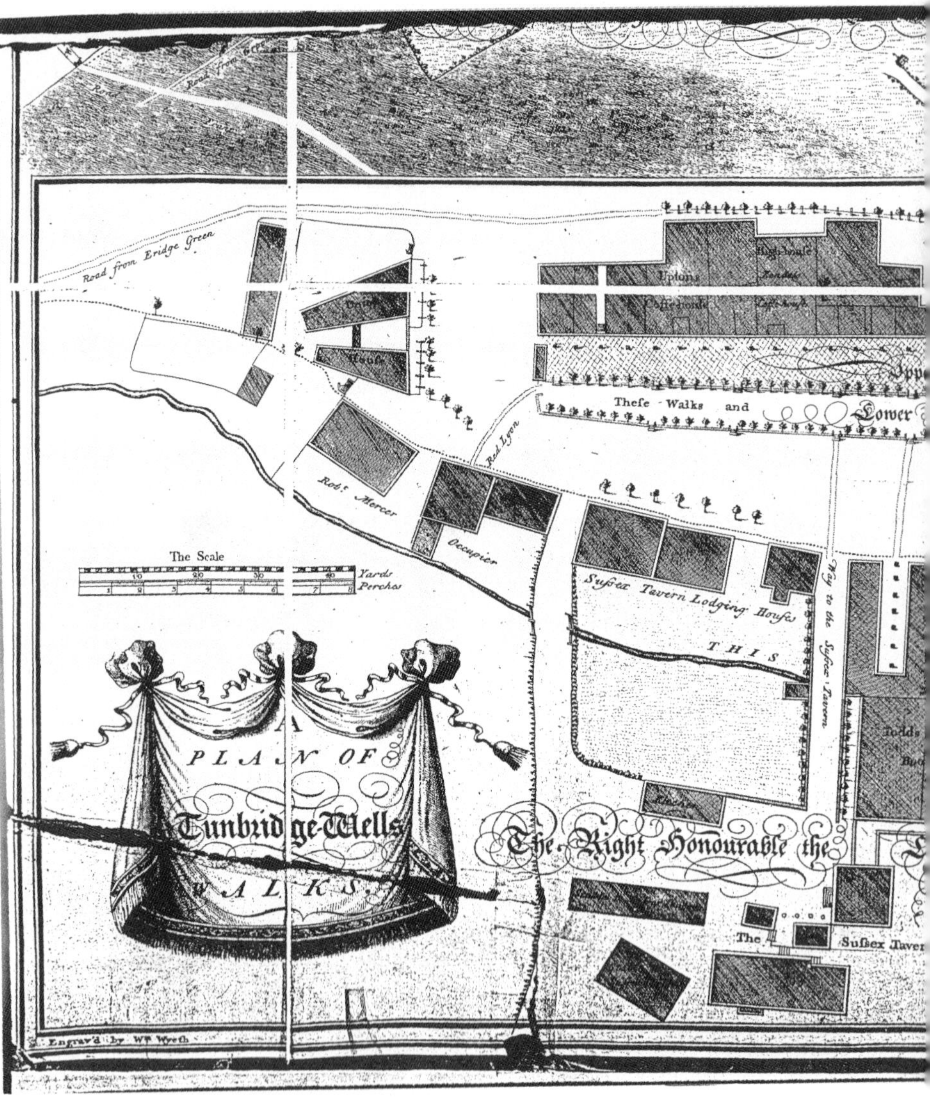
Road from Eridge Green
Uptons
Coffee house
These Walks and
Lower
Red Lyon
Robt. Mercer
Occupier
The Scale
Yards
Perches
Sussex Tavern Lodging House
THIS
Way to the Sussex Tavern
A
PLAN OF
Tunbridge-Wells
WALKS
The Right Honourable the
The
Sussex Tavern
Engrav'd by Wm Wyeth

only one or two. It proved to be a very good investment for them. It gave them also, as shareholders, a share in the enterprise of the Spaw of Tunbridge Wells – a share in the equity, as modern financiers would call it – and a further interest in the running of the place. The shares could be, and were, bought and sold – as property; a legal arrangement perhaps unique.

The freeholders were also to receive a third share in any manorial dues arising from the waste or common of the manor: e.g. the rent for circuses or fairs on the Common, and the 'encroachment rents' charged for way-leaves, etc, to or from adjoining properties. In the 19th and 20th centuries, when houses, shops, and other buildings came to be put up on lands adjoining the Common, these became numerous and sub-

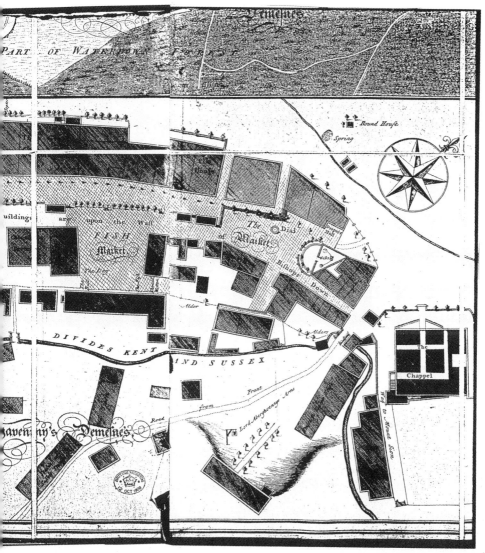

The Walks from Bowra's map of 1738.   (Tunbridge Wells Reference Library)

stantial, and sometimes, it seems, vexatious. The freeholders retained their grazing rights: sheep were to be seen on the Common in quite recent years. The 1863 Act, and another in 1902, dealt with manorial procedure, such as the registration of freehold tenancies, freeholders' meetings, bye-laws, etc. The freehold tenancies, like the shares in the walks, have changed hands during the years: thus Lord Abergavenny's interests as a freeholder have been sold off, but he remains a share-holder in the Walks Estate.

The original lease had contained, as we noted, some strict covenants. These, revised and extended in the new agreements embodied in the Act, were thus given the full sanction of a statute; a point of vital

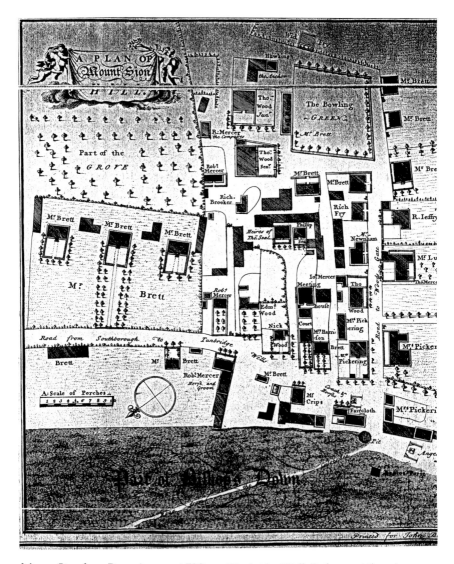

Mount Sion from Bowra's map, 1738.　　(Tunbridge Wells Reference Library)

importance to the future integrity of the Common, the Wells, and the
Walks. The Walks were to remain 'always open and free for the public
use and benefit of the Nobility and Gentry, and other Persons resorting
to or frequenting Tunbridge Wells.' No new building or improvement
or repair of existing buildings was to take place on the Walks except upon
the existing foundations. The pillars and colonnade were specifically
included in the scope of the agreements. Dippers were to be appointed
by the lord, preference being given to the freeholders' womenfolk. No
more enclosures should be made of the waste or common of the manor

except with the agreement of the lord and a majority of the freehold tenants, holding the greater share in the property. The Rusthall Manor Act is hailed by Lewis Melville as the charter of the town. He quotes Amsinck, in 1810 – 'To this Act Tunbridge Wells may be said to owe its continued prosperity; without it, it might have been increased by buildings, rivalling those of St George's Fields; and the houses tenanted by company issuing from the deserted brothels of the metropolis; but it would not have continued to yield attractions to the lovers of pure air and romantic scenery; nor would it be distinguished, as is now the case, as the resort of the best and most accomplished families.' We should not write thus today, and we note that the Act did not prevent the great development of the town which was beginning even as Amsinck wrote. But it did keep the wells open to the public, confirm the character of the Walks, Parade, Pantiles, and preserve the Common, the town's green lung and the third of its essential features; and it set an example, a precedent, to later development. The modern citizen of Tunbridge Wells, whether flattered or not by Amsinck's compliments, would neglect at his peril, and posterity's, to defend and preserve this heritage.

FOOTNOTES

1. KAO, U749, T2.

2. Quoted by Luke Pearce. The MS, which came to light in the 19th century, is now in the BM.

3. The dating of buildings by reference to architectural styles or structural features and materials is a fascinating but, in the absence of more direct evidence, a notoriously tricky exercise. The whole Mount Sion area would repay special study, No 9 High Street, previously The Hole-in-the-Wall, once displayed a leaflet taken from *Kent Pubs*', by DB Tubbs, Batsford 1966, claiming that Charles II granted a charter for it to 'stay open during his royal pleasure; the tradition being that he wanted a drink when passing through. It sounds a very far-fetched story, for which I have been unable to find any evidence. Another tradition, still regularly re-appearing, is that Charles II hid, presumably during his flight after the battle of Worcester, in a secret chamber cut in the rock of the cellars at Mount Ephraim House; and also that a tunnel once connected the house with King Charles' chapel. Most tunnel-tales, which are very prevalent, turn out to be either baseless or related to drains, or deep cellars. The house does appear, from a silver coin found in the foundations, to have been built in the reign of Charles I. Why anyone should want to dig a tunnel under the steeply falling Common for half a mile is not clear.

4. The Act actually received the Royal Assent on 27 April 1740, which has led some writers to give it that date; but by Sect II of the Rusthall Manor Act, 1863, the first Act was designated The Rusthall Manor Act, 1739.

Bowra's map of the town, 1738.   (Tunbridge Wells Reference Library)

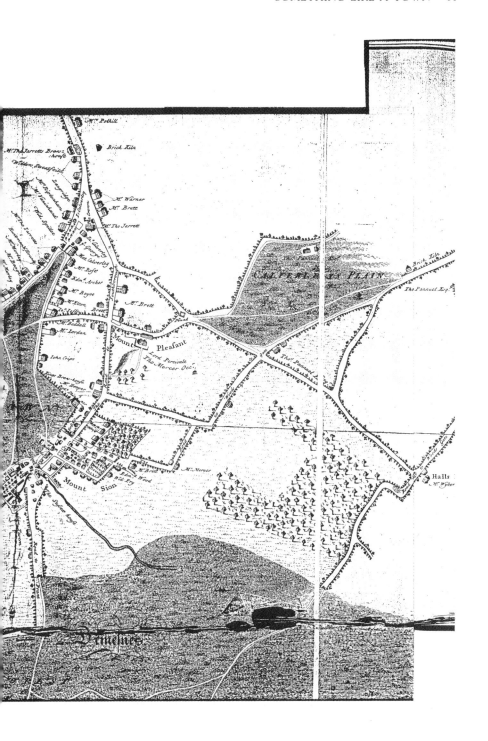

CHAPTER FIVE

GEORGIAN NOON: BEAU NASH

Beaux, belles and bishops – nay the judge and wit
To his decision nod, at once submit;
Both court and country partizans unite,
And every season deem their Dick the Knight.
Not the red ribbon more respect can claim,
Than the White Hat of everlasting fame –
At balls, the pump, parade, or at the play,
Each sex, all ages, ready homage pay;
A bow, a smile, a whisper, or a hand,
By turns employed, does every heart command.
O! would that ruby face for ever shine,
The fair, as now, might still appear divine.

From verses in the *Gentleman's Magazine*, 1743.

In Baker's play of 1703, a character explains, 'I am the Master of the Ceremonies here, appoint all the Dancing, summon the Ladies and manage the Musick.' There seems to be no local evidence of any such person at that time, nor of any formally arranged routine for the day. Yet a routine had clearly grown up, and conventions established themselves. The company, says Macky, writing of about 1708, 'rise in the Morning and go to the Wells, where Gentlemen and Ladies mix together in dishabille, to drink the Water: at Nine we go home to dress; and at Ten, the company returns, some to go to Church and others to the Coffee Houses, where one is very well informed of what passes in the world. After Prayers, all the Company appears on the Walks in the greatest splendor, Music playing all the time; and the Ladies and Gentlemen divert themselves with Raffling, Hazard, Drinking of Tea and

Walking till Two, when they go to Dinner . . . In the Afternoon there are the Bowling Greens for those that love that Diversion; and on those Greens are Balls four Times a Week for the Young People; and where any Gentleman may Dance if he pleases. At night the Company generally returns to the Shops on the Walks, where is all manner of Play till Midnight.' Like Baker he stresses the informality: 'there is as little ceremony here as at Montpelier. You engage the Ladies at Play without any introduction, only they do not admit of Visits at their Lodgings; but every Gentleman is equally received by the Fair Sex upon the Walks.'

This liberty had, Macky admits, 'an Inconvenience, that Sharpers, whose Trade is to go Genteel and with a fine Address, mix Themselves in all the Diversions here; and with their false Dice very often send People from the Walks sooner than they would otherwise go. These People are easily discovered by their more than ordinary Assiduity to Strangers. They are the first that bid you beware of Sharpers when they design themselves to pick your Pockets. All shopkeepers are in Fee with these Fellows, and it is they who furnish the Dice for them.' Ned Ward, a humorous writer in letter form, was pretty rude about the whole place, in 1718: 'A Valley of Pleasure, but a sink of Iniquity', he called it. 'The Fidlers are as saucy as Bum-Bayliffs at a Sessions House, and tug you by the sleeve for Half-Crowns the very first time of your appearance;' at Rusthall bowling-green 'Fools lose their money and Knaves win it . . . Lodgings are so dear and scarce that a Beau is sometimes glad of a Barn, and a Lady of Honour content to lie in a Garret . . . A pack-saddle of Mutton and Wheatear Pye cost nearly as much as a journey to Amsterdam, a fish dinner for six, and back again.' and so on. Defoe warns the ladies: 'And yet Tunbridge also is a Place, in which a lady, *however virtuous*, yet for want of good Conduct may as soon Shipwreck her Character as in any part of England.' Macky believed that 'There is no Place in the World better to begin an Intrigue in than this, nor than London to finish it.'

The diversions of the ladies received notice also in the *Spectator*. Sir Richard Steele had been to the Walks and published on 24 September a letter purporting to come from Matilda Mohair, a young lady of eighteen, a Maid of unspotted reputation. She complains of 'a set of familiar Romps, who have broken through all common Rules, and have thought of a very effectual Way of showing more Charms than all of us. These, Mr Spectator, are the Swingers. You are to know these careless pretty Creatures are very Innocents again; and it is to be no Matter what they do, for 'tis all harmless Freedom. They get on Ropes, as you must have seen the Children, and are swung by their Men Visitants. The Jest is that Mr Such-a-one can name the Colour of Miss Such-a-one's stockings; and she tells him he is a lying Thief, so he is, and full of Roguery;

The Pantiles in the eighteenth century. (*Up and Down the Pantiles*, Mrs Marshall)

and she'll lay a Wager, and her Sister shall tell the Truth if she says right, and he can't tell what Colour her Garters are of. In this Diversion there are very many pretty Shrieks, not as much for fear of falling, as that their Petticoats should untie: For there is a great Care had to avoid Improprieties; and the Lover who swings the Lady, has to tie her clothes very close with his hatband before she admits him to throw up her Heels.'

From all this we get the impression that the company resorting to the wells at this period, from courtiers, beaux wishing to cut a dash, local gentry, to aspiring citizens, tradesmen there for the takings, adventurers of all kinds, hangers-on, and tricksters, were what you would expect of a fashionable holiday-resort at a time when such were becoming popular with a new affluent society; patronised by royalty from time to time, and with a reputation for 'the cure'. The Prince of Wales, the future George II, paid a flying visit in 1716, when he took one turn on the Walks, 'gave 5 guineas to the Coffee House, tasted the Water, and gave the same to the Dippers and 5 to the Musick, and 9 or 10 to the Chaplin.'[1] He came again in 1724, evidently expected, for Defoe could hardly find a room in the place. His son Frederick when Prince of Wales was there with his princess in 1739. Marlborough, broken in health by a stroke and seeking the cure, was here with his duchess in 1717: Sarah liked the Wells as much as Bath and came often to both. Princess Amelia was another frequent visitor. There were certainly plenty of hypochondriacs. Lord Boyle, writing to Lady Salkeld in 1728 of the visit of Princess Amelia, remarks how 'in all reasonable Pleasures, nay in Pains as far as the Toothache and the Vapours, we humbly imitate her . . . Under the Rose, I believe the renowned Wells are not of any great use. We are ordered down here commonly pour la Maladie Imaginaire, for the spirits and the melancholy to which our whole Nation are too subject. The Diversions and Amusements of the Place send us home again cheerful, and the foggy Air of London with the common Disappointments of Life urge our Return the following Year.' Macky found the manner of living 'very diverting for a Week; but as there is no Variety but in new Faces; it soon proves tiresome to a Stranger.'

Other contemporary spas seem to have followed a similar pattern – the spring, the promenade, the bowling-green, sometimes the church and the assembly hall, the shady walks like Ned Ward's Grove at Tunbridge, 'where the Ringdoves coo above, whilst the Lovers bill below.' Epsom and Hampstead had them all; but Defoe thought them not quite for the best people, in spite of early visits by royalty. The other London spas, from Islington to Dulwich and Streatham, tended to become tea gardens and rowdy amusement parks. At Cheltenham, already a small town, the streets were dirty and the entertainments 'not genteel' – jigs, football, cock-fighting, cudgel matches, letting-off fire-works by the local peasantry.

Bath, the queen of spas, boasted at that time four open-air baths, the hottest at 103°F, as well as chalybeate water to drink. As with Tunbridge Wells, the visits of the Stuart royalty, from Queen Anne of Denmark to Queen Anne of England, had established the city in fashion 'at the head of English watering places' in Macaulay's opinion, 'without a rival'. But although already a city of some 250 houses, it was no better prepared for the invasion that followed them than the wells near Tunbridge had been. At the end of the 17th century, the lodgings were mean and dirty, the charges outrageous, the sedan chairmen rapacious, the streets unlit and unpaved, infested with beggars, the high roads founderous and beset with highwaymen. The baths, said John Wood the elder, were 'like so many bear-gardens, and modesty entirely shut out of them;' the visitors cared little for the proprieties, the ladies dancing in aprons (à la fashionable milkmaid) and the gentlemen in boots muddy from riding, and wearing swords which were often drawn at the gaming tables in hot blood. The master of ceremonies, Capt Webster, was himself killed in a duel. He was succeeded, in 1705, by another gambler and adventurer, who was to prove one of the most considerable and influential men in the social history of 18th century England.

Richard Nash was born in Swansea in 1674. His father was a glass bottle manufacturer, his mother came from a family of mark in South Wales. He went to Queen Elizabeth's Grammar School in Caermarthen, and thence to Jesus College, Oxford, to read law; but he left before a year in a hurry, probably to escape a woman. His indulgent father bought him a commission in the Guards, equally short-lived, and then entered him at the Inner Temple. Here he was much more successful, not at law but in society, where he developed, at the tea and gaming tables, a carriage and manner which earned from his comrades the nick-name of The Count. In 1695 he first showed his genius for showmanship in organising a pageant for William III, who was so captivated that he offered the young man a knighthood; to which Nash replied that he would need a pension to support such a dignity; and heard no more. His reputation in society was enlivened with a whole saga of intriguing stories of his adventures. Only money was lacking. He was, says his first biographer, Oliver Goldsmith, 'very poor, but very fine.' Scorning to seek patronage, then the accepted route, he staked his fortunes on his flair at the gaming tables. Out of luck here, and already over thirty, he decided to follow Queen Anne, the fashion, and the gamesters, to Bath. There, he made a friend of Webster, and on his death, the city corporation was persuaded to appoint him Master of Ceremonies, without a salary, but drawing perquisites from the patronage.

In a very short time, Nash transformed the motley, unruly gatherings of the city into something more resembling the court of Versailles under Louis XIV. There was, indeed, a good deal of the *Grand Monarque* about him. This 'philosophic beau', said Meredith, putting him as Beau Beamish in his *Tale of Chloe*, 'held it axiomatic that the social English required tyrannical government as much as the political were able to dispense with it.' Pope and others thought him high-handed and ridiculous, but Nash judged his company rightly: they welcomed the formality, the style, the ceremony. In a series of pungently phrased edicts, he transformed public manners, banishing swords, aprons, and 'Hog's Norton squires in boots', and regulating the dancing. This would begin with minuets, danced one couple at a time, the first lady led out by the Master himself. After the interval, country dancing; but the ball would end at eleven – even when Princess Amelia herself, George II's mannish daughter, wanted another dance. He also improved the amenities with a theatre, a new pavilion and pump room, an assembly room, good musicians from London; cleaned up the lodgings, fixed charges, lit the streets and improved the roads, rounded up the vagrants and scared off the highwaymen, and with an often quixotic generosity to those in need which was one of his most endearing qualities – and the subject of many romantic stories – set about raising money for his mineral-water hospital for the poor, which became the Royal National Hospital for Nervous Diseases. Under his rule, a new and glorious epoch followed at Bath, as men of vision like Ralph Allen and the Woods proceeded to build a Georgian city without rival in Europe.

According to Nash himself, in what might be called his anecdotage, he first came to stay in Tunbridge Wells on the advice of Dr Pellet at Bath, who recommended the place when he was out of health; not for the waters, which Nash protested he could not drink, but for a daily regimen, a change of scene, a rest cure; it was the air, said Nash, that cured him. It is more likely that he had his eye on the place for some time, as a further outlet for his talents, an extension of his kingdom. He appears to have spied out the land as early as 1721, and to have made a practice of attending the first ball of the season, on Mount Sion; no doubt to show his flag, and to demonstrate to his friends how much better things could be done by a skilled organiser – but very discreetly. For some years, he was prevented from going further, by a woman. According to the anecdotes in *Sprange's Guide*, 1780, a certain Bell Causey, established at the Ring in Hyde Park with her 'nymphs' who sold oranges and conveyed *billets doux*, and expert at 'promoting friendship between persons of the highest rank', became established also in the season, from 1725 to 1734, as 'absolute governess at Tunbridge Wells

Bell Causey still visits the Pantiles, as witnessed here, Easter 1992.

(Charlie Bell)

. . . and directed the company in all its pleasures and amusements.' She was 'a fine but very large woman'. When money was to be raised for entertainment or charity, she would post herself outside the chapel as the company came from morning prayer, her apron spread in both hands, a barrier impossible to pass untouched; and a newcomer of rank or fortune was liable to find himself singled out for special greeting and wheedled into playing host at a public breakfast or tea-drinking. Formidable, but affable and generous, she had, says Sprange, an 'astonishing influence' upon the nobility and gentry, spent her allowance (two guineas a day for conducting the gaming-room) on refreshment for the company, kept a good table, and gave what was left to the poor, 'by whom she was adored.' Her influence at the Wells was strong enough to keep 'the great Beau Nash' from any power there while she lived. She seems to have been a queen for his king, though probably less formal and autocratic.

Manners at Tunbridge Wells appear to have been better than those described at Bath; but they were not always good enough. In his letter above-mentioned, Lord Boyle describes 'a Madman, surnamed Drapier, a half-pay Captain apparently, who strikes us all with pannick Fear, and affords us Diversion at the same time. He has raised a Regiment and enlists his soldiers in a manner not a little extraordinary. He fixes on any Gentleman whom his wild Imagination represents as fit for martial Exploits, and holding a Pistol to the pore Captive's Breast obliges him to open a Vein and write his name in blood upon the Regimental Flag. Some have leapt out of Window to escape the Ceremony of bleeding but many others have tamely submitted, and they march every morning in Military Order at his Heels . . . I wish he were chained up, for the Women are all frightened out of their Wits at Him; thank Heaven I have not the Honour of his Acquaintance.' The chapel vestry trustees paid next year for a cage to lock up sturdy beggars, and 'drunken fellows who commit disorders'.

Not until 1735, after Bell Causey's death, was Nash able to move in. With none to appoint him, but probably a fifth-column of friends prepared the way for him, he declared himself Master of Ceremonies. He was by now over sixty; still younger than the figure whose portraits hang today at the top of the main staircase to the town hall at Tunbridge Wells and in the Pump Room at Bath; the latter by William Hoare, RA and the former, a particularly good one, also now attributed to him. Taken together, they show the red, lined face with its long nose and double chin, and the famous white or cream hat which Nash uniformly wore – apologising for such singularity that this was purely to avoid its being stolen. The rest of his dress was equally distinctive; showy but perhaps deliberately 'not quite genteel', says Goldsmith; 'He might be considered a beau of several generations, and in his appearance he, in some measure, mixed the fashions of the last age with those of the present.' His equipage, in which he usually made the journeys between Bath and Tunbridge Wells, was magnificent; a post chariot and six greys, with postilions, outriders, footmen, French horns, and every other appendage of expensive parade. Sheer, superb swank. When he arrived, wrote Elizabeth Scribe, a young milliner's assistant to her brother, on 21 July 1754[2] – towards the end of his reign – 'the guns keep firing off although we was at church, there was not a face but what a smile overspread so joyful was the news to all the talk was Nash is just arrived now trade must flourish.'

Nash's installation was followed in 1736 by the finest season, according to Thomas Wilson, for many years. Staying for six weeks in July and August, he wrote that some 900 gentlemen and ladies were there, and named 72 'Persons of Quality', present in his first week: 7 dukes, duchesses and their daughters, 33 marquesses, earls, barons, their wives, children and relatives; 16 knights, their ladies, children, etc; 3 MPs; 3 colonels, and 10 other persons of social distinction. Further, Sir Robert Walpole the Prime Minister came down for a few days to see his mistress, Miss Skerrett, who was ill. No doubt she took the waters seriously, as did Wilson.[3] With most of these social lions already familiar with Nash's code at Bath, he would have found little difficulty in imposing it upon the Walks; mainly a matter of introducing improvements and tightening up manners. He would have tolerated no Drapiers. As at Bath, he improved the music with an orchestra from London. Burr, writing just after Nash's reign had ended, says that 'each family on the first morning after their arrival are early saluted by the music.' At Bath, with a characteristic piece of showmanship, he had the Abbey bells pealed for new arrivals – at a customary fee of a guinea for the nobility or half for commoners; and according to some writers, the same welcome greeted them at Tunbridge Wells, but they do not say what bells were pealed: the single bell of King Charles chapel would hardly have been appropriate. Burr's more modest account looks the more likely; though guns on the common, as Elizabeth Scribe heard saluting Nash, may have sounded for the really great. It seems that in later days in that century at any rate, a newcomer's arrival was announced by a crier in the street ringing a bell.

For dancing, the Bath programme was established, of minuets followed by country dances, with an interval for tea-drinking: all over by 11pm. The public room on the Upper Walk was enlarged in 1739 as an assembly room to supplement or supersede the one by the bowling-green on Mount Sion. Nash's regime, however, brought to Tunbridge Wells no public or private building comparable with that of Bath to dignify the town – if it was a town. Burr in 1766 still saw four villages: the Walks and the three Mounts. The Act of 1739 stood in the way of any development of the Common; and for the rest, it appears that the Wells near Tonbridge, though now become a settlement of some size, appealed to those staying there for its rusticity rather than its urbanity. Mrs Elizabeth Montagu writes to the Reverend Mr Freind in 1749 – 'In many respects this place is inferior to the Bath, in some it is better. We are not confined here in streets; the houses are scattered irregularly, and Tunbridge Wells looks, from the window I now sit by, a little like the village you see from our terrace at Sandleford, only that the inhabitants, instead of Jack and Joan, are my Lord and Lady.' Burr remarks how 'at a little distance, it bears the appearance of a town in the midst of woods

A fine portrait of Richard (Beau) Nash presented to the Corporation by Mr William Nash. (Tunbridge Wells Museum and Art Gallery)

and conveys to the imagination the soothing idea of a rural romantic settlement, while it actually affords all the conveniences of a city life.' In this he comes nearer than the analysts and advertisers of the water, from Dr Rowzee onwards, to the secret of the appeal of the place to the jaded courtier and townsman: an appeal which, *mutatis mutandis*, has remained valid to this day.

The visitor to a watering place faced a long round of subscriptions and dues. A full list, given in a letter in 1767[4] begins the local round

Sarah Porter.   (Tunbridge Wells Museum and Art Gallery)

with a 'small present' to the Music for serenading in the early morning of the first day, plus half-a-crown to a guinea, according to rank and circumstances, from every family or single gentleman, for their playing in the music gallery and at the balls; a crown to a guinea in each of the two 'great rooms' (on the Upper and Lower Walks) for walking and talking therein, enjoying the fire, reading journals, writing letters, and cards and conversation in the evenings, alternately at each room; for the balls, once a week at each room, half-a-crown at the door for the gentleman and a shilling for his lady; a crown for the gentlemen's coffee house; a crown at the booksellers for borrowing books; half-a-guinea to two guineas per family for the clergyman, 'collected by some Person of the Company'; a collection and voluntary subscription for the Dissenting minister; a shilling or more for the sweeper of the Walks; a crown to a guinea or more to the water-dippers on leaving, and something to the waiters at the rooms. At this time, Derrick the MC had the proceeds of tickets for a ball, twice a season. Nash at Bath appears to have been paid by commission; but we do not hear of this at Tunbridge Wells. Finding that the assembly rooms needed a Bell Causey if the dues were to be effectively collected, he brought in another dragon, Sarah Porter. Her portrait, engraved by William Pether, shows a lady much less ample than her predecessor, but businesslike; she is said, indeed, to have been most efficient. 'There was not a person of the least rank she let escape,' says Sprange. She stood at the ballroom door, curtseying and accosting new arrivals, with respectful familiarity, inquiring after their relatives – all of whom she affected to know – and exacting cash down. Failing this, she would follow the defaulter all round the room, book and pen in hand, politely but inexorably, until he paid up. The portrait describes her as 'The Queen of the Touters' – aptly but not quite accurately, for these were a horde of agents operating not as collectors for the public amenities but as touts for the tradesmen, who pestered visitors before they had even set foot on the Walks; winning for themselves a notoriety of which more in the next chapter. In raising funds for good causes as he saw them, public or private, from the nobility and the well-to-do, Nash's own effrontery had no rival, as witness his getting 40 guineas for his hospital at Bath out of Sarah, Duchess of Marlborough – and remaining her friend.

In the classic age of fashionable literacy, versifying by the Water Poets, as they were dubbed (with a title taken, it seems, from Horace), was another popular diversion at the watering places. It became the custom at Tunbridge Wells to write the verses into a book kept at the bookseller's on the walks, to be read daily, especially by the ladies, in whose honour most of them were written, though there were many lampoons as well. Appeals to Horace, and to the Muses and classical mythology were to be expected, and the heroic couplet flourished: some were in Latin. The season's verses, or some of them, came to be published, intermittently it seems, over much of the 18th century, in pamphlets: thus *Tunbrigialia* (variously spelt). *The Tunbridge Miscellany, Tunbridge Epistles*. A collection of Water Poetry from several resorts came out in 1775. There was also a steam of verses separately published, most of them descriptive of journeys to the Wells and what went on there: *Metellus, His Dialogues*, was an early example in 1693. John Byrom, FRS, inventor of a system of shorthand and prolific writer of facile, rather doggerel verse, published *Tunbridgiale* in 1726. For a century or so the verses poured out, noteworthy for quantity rather than quality. Lewis Melville has a selection. Congreve in 1695 thought them execrable, though he wrote some himself to Miss Temple. Steele, more kindly, writing from Bath in the *Guardian* in 1713, defended the Water Poets as 'an innocent tribe'.

At Bath, and at Tunbridge Wells, the main centre of attraction was not now, it appears, the healing springs, nor yet the nymphs of the poetasters, but the gaming tables, at which, as in London, both sexes in society found their chief amusement. Immense sums of money, says GM Trevelyan in his *English Social History*, changed hands over cards and dice. To Nash, and to Bath and Tunbridge as he saw them, this gaming, and in public, was vital. 'The Wells, your houses, and every beneficial cure attending the place', he is said to have told a lodging-house keeper who had dared to obtain from London an EO table (even and odds gaming table) for private play by his guests, 'depends entirely on the Company's frequenting the Rooms. When once that ceases be assured the Wells will drop.' Throughout, he relied upon his flair at the tables. Did he win, or lose, over the years? He kept no accounts, but there are spectacular stories of gains and losses. Chesterfield, hearing him complain about the latter, said he wondered not that Nash could lose, but where he got the money to lose. Had he also a secret interest in the takings of the bank? At the time of his rebuke just quoted, he certainly had, as will appear; but when the EO affair became public knowledge, no firm evidence seems to have come to light of any previous interest. Nor was he a sharper, nor did his quixotic instincts desert him at the tables. Among the multitude of stories that grew up around him, as with all great showmen, are several of his solicitude for the young and comparatively innocent, his attempts to restrain rash young aristocrats from ruining themselves at play; and not only at play: there was a Dutch uncle in him.

Goldsmith gives the story of the young Duke of Bolton, who, 'being chagrined at losing a considerable sum, pressed Mr Nash to tie him up for the future from playing deep.' Nash gave him a hundred guineas, on condition that he should forfeit to him £10,000 whenever he should lose such an amount at play, in one sitting. It was not long, however, before he lost 8,000 guineas at hazard, and he was about to throw for another 3,000, when 'Nash, catching hold of the dice-box, intreated his Grace to reflect upon the penalty if he lost. The Duke for that time desisted, but so strong was the furor of play upon him, that soon after losing a considerable sum at Newmarket, he was contented to pay the penalty.' It was this duke who, married against his will to an Irish peer's heiress and by now parted from her, fell in love when in his forties, like other noblemen after him, with an actress; Lavinia Fenton. She was the daughter, it was said, of a naval lieutenant, Beswick, and a coffee-house keeper. A charming, witty woman, she was at that time playing Polly Peachum in the *Beggar's Opera*. John Gay, the author, wrote to Swift from Bath, 'The Duke of Bolton, I hear, has run away with Polly Peachum, having settled £400 a year on her.' She remained his mistress, bearing him three sons, till his wife's death in 1751, when he married her, and they settled in Tunbridge Wells, where he died in 1754. She followed him, at Greenwich, in 1760; and in her will left £66, the cost of a 'new best 8-day Clock' for King Charles chapel, with an hour hand only, till 1799. It is still at work, its chimes a little uncertain. Altogether, with its various *nuances*, the story makes a good 18th century specimen. On another occasion, having just won £200, Nash overheard a bystander tell his neighbour how happy such a sum would make him. Recalling perhaps how in his early days he had once given a man £10 on the same plea out of the Temple funds, Nash at once handed him the money, saying, 'Go and be happy.'

The excessive indulgence of the aristocracy with gaming, brought upon it, as the century proceeded, a growing opposition among others. In 1706, Theophilus Dorrington, Rector of Wittersham, in a sermon on the *Regulation of Play*, preached in King Charles chapel itself before a congregation in which no doubt players were numerous, condemned games of chance altogether. The Kent justices in 1729 were concerned with the disorderliness of 'illegal' gambling at the Wells. There was however, a powerful gaming lobby at Westminster, and for some years, the government would go no farther than to gather in a tax on dicing and cards (1712). But in 1739 an Act was passed banning Pharaoh (Faro), basset, ace of hearts, and hazard, with a £200 penalty – a considerable sum in those days. The following year the statute was extended to cover all games 'with numbers thereon'. The players set about evading this by devising games of chance in which numbers were not used, e.g. rolly-polly, and Marlborough's Battles.

Then a certain Cook, at Tunbridge Wells, invented EO, Even and Odd, a form of roulette in which letters were substituted for numbers round the table and the spinning cone. The game caught on at once, but a quarrel broke out between Cook and the manager of the gaming room, Joye or Joyce. Each appealed to the Master of Ceremonies, offering shares in the bank's takings. Nash, no doubt much disturbed by the recent legislation, lent himself to this, and being assured by counsel that the game was legal, secured a compromise whereby the three of them shared the profits. He then took the game to Bath, and took a fifth share there. The money rolled in; but after a time Nash, who was no accountant and had kept no checks, discovered that he was being quietly cheated at both places; of £20,000 he said. Very foolishly, he went to law; and the whole sordid business came out. The courts non-suited him, and fined one of the Bath proprietors £500. In 1748, all play was declared illegal except cards, and no house could be kept for gaming. Whist came in, and noblemen gambled in privacy, at home.

Tunbridge Wells and Bath survived; but the decline of Nash set in. He was, after all, over 70, an old man for those days: his portraits date from this time. He moved into a smaller house, sent home his country mistress Juliana Papjoy, sold off his grand equipage, and one by one, the snuff boxes he had been given by royalty and others, and the treasures he had collected; and carried on. He appears in Loggon's picture of the Walks in 1748 with Richardson and other celebrities. In 1752 he was taken ill at the Wells, with apoplexy. 'Poor Nash has had a fit,' wrote Lady Jane Coke to Miss Eyre,[5] 'but does not seem to mind it, tho' he looks just-a-going.' A lady vented the general anxiety in the water-poetry book, in verses ending –

> Come then, kind Health! O quickly come away,
> Bid Nash revive, and all the World be gay!

When Elizabeth Scribe reported his arrival he was 80. 'I was very impatient to see the man I had heard so much tell on but how great was my surprize at the sight for if I may speak as I think I never saw such forlorn hopes in my whole life.' In the same year his friends got up a subscription for a 'History of Bath and Tunbridge Wells for the last forty years by Richard Nash Esquire, with an Apology for his Life'. No one expected the book to be written, but money flowed in, and helped to keep him afloat.

Next year, 1755, he was off again to Tunbridge Wells, taking up an appeal by one Henderson, a Quaker, on behalf of a young man deprived unjustly of a share in a large estate, and pursuing it next year at Bath, where, according to Henderson, he had promised he would do better than at Tunbridge. This appears to have been his last recorded visit, and his last public effort – in which he headed the subscription list – on behalf of those, well-born or lowly, whose needs touched him. He was more and more confined to his house, where Juliana had returned to take care of him. In 1760 the corporation of the Bath he had made possible voted him the scarcely royal pension of ten guineas a month: next year, they found £50 towards what was indeed a kingly funeral; he died on 3 February 1761, aged eighty-seven, having lived in seven reigns and to the beginning of an eighth.

In the golden age of epitaphs, Nash received his due in laments from many writers, and in two long ones by his old friends Drs Oliver (of Bath Oliver biscuit fame) and King. The latter's runs to a hundred lines of Latin, on the tomb in Bath Abbey, where Nash, though no believer, had regularly attended morning prayer, as no doubt he did at King Charles chapel. In this epitaph Tunbridge Wells appears, as translated by Goldsmith:

> To his empire was added
> By the consent of all orders
> A celebrated province
> Which he ever swayed with great prudence,
> Not by delegation but in person.
> He deigned to visit every year
> And while the necessities of state demanded his presence
> He usually continued there.

As Steele had pointed out and the epitaphs repeated, he had found the happy secret of mixing the vulgar and the great, the poor and the rich, the learned and the ignorant. His faults, they wrote, 'were rather obnoxious to himself than to others'; and so on. One good touch by Dr King was that the whiteness of Nash's hat symbolised the candour of his mind.

The impact of Nash on Tunbridge Wells was clearly less dramatic than on Bath. He was not there so long – though it was 26 years – nor so often. Like the Romans in Britain, he annexed the place late in life – a celebrated province to his empire, as the epitaph had it – and treated it rather as a summer retreat, a place for royal visitation. He did not, for instance, exert himself to curb the troublesome touters, as he would surely have done at Bath. Someone called him King of Bath, Duke of Tunbridge Wells. He himself told Henderson that the Wells was 'not within the limits of his province'; but by then, he may have resigned it to the man who was, according to Elizabeth Scribe, already there to succeed him. He had followed Queen Anne to Bath. Perhaps if she had continued to patronise Tunbridge Wells he would have come here first, in the vigour of his youth, with what results we can only speculate. As it was, he does not seem to have assumed here the arrogance he had put on at Bath: he had become less rude and saucy to strangers, wrote Dr Holmes to Thomas Wilson in 1736. It may be that Tunbridge Wells, nearer the metropolis and more open to its influence, was already more civilised, in the strict sense, than the rather remote west country, and needed less training in manners – or that its leading figures had had it already from Nash, at Bath: no Hog's Norton squires, as far as we know, wore boots in the ballroom. Burr remarks of his mastership that 'Tunbridge Wells, amongst the rest, has from that period become the general rendezvous of gaiety and *politeness* during the summer' – a significant change from Count Grammont's 'gallantry'.

Nash, it may be said, made gaiety compatible with order. To him, there was a time for everything, and a way of doing it which all must follow, from which all would benefit. His own way of life was similarly ordered: he rose very early, worked hard, ate and drank moderately. It is easy to decry its essential triviality, and his supreme arrogance. We may set against his banishment of swords and duelling, no mean achievement as it was, his encouragement of gambling and his percentage of the takings. But we note Burr's appreciation. Nash, he said, 'first taught the people of fashion how to buy their pleasures, and to procure that ease and felicity they sought for, without diminishing the happiness of others'; and we may accept GM Trevelyan's judgement; 'During his long supremacy as Master of the Ceremonies, nearly covering the reigns of Anne and the first two Georges, Nash did perhaps as much as any other person even in the 18th century to civilise the neglected manners of mankind.'

The Fishmarket, the Pantiles, 1978.
(David Addey)

FOOTNOTES

1. Elizabeth Twisden to Mary Hammond: Arch. Cant., 5, 87.
2. MS letter in local museum.
3. *Diaries*. Wilson, son of Bishop Wilson of Sodor and Man, was a well known London clergyman.
4. *A Particular Description of Tunbridge Wells, in a Letter from a Gentleman at that Place to his Friend in Town*; signed Marinus.
5. *Letters*, ed FC Rathbone, 1899.

CHAPTER SIX

GEORGIAN AFTERNOON

All you who wish the World to learn
To Tunbridge Wells repair – a,
Where you will learn more in a Day
Than elsewhere in a year – a.
Not that our Numbers do surpass
What you may elsewhere find – a,
But here no mortals you can meet
An hour in a mind – a.

From a mid-18th century song; in *Notes and Queries* 24 July, 1858,
quoted by Lewis Melville.

With the death of Beau Nash in 1761, Tunbridge Wells, the fashionable spa, passed its zenith; but a long afternoon still stretched before it, prosperous and populous, decorated by high society with Georgian elegance, fading, as the 18th century came to its end, into a transformation scene.

Unlike Bath, where a similar process went on but the city continued to be enlarged and adorned with buildings as gracious as those of the Woods, Tunbridge Wells remained essentially as Burr saw it, until the end of the century. On the Walks, major structural repairs were done in the 1740s, about 1750, and 1779–81. These gave the chapel its present cupola and turret, with Polly Peachum's clock in 1769, and no doubt had some effect upon the appearance of the houses of the Upper Walk; but Loggon's picture of 1748, and Green's watercolours of 1793 are not markedly different from Kip. Loggon shows the palisade which now divided the Upper from the Lower Walk, the latter 'chiefly used by country people and servants', and in 1786 still unpaved. Green does

From a map of 1768.

show the musicians at play in a gallery[1] projecting from a house in the middle row. Sprange's guide of 1786 says that all the principal taverns – the Sussex, Kentish New Inn, and Angel – had been improved, the first especially, with the Assembly Room adjoining it. But no new building appears to have been done until the beginning of the next century.

Barrow's map of 1808 shows two buildings in the gravel pit on the Common, Mount Edgcumbe and Gibraltar, none of them in Bowra, although it is said that the Burrows family began their manufacture of Tunbridge Ware in a cottage at Gibraltar as far back as the 1680s or early 1700s. On Barrow's map they appear in the works behind Jordan's Cottage, in Jordan's Lane (now Church Road); and in 1822 a picture shows their sign on Jordans itself, claiming this to have been the original manufactory. Tunbridge Ware was very much a family business, and there is some mystery about its origin and development. The Pintos (see bibliography) are inclined to give Burrows priority. They also mention Sharp, whose works appear in Barrow, at the top of

Mount Ephraim-Culverden. 'Were this smuggled abroad and then imported as a foreign commodity' complained Derrick in 1762, 'I am persuaded that people would run after it, but, alas, everyone knows it is English, and the encouragement is therefore poor'; but by the 1770s, Tunbridge Ware appeared for sale not only locally but in London. The principal woods used at this time appear to have been holly, cherry, plum, yew, and sycamore, and the toys, such things as small cabinets and souvenirs, built up by highly skilled workmanship. When the change to mosaic and marquetry took place is not exactly known, but by the end of the century this was in fashion, and was to flourish in the first half of the 19th century. Fitted work-boxes for ladies were popular: Queen Charlotte had one.

The great and continual increase in trade and communications which went on all over the country in the 18th century demanded better roads; nowhere more than in the clay of the Weald, which made them, as Celia Fiennes discovered, unusable in wet weather. In 1709–1711, two of the first Turnpike Acts, which set up bodies of local trustees charged with the maintenance of a stretch of road from the proceeds of tolls levied at the turnpike gates, were applied to the Hastings road through Sevenoaks as far as Woodsgate and Tunbridge Wells; no doubt because of the quantity, and we may suppose the quality, of the travellers who used it. In 1762 Derrick still found the road from Tonbridge to the Wells in very bad order, and in 1774 Fanny Burney reported it 'so very sidelum and jumblum'.[2] Burr in 1766

The Music Gallery, 1990. (Charlie Bell)

pleaded for a good road from Wells to Woodsgate, which would lay open that area to communication with the Wells, and 'an effectual amendment of all the roads in and near the place . . . a necessity every year more evident.' The chief internal roads should be well paved, in the manner of other country towns. He had far-sighted ideas, also (which were to turn up again a century later) for forest drives and walks, ornamental water, tree planting on the common, an orchestra for the Grove. Marinus told his friend George in 1767 that 'we have been this season particularly well accommodated by two Flys, which run in opposition to each other, which carry four Persons only, and are never more than five hours and a half on the Road; one sets out at Five in the Morning from hence, and gets into London at Eleven, and returns from thence at One. The other sets out from London at the same time in the Morning, and returns from hence at One; by which the Company have an opportunity of having Turbots, Fruit, etc in Time for Dinner and of sending Wheat Ears from hence to their Friends in London: the Fare is Half a Guinea.' In the 1780s, John Sprange does not mention the fly, but advertises Parman's stage coach, now every weekday in the year, to and from the Golden Cross at Charing Cross: fare 9s, 'outside Passengers and Children in Lap, Half Price', and two carriers, running to and from the Queen's Head and the Nag's Head in Southwark respectively in the season; no doubt with many calls on the journey, which took twenty-four hours. The mail from London arrived every morning except Monday at 11am, and went out at 6pm except on Saturdays: a letter to London in 1779 cost fourpence. Immediately after the arrival of the mail, the Cross-Post set out on local deliveries in Kent and East Sussex. Most travellers probably had their own means of transport, from Nash's coach and six, and the carriages of the nobility, to Celia Fiennes' horse.

To the state of the roads and the risk of highway robbery which all had to face, a journey to Tunbridge Wells added another trial. On reaching Tonbridge, or even at Sevenoaks, the traveller would be waylaid, as far as the Wells themselves, by a succession of 'touters' or touts, on horse and foot, soliciting his custom for their particular tradesmen and his provender or services. One verse in the Touting Song written about them runs:[3]

> The Brewers, the Butchers, and Dippers
> Are most of the Clamorous Rout;
> The Pastry-Cook, and the Shopkeepers
> Are not unmindful to Tout:
> But if unsuccessful in this,
> To Billingsgate Rhet'ric they fall,

And would fain scandalise one another,
But that they are Proof against all.

Derrick and his fellow travellers were alarmed at the appearance of the touters: who were troublesome and intimidating. Thackeray's Harry Warrington in the *Virginians*, riding over with Colonel Wolfe from Westerham, 'was for charging, pistol in hand, supposing them to be highwaymen,' but the future hero of Quebec laughingly dissuaded him.

A succession of Masters of Ceremonies followed Nash, but none ruled as he did, nor lasted as long. The first two reigned at both Tunbridge Wells and Bath. The first of these, a French dancer and fencer named Caulet, Collette, or Collett, who may have been acting already in Nash's later days, and the successor mentioned by Elizabeth Scribe, threw up his job in 1763. He was succeeded by Samuel Derrick, the writer of the *Letters* already cited, in which he made a greater contribution to the history of the two spas than in an office whose emoluments, which he badly needed, proved hard to earn. An Irishman, born in 1724, former draper's apprentice and failed actor, he took to hack writing. 'I dont *live* anywhere,' he told an inquirer, with Irish wit, 'but I *starve* in a Garret at a Chandler's shop by the side of Fleet Market.' Then he met Boswell, and Johnson, who employed him to collect material for his life of Dryden, and won his sympathy: Johnson had lived in a garret himself. His *Letters*, remarked Johnson, would have been thought 'very pretty' had they been written by one of a more established name'; but his poetry, said the great man, was lousy. Derrick, a little man, lacking in social presence or dignity, too eager to please, was not a very likely person to preside over the ceremonies of the two most fashionable watering-places. He made some gaffes at Bath, and became the butt of the wits. Smollett referred to him in *Humphry Clinker* as Tom Thumb, and 'a pretty little gentleman'; Garrick addressed rude verses 'To Mr D, upon his recalling his order against dancing Minuets in Socks.' Nash must have turned in his grave.

At Tunbridge Wells, however, Marinus thought he gave 'so much Satisfaction in this important Office, that very few gave him less than Gold for his Tickets' for the MC's benefit ball. Perhaps they were more kindly here than at Bath – though his attempt to become MC at Brighthelmstone as well, 'gave some umbrage.' After his death in 1769, and his successor Major Brereton's departure in the same year, the two spas made separate arrangements. Who made them at Tunbridge Wells is not clear: there may have been some form of election or selection by the Company at the start of the season. Blake, the next man (1769–79) had a dispute with Pinchbeck, son of the inventor of the alloy named after him, who was at one time master of one of the assembly rooms on the Walks, and built the bath at Adam's Well. It appears that Blake upheld his dignity and came off best with the Company; for George Selwyn wrote to Lord Carlisle – 'Pinchbeck is in disgrace for having behaved ill to the MC at Tunbridge, and says he is many hundred pounds worse off for his close connection with the King and the Royal Family.' The king was George III: Pinchbeck was one of the political group of 'King's Friends'. Richard Tyson (MC 1780–1801) issued a code of Rules, very much more gentle than Nash had imposed upon Bath, which are worth setting out in Appendix III, for the information they give. Of the remaining MCs little is known: Fotheringham (c1801–05); Paul Amsinck, (1805–17), author and illustrator of *Tunbridge Wells and its Neighbourhood*, from which we have quoted; 'the only one of his kind I ever saw very like a gentleman, and not at all a coxcomb', wrote Mary Berry.[4] Then, after a brief return by Tyson, GT Roberts, (1817–22); Captain Merryweather (1822–5); and H Madden, Royal Marines officer, last of the line, who resigned in 1836, by which time this office had become redundant.

Our knowledge of the Wells and its Company continues to be derived from the very plentiful letters and diaries of this age of literary expression. As many more may still be awaiting discovery. Inevitably they contain much gossip and personalia, very seductive, but for us here, too discursive. The lords and ladies, it appears, continued to come; still, as in Boyle's time; more for society than for therapy, though many drank the waters and said these did them good. By perseverance and a gentle daily ride, Marinus got rid of the vast depression, a severe fever of the previous winter, and a nine-month's ague, acquired an excellent appetite, and felt 'as well as ever I was in my life.' Lady Jane Coke and Mrs Montagu, two more who might excusably be called well-satisfied customers, wrote that the waters made them feel giddy, and the latter made this an excuse for not writing more often 'as it is apt to make the waters get into the head' – a difficulty which did not prevent her becoming the most articulate as well as the most assiduous and one of the most colourful of all who resorted to the Wells.

This most extraordinary woman, as Johnson called her, came here first in 1733, when she was thirteen, and often afterwards, until at least 1779. On her first visit she reported that 'a great part of the company, and especially of the Gentlemen, are vapoured,' ie hypochondriacs. She became one herself; suffering, one gathers, from migraine; and tried all the spas. From them she addressed her celebrated letters, mostly to her lifelong friend Lady Margaret Harley, later Duchess of Portland, and to her husband Edward Montagu, who had no time for the Wells and society. A founder-member of the Blue Stocking Club, she became London's leading hostess – the Madame Deffand of the English Capital, as Wraxall called her. A blue-stocking in the accepted sense she was not. Nor was she a beauty, as Reynolds' portrait makes clear; but a woman of fashion, who was also a prolific reader, with a great attraction for and to intelligent men. She flourished at a time when women, like her more brilliant cousin, Lady Mary Wortley Montagu (who incidentally thought Tunbridge Wells beautiful, and had 'a great opinion of its mineral waters') were becoming articulate, and entering the field of literature.

Her letters, flowing in a steady stream, sparkling and amusing, if perhaps after a while a little tedious, light up the social life of the Wells, among other places where she shone. We hear of the men who fell under her spell, from Edward Young, DD, the serious minded author of *Night Thoughts*, to the adoring Lord Lyttleton, a minor poet, the very elderly statesman Lord Bath (William Pulteney, now in his seventies and infatuated by her) and Dr Messenger Monsey, the sardonic Whig physician, who remarked, of the two last and himself 'so now there are three fools of us.' In 1772 she collected Richard Cumberland, not yet a resident – 'a very agreeable Bard for my choir.' She gives lists of the best people who have arrived, and is brilliantly rude about some of them – 'one of the ladies looks like a state bed running upon castors, she has robbed the valance and tester of a bed for a trimming'.

A snob she certainly was: to Richard Church 'a detestable woman'; but she must have had charms and wit to fascinate men like Burke and Reynolds, Garrick and Johnson. She prattles on about her diversions: how Young took her and another lady for a ride to the 'fine old ruins' of Tonbridge Castle, how the townspeople stared, how the ladies went scrumping in the parson's orchard – and roped him into the party; how in 1753 she vacated Stone House on Mount Ephraim, where she was staying with a party, for the rising young politician William Pitt, who was ill with insomnia and depression, but soon got over that with her to listen to, and went sightseeing with them to Penshurst and 'to a place called New Vauxhall . . .' 'We drank tea yesterday in the most beautiful rural scene that can be imagined, which Mr Pitt had discovered in his morning's ride, about half a mile from hence; he ordered a tent to be pitched, tea to be prepared, and his French horn to breathe music like the unseen genius of the wood. The company dined with me; and we set out, number eight. After tea we rambled about for an hour, seeing several views, some wild as Salvator Rosa, others placid, and with the setting sun, worthy of Claud Lorraine. These parties are good for health and pleasure, and break the dull line of Tunbridge life.' Another time, in 1761, the party went to the High Rocks. Among them was another Elizabeth she had collected, Miss

The remarkable characters who were at Tunbridge Wells with Richardson

'1748 Aug:
1 Dr. Johnson
2 Bp. of Salisbury (D: Gilbert)
3 Ld. Harcourt

4 Mr. Cibber (Colley)
5 Mr. Garrick
6 Mrs. Frasi (The Singer)
7 Mr. Nash.

8 Miss Chudleigh (Duchs)
9 Mr. Pitt (Earl of Cha
10 A. Onslow (The Spea
11 Ld. Powis

Printed 20th May 1804. for Ric

Loggon's famous illustration of the Walks, 1748.
(Tunbridge Wells Museum and Art Gallery)

a drawing in his possession with references in his own writing

...op of Norfolk
P.294
Banks
Lincoln
Littlen (Afterwards
Lord Lyttleton)
...uls Church Yard.

16 *The Baron* (A German Gamester)
17 *Anonym.* (M.ʳ Richardfon)
18 *S.ʳ M.ʳ Onflow*

19 *Miss Onflow*
20 *S.ʳ M.ʳ Johnfen* (The D.ʳˢ Wife)
21 *M.ʳ Whifton.*
22 *Loggan the Artift*
23 *The Woman of the Wells*

Carter, the pious, modest daughter of a parson, who spoke several languages, could 'talk Greek faster than anyone in England', and earned her pin-money by translating – a true blue stocking. 'All was wild, spontaneous beauty,' wrote this young lady. 'We drank tea in the wild region after sunset; and waited to see the effect of moonlight on so solemn a scene.' As Christopher Hussey points out, they represent the awakening interest of the educated classes in 'The Picturesque', the appeal of romantic scenery, especially with ruins. We note also their interest in tea.

Then her coach and six nearly overturned in the lane behind the Walks, after the Friday night ball. 'It had like to have been fatal to me,' she wrote to her husband . . . The footmen were thrown off from behind, but several people being by, the coach was held up, and I got safe out.' There was of course a considerable to-do about it. The coachman was sacked for having taken drink, Mrs Montagu was reduced to a chaise and pair while the coach was repaired, everyone inquired after her nerves, and the proprietor of the Public Rooms undertook to have the roadway levelled, in the hope she would come again. A decade later, when she was in her fifties, she was addressed as 'The Naiad of Tunbridge Wells' in verses by an anonymous author (suspected to be Garrick) in a London journal: he prayed for her recovery there from her malady of the moment.

Among other men and women of letters who trod the Walks, we know of Lord Chesterfield, Samuel Richardson, David Hume (recuperating with his wife in 1759), Garrick, Fanny Burney . . . Pope, Goldsmith, Burke, Reynolds, may well have come here as to Bath; but we have no record. Loggon's picture of 1748, with names written below by Richardson, shows Dr Johnson himself; but was it *the* Dr Johnson? Margaret Barton objects that he had not received then his doctorate, and asserts that the man in the picture is Dr James Johnson, the future Bishop of Rochester, with his spinster sister, known (as was common in those days) as Mrs Johnson, who came later to live on Mount Ephraim. There was no bishop Johnson at Rochester in the 18th century; but there was one at Worcester. Boswell is silent, but Richard Church counters with a footnote by Malone, who knew Boswell and edited the third edition of his *Johnson* in 1799, stating definitely that Samuel and his Tetty were at the Wells in 1748 and were in the picture. Malone however could have been relying on Richardson too. The picture does not help much: the only man in it who looks ecclesiastical is the Bishop of Salisbury; nobody looks particularly like Samuel Johnson. All we can say is that if he was not at the Wells he ought to have been: did not Thackeray's Lord March point him out on the Walks, and Richardson and Chesterfield too, to young Warrington, in *The Virginians*?

Richardson: Heaven bless my soul, Mr Johnson, I ask your pardon if I have trodden on your corn.

Johnson: You have done both, sir. You have trodden on the corn and received the pardon.

Richardson went to the Wells for his giddiness, but was not cured: nor was he at home in a society too aristocratic and frivolous for his taste. He moralises in his letter to Miss Westcombe of 2 August 1784: 'Methinks I would wish that wives (particularly some that I see here) would not behave as if they thought themselves unmarried coquettes, and that it were polite to make their husbands the last people in their notices.' Among scores of belles, flatterers, triflers, he found a pretty woman as rare as a black swan, and when one came, she reigned as a beauty – Miss Banks, Miss Chudleigh (both in Loggon's picture), Miss L of Hackney – all had their turn and were forgotten for the next.

Colley Cibber, who walked the Walks with Nash and struck up an unlikely friendship with Young, was now 'head over ears in love with Miss Chudleigh'. 'This lady was an adventuress of the Manon Lescaut-Becky Sharp class. Having married, secretly, a sailor who turned out later to be the next Earl of Bristol, and then bigamously, the Duke of Kingston, she was convicted, after a fashionable trial, by the House of Lords. There was however no precedent for sentencing a peeress for bigamy, so she got off, with the Duke's money, and went abroad. There is more than one book about her; including the one by Doris Leslie, *The Amazing Duchess* (Heinemann, 1974).

Frederick Handel is reported here more than once, in 1748 and 1755 (when his name appears as a subscriber in the chapel accounts) but no artists seem to have practised here as did Hoare and Gainsborough at Bath. Thomas Loggon,[5] the nearest we have, was court dwarf to Frederick, Prince of Wales, and later established himself as a fan-painter, in Bath and Tunbridge Wells and the Hotwells at Bristol. In his shop at the extreme end of the Walks he observed the passers-by, and put them into his topographical fans and views, which he sold as souvenirs. He appears in the corner of his 1748 picture. One of the water-poets addressed some verses to him with satirical directions on how to present certain well-known people; to which Loggon (who had his clients to consider), replied in more respectful verse. He seems to have had a good eye for business; 'he died recently, much respected', says Sprange in 1780, 'at the Hotwells.'

Loggon was not the only odd character on the Walks. Sprange describes several: 'Sir Robert Walpole', supposed bastard son of the statesman, 'who cleaned shoes . . . and said a thousand small things to the Company, and was reckoned more like Sir Robert than any of his

The Pantiles en fête 1973 with some historic characters: Beau Nash, Elizabeth Chudleigh and Colley Cibber in centre; Loggon the dwarf on left. (Alan Savidge)

children'; Lady Tunbridge, the mad woman, presumably 'the woman of ye Wells' shown with Loggon in his picture; 'Lord Rawlins', the town-crier, 'who gained his title by being taken to London by the famous Duke of Wharton, ridiculously but richly dressed, and introduced by him into some of the first clubs in London.' The Duke also taught him to sing the Touting Song and to make speeches about the Wells, 'but he remained so proud after from this acquired title, that he went mad, and died so in the parish workhouse' – forgotten, no doubt, by the Company he had been taught to amuse. Two beggars, known as Dame Fortune and Berwick Jack, used their scandalous knowledge gained from the servants of the great to sponge upon them and the Company. Every writer repeats Sprange's story, c1737, of William Okill, 'a very singular character', then Clerk to King Charles chapel, who kept a small lodging-house on Mount Sion, and when he wanted to let, would give out Psalm 48, with the telling words in the second and third verses:

> The hill of Sion is a fair place and the joy of the whole earth;
> Upon the north side lieth the city of the great King;
> God is well known in her palaces as a sure refuge.

According to Sprange, two noted card-sharpers, Gilbert and Sidney, had a bet on whether Okill would read the psalm next Sunday, his house being let: Gilbert tricked Sidney by bribing Okill to do so.

Gambling for gambling's sake being now illegal, at least in public, the card games mentioned in Tyson's notice replaced the casting of dice and the rolling of balls in the two assembly rooms; on alternate evenings except Tuesday and Friday, the ball nights, and Sunday when, according to Sprange, 'the Company in general meet to drink tea at the Great Room on the Walk.' Some of the games, eg. Lottery, forerunner of Lotto and today's Bingo, were scarcely games of skill and judgement; but they passed, and as Dr Arbuthnot discovered, money passed with them, though not in the blatant manner of the previous era. There was also a race-course on the Common, shown on Bowra's and later maps, its origin unknown, its track still surviving as a ride among the groves that have sprung up since. Handbills printed by Sprange in the 1790s announce an annual event in August or September, with purses or cups given by the Lord of the Manor and local gentry, and cock-fighting. The gentry appear also to have had subsidised fun and games on the Common, held annually or on special occasions, and known as 'Diversions'. The visit of the Duke of York and Gloucester in 1765 was celebrated by a triple discharge of 18 pieces of cannon on the Common, and the illumination of the Walks. Cricketing appears in Lady Jane Coke's description of the day's programme in 1750; Thomas, son of Edward Strange who kept a lodging-house on Mt Sion in 1767, played 'in the first recorded game with a full score,' says CH Strange, on 13 September 1790, for Tunbridge Wells on Brighton Level, against that town. A handbill of 1795 advertises a match on 19 August, on the Common, Hoskins and Strange against two gentlemen of Sevenoaks for ten guineas: the wicket to be pitched at ten o'clock.

Besides such amusements there were lectures, 'superficial enough to entertain the imagination', says Burr, 'without fatiguing the under-

Mrs Baker's theatre from an engraving of 1804. Notice the previous site of the Sussex Tavern. (Tunbridge Wells Museum and Art Gallery)

standing.' Nash's friend Dr William King was given a series on astronomy when William Pitt escorted Mrs Montagu to listen, and put searching questions to him. Whiston, the translator of *Josephus*, lectured on Moses' tabernacle and the Temple of Jerusalem. Burr in 1766, and Sprange copying from him in 1786, mention 'frequent concerts attended by the most eminent performers in London, where all those who are happy in a taste for music, may be entertained . . . at the expense of a crown.' Sometimes there were breakfast concerts, at 3s 6d: talented amateurs might take part. In theatrical entertainment, Tunbridge Wells was far behind Bath, which rivalled London itself. Lewis Melville records some strolling players in 1737, and the company of 'Canterbury' Smith in the fifties. In 1773, a disgruntled correspondent reported 'a set of players down with us, the vilest miserables who meet with no encouragement but from the affable, beautiful Countess of Tyrconnel, who kindly bespeaks a play now and then to keep them from starving.' Then there arrived on the scene Mrs Baker.

Sarah Baker was another of the remarkable women in the history of the town, and a notable character in the colourful history of impresarios. It is not easy to date with certainty the events in her career. She was born in 1736 or 1737, to an acrobatic dancer, Ann

Wakelin, and spent her youth touring the fairs with her mother's company, in which she met and married the acrobat Baker. She had no education at all, and to the end of her life she could not read or write. On her husband's death, about 1769, leaving her with three young children, she is said to have mounted them all on donkeys and toured the fairs, probably with a puppet show; she was at Bartholomew Fair in 1780 and 1782, and often in North and East Kent. Some put her 'Temple of the Muses', as it was nicknamed, on Mount Sion, as early as 1770: but it is clear from Norma Hodgson's recent researches[6] that although Mrs Baker and her company had been touring the Wells many times before, it was in 1786 that she first set up in a theatre here. She found a rival, Glassington, who made his theatre in a warehouse in Castle Street, and played on the same evenings; but by 1789 she defeated him. By this time, she had apparently lost East Kent to other rivals, but had beaten all comers at Canterbury, Rochester, and Faversham, and was becoming established as 'The Governess-General and Sole Autocrat of Kentish Drama, erecting no fewer than ten different theatres at her own expense without running into financial difficulties.' This was the golden age of the provincial theatre.

It was, it seems in 1789 that Mrs Baker pulled down the Temple and rebuilt it, largely with the same materials, on the Lower Walks. Carey in his *Balnea* of 1801 wrote that the theatre was very small, but well patronised: the actors were almost in the audience's lap. Soon after this, Mrs Baker rebuilt again. Sprange's playbills of the 1790s indicate shows two or three times a week in August and September, some 'by desire' of a distinguished visitor, one of them the Duchess of York. In that year, *The Jew* had its first performance. Richard Cumberland, author of this and a plethora of plays, none of them known today, had come to live at Mt Sion, and his son used to tread the boards. A more distinguished member of the cast, William Dowton, Mrs Baker's son-in-law, made his name when Sheridan put on *The Jew* at Drury Lane. As the original playbill showed, the evening's entertainment ran to three numbers; the main play, a dance or song interlude, and usually a farce to finish. *The Rivals, The School for Scandal, She Stoops to Conquer,* the *Merchant of Venice, As You Like It,* and other famous plays took their turn with several of Cumberland's and other less memorable ones.

Sarah Baker was a hard worker, had a finger in every pie, and was a past mistress of economy, keeping prices down and her money in a row of punchbowls on her desk rather than in the bank. She ran the box-office herself, and thus got to know everybody: her standard greeting to customers, of whatever class, was 'Pass on, Tomfool' – but all admired her elegant bearing and graceful curtsey. She relied on the local trades-people and on local taste – Cumberland especially at Tunbridge Wells –

though she had her distinguished patrons. Grimaldi, the great clown, who played a few times for her to packed audiences, recalled how easily the company could pack up and move to her next theatre, which was identically planned. In 1797 she is said to have put on 53 different pieces at Tunbridge Wells. One of her stalwarts, Gardner (who died here) played all the parts, in his career. By that time, the French war was making patriotic songs and plays more popular than Shakespearean tragedy: Dibdin's *Mount of the Nile*, celebrating Nelson's victory of 1798, had a great reception everywhere. During his time with her company, he often ran up quick farces and songs, and painted scenery. A rich unpolished gem was his description of her in the epitaph he wrote for her tomb at St Nicholas, Rochester, when she died, leaving £16,000 in 1816.

FOOTNOTES

1. The 1739 Act refers to 'the Musick Gallery over the two other shops occupied by Brooker and Bridget Byrne, which is to be maintained by the Lord of the Manor or his tenants, and continue free and open for the use of the Musick in the manner it is at present used without paying anything for the same.'

2. Diary and letters of Mme d'Arblay, ed Dobson, 1904.

3. *Tunbrigalia*, or the *Tunbridge Miscellany*; T Webb, 1739. 'Tooters or Touters', wrote Derrick, were so called 'from the people of Tooting in Surrey, who set the example by way-laying the Company formerly resorting to the mineral waters of Epsom Wells in that county'. There was certainly a touting tradition there: I spent my youth there, and remember the children, in the first quarter of this century, running beside the cars and brakes of race-goers in Epsom's Derby week, crying 'Throw out your mouldy pennies!' But the dictionary does not support this derivation.

4. Authoress (1767–1852); with her sister Agnes well-known in Society. Horace Walpole left his house in Strawberry Hill to them. Occasional visitor to T.W.

5. His own spelling: others have Loggan and Logan; Harleian MSS 7190, biographical details.

6. *Studies in English Theatre History*, 1952. Also PP Mander, in *Country Life*, 22 Dec. 1950.

CHAPTER SEVEN

WINDS OF CHANGE

The houses are so many bijous made up for the occasion . . . and the whole an air of such simplicity that I am delighted with it, as much as when my amusements were, as they were formerly, at the Rooms and upon the Pantiles, which are now to me detestable.'

George Selwyn to Lord Carlisle, 1774.

Your prudent grandmammas, ye modern belles,
Content with Bristol, Bath, and Tunbridge Wells,
When health required it, would consent to roam,
Else more attach'd to pleasures found at home.
But now alike, gay widow, virgin, wife,
Ingenious to diversify dull life,
In coaches, chaises, caravans and hoys,
Fly to the coast for daily, nightly joys,
And all, impatient of dry land, agree
With one accord to rush into the sea.

from William Cowper, *Retirement*, 1752.

We have noted as early as 1707 Dr Browne's advocacy of bathing in water rather than drinking it. In 1750 Dr Richard Russell of Lewes brought out his book on the remedial effects of sea water, with such results that four years later he moved to Brighthelmstone (pronounced Brighton) to be at hand for the flock of new patients: the latest thing in cures was launched. Burr in 1766 was welcoming the proposal of a turnpike to Lewes, which would make Brighton more easily accessible from the Wells, so that visitors could go to both. He had no fear that this might be bad policy; 'As Tunbridge has confessedly the great advantage of her rival in every respect, she cannot suffer, but must on the whole be an infinite gainer by the comparison.' The new watering place indeed modelled itself on the Wells; the Steyne and the Grove, its Walks, even a chalybeate spring conveniently discovered nearby. But Burr reckoned without Prinny; George, Prince of Wales, Prince Regent, the First Gentleman in Europe, George IV. He did indeed visit Tunbridge Wells, more than once, it appears; and breakfasted at the High Rocks, (where, reports Betsy Sheridan, he forgot to tip the staff); but by the time she wrote in 1785 the young prince, then 23, had fallen for Brighton, bringing Holland to do the first classical rebuilding of the Pavilion, and all the gay and gallant, the future Regency rakes, to the Steyne, where fun and games, more riotous, probably, than the Wells ever offered, went on by day, and there and elsewhere by night. From this, Brighton and Hove went ahead, in the days of his Regency, to outdistance their former model. More sedately, the Prince's father George III was bathing at Weymouth.

The English, as Horace Walpole remarked, were waddling like ducks to the water; but not all of them to the seaside. Cheltenham was entering upon its most fashionable period, Dr Holyoake was laying the foundations of Royal Leamington Spa, and a galaxy of inland watering places was to become prominent in the coming century. Tunbridge Wells however, perhaps more vulnerable because Brighton was so near, began to look, in some eyes, rather jaded. In July 1773 it was still, wrote our disgruntled correspondent of the previous chapter, 'extremely full, but the company consists of an odd olio of old maids, lively widows, polluted batchelors, Jews, parsons and some few nobility.' The Walks were paved with broken flat tiles, with some trees confined to one side, and a set of shops little better than shambles. In 1779, Fanny Burney, staying at the Sussex with the Thrales en route to Brighton, could see in the Pantiles 'no beauty in itself – only common houses at one side and little millinery and Tunbridge Ware shops at the other and each end is choked up by buildings that intercept all prospect. How such a place could first be made a fashionable pleasure walk, everybody must wonder.' The houses of the place were all scattered about in a strange wild manner, except for the shopkeepers, who had 'two or three dirty little lanes, much like dirty little lanes in other places.'

There was by now another element in the place; new, though not indeed young. The rising national prosperity of the 18th century was producing a steadily increasing number of what may be grouped as professional people; not only the army or naval officer, the lawyer, the physician, but the official from the governing and mercantile institutions – like the East India Company – of the expanding empire; men of letters and art too, and soon to follow them, bankers, merchants, industrialists. By the latter part of the century, many of them were finishing their active careers, thinking of taking life more easily, and looking for congenial surroundings in which to do so. They found increasingly in Bath and Tunbridge Wells, and soon in Cheltenham, an atmosphere to their taste, and the cost of living cheaper than in London. In the late 1750s a successful physician from Portsmouth, Dr George Kelley, established himself as the first really local resident magnate. He bought the Manor of Rusthall, the lord's houses on the Walks, some more on Mount Ephraim, and 250 acres of land in Speldhurst parish, for a total of £19,000, leasing more lands and farming himself. By 1762 he had become Sir George Kelley, of Bishop's Down Grove (where the Spa Hotel now is), active in local affairs, magistrate, and sheriff of Kent.[1] There were elderly aristocrats too, who liked to pass their summers regularly in the rural, 'well-appointed' scenery of Tunbridge Wells, wintering in London or Bath. One of these was the Duke of Leeds, who rented Mount Pleasant House for ten weeks annually for about twenty years from Grattan of the Gloucester tavern, who had acquired it from the builder, Lord Egmont. A nobleman of the old school, he always dressed ducally, never walked, appeared every morning on the Walks, where he took his glass of the water and was nobly gracious to all, and again once a year, on 12 August, the birthday of the Prince, when he held a public tea-drinking and a ball, and received compliments in Latin verse. For the rest, he had his friends to dinner, and drove daily, in a coach and six with full appanage, along the turnpike to a point he called Turnham Green, where the equipage turned for home.

By the 1780s there were a number of such regular distinguished visitors or permanent residents: among them Joseph Hiller, successful wool draper of Southwark, at Chancellors on Mount Ephraim (by tradition, but without direct evidence, built for James II's notorious Chancellor Jeffreys, but never occupied by him); he later sold the house to Sir Richard Heron, Bt, retired government secretary, who much altered it. On Bishop's Down, Martin Yorke, clergyman's son, major in the East India Company force and veteran of Plassey, retired rich from India, bought Sir George Kelley's house and spent the last twenty years of his life there. On Mount Sion, Sir James Bland Burges, veteran of Culloden, statesman and literary man in his later days, came to live at Burlington House; and close by, in a house on part of the site of the old assembly room and bowling-green on Mount Sion, was the other literary man, Richard Cumberland. He too had held a government job, as Secretary to the Board of Trade and Plantations, but lost it in a political upheaval, found himself a half-pay pensioner with a family to support and retired to retrench at the Wells. He cultivated his garden,

The Walks 1793. The building on the extreme right has a sign saying HARBROE.
SURGEON AND APOTHECARY.   (Tunbridge Wells Museum and Art Gallery)

wrote some more plays and novels and took an active part in local affairs. The place suited him very well, he says in his *Memoirs*. 'It is not altogether a public place, yet it is at no period of the year a solitude. A reading man may command his hours of study and a social man will find full gratification for his philanthropy.' He lived on till 1811, when he achieved burial in Westminster Abbey. 'The Terence of England, the mender of hearts' someone called him; but his works are all forgotten now.

Lord North, the prime minister himself, forced finally from office on the fall of his egregious coalition with Fox in 1783, retired to the town his great-grandfather had founded, and took up residence below the Grove. Lord Chief Justice Mansfield, whose town house had been burned down by the mob in the Gordon Riots of 1780 because he had supported a bill to relieve the disabilities of Roman Catholics, came to Mount Sion, and later to stay with Mrs Johnson, with whom he had once been in love. He was said to be in very poor health; but he lived till 1793, and was often to be seen on the Walks. Lady Jerningham, staying annually nearby in the early 1800s, and Samuel Rogers the banker-poet, found the company delightful: Rogers in 1805 could hardly leave 'this Castle of Indolence'.

This latterday rustication, a calling-in of the old world to redress the balance of the young, gave the place a new aspect and new prospects, and was good for the traders, who had been dependent on the visiting Company, and faced a decline. Benge Burr, alert to social and economic questions, had pointed out how vulnerable they were to a bad season, and advised them to get together, as the butchers had done, to stabilise prices and put an end to their feverish seasonal competition, and to 'that mean and scandalous practice of touting, which the greater part of the tradesmen had so preposterously fallen into': to buy from local farmers, to set up a regular market. He appealed also to the Abergavennys to develop some of their forest to the south of the town as small holdings, for the subsistence of 'innumerable families of industrious poor' – successfully, as appears from Sprange. The latter had a sententious welcome to the newcomers, 'from whose munificence . . . the neighbouring poor are greatly relieved, and kept in full employ; and the trades-people likewise reap a benefit extraordinary during the winter season.' These *obiter dicta* reveal that poverty and hardship existed behind the display, in those 'dirty little lanes', especially in the winter. But to Burr and Sprange it was probably a relative term. The poor-relief administration at Tonbridge does not appear to have been troubled much with this end of the parish.

The winds of change were blowing in religion also. After a century and more of religious controversy, the establishment had arrived by the time of George I at an attitude, reflected no doubt in the sermons at King Charles chapel, of greater tolerance and less fervour. Reasonableness was the way: 'enthusiasm' was to be abhorred. This meant a more civilised society, as did Nash's reforms in manners; but not zeal for social reform as later understood. There were many good works; but the poor in general were neglected. Against this attitude of mind broke, in the 1730s and after, the fervour of the Methodists, believing that religion was not a matter of reason or ritual but of conversion, 'a sudden assurance of salvation'; and of discipline in daily life. To the establishment, to the respectable classes in general, their methodism with its preaching to mass meetings, the convulsions and raptures of the converted, were odious. In 1739, John Wesley, coming to Bath to preach – and to take the waters which he approved – was challenged by the king of that fashionable city for his authority: he replied that it was that of Jesus Christ. Nash protested that Wesley's preaching frightened people out of their wits, but had to admit that he had never heard it, but judged it 'by common report'. 'Sir,' replied Wesley, 'is not your name Nash? I dare not judge you by common report.'

Meanwhile, the toleration of Dissent and the building of the chapel for the Presbyterians on Mount Sion had brought Nonconformist groups into quiet activity. The ministry of the word, it appears, produced memorable sermons there as in the chapel of the establishment. Isaac Watts the hymn writer is reported to have preached at Mount Sion in 1729 from Revelations 6, v 15-17, on 'the vain refuge for sinners; a meditation on the rocks of Tunbridge Wells.' Two scholarly men, Thomas Bayes, FRS and William Johnson, ministered with distinction between 1731 and 1776. The Duke of Leeds and others of the nobility and gentry are said to have listened to them. About 1750, a group of some 34 Independents established themselves in a meeting-house on the London Road. They had earlier come together privately on Sundays, after attending, and duly receiving the sacraments at Speldhurst church; where however, it appears from the *Church Book* of the spiritual experiences of the founding fathers,[2] 'sermons were preached against us, and we began to be accounted a strange sort of people.' They had then, in 1749, arranged with the Presbyterians, during a partial retirement of Bayes, to supply the pulpit at Mount Sion with morning preachers; but after a time Bayes objected and the arrangement broke down. Their first pastor, aptly named Shepherd, ministered in their new house until 1780, when he moved to Tonbridge. The group then fell into decline, and the meeting house was sold, becoming Durham House (behind Sydenham Villa in Vale Royal: long demolished). Of the Baptists who became prominent in Rusthall and Pembury during Commonwealth times, not much is known at the Wells until 1770, when they built a chapel on land adjoining Mount Ephraim House. Joseph Haines was their pastor for upwards of thirty years. It is said that Archbishop Secker (himself of Nonconformist origin) liked during his visits to the Wells to walk across the Common for a good theological argument with him at Gilead Cottage on Mount Ephraim. They retained their old burial-ground, two miles away, in an orchard off the Langton-Speldhurst road, at Burying Ground Farm.

Upon this scene the Methodists descended in the 1760s. They marched in two columns. One was led by John Wesley himself; the other, by now in an uneasy relationship with him, had George Whitefield as its herald, and its captain and paymaster the redoubtable Selina, Countess of Huntingdon. It is not clear when Wesley paid his first visit to the Wells, but he is reported at New (Little) Bounds in Southborough, the home of Sir Thomas I'Anson, in 1762/3, preaching in the parlour, and starting a Methodist Society there. Certainly in 1763 Selina arrived with Madan and Ferrer, two of the Anglican clergymen she had attached to herself as chaplains, and applied for the use of King Charles chapel. This being refused, she took the Presbyterian chapel on Mount Sion, and held a meeting which soon overflowed outside. 'So strong and general an influence over a congregation,' she wrote, 'I seldom remember to have seen. Many were melted to tears, and seemed resolved to fly from the wrath to come.' As

Venn gave out his text – 'Come unto me, all ye that labour and are heavy-laden, and I will give you rest,' one of the crowd, overcome by the occasion, collapsed and died. Believing in 'attacking Satan in his headquarters', Lady Huntingdon had begun to build chapels of her own at Bath (where Nash went to one of her meetings, and was lampooned by the water-poets for doing so) and another at Brighton; and in 1768, she decided that her call to set up at Tunbridge Wells had come. She took the lease of Culverden House and next year her chapel, a timber building in the new Gothick style, was opened on Saturday, July 22 by Whitefield, greatest of the mass-preachers, with a crowded congregation, including some society ladies: he addressed an overflow meeting from the stump of a tree outside.

The Methodist movement had begun within the established church, and the Wesleys, Whitefield, and many of its prominent men were ordained clergymen. Some of them Selina had taken under her wing as chaplains. But her assumption that they could thus go anywhere and use Anglican pulpits, or be set up in private chapels where she chose, virtually independent of the bishop, proved over the years too much for the establishment. A consistory court decision left her and them the choice of going along with the diocesan and parochial system or leaving the church. As JH Newman later said, Selina had to be pope or nothing; and she went forth, setting up with her considerable means, her own 'Countess of Huntingdon's Connexion', her ministers taking the oath as Dissenters: she founded her own seminary in Wales to supply future ones – though students there were not bound to join her Connexion. Meanwhile Wesley, operating separately from her, paid several visits to his local Methodist society, and like Selina, made use of Mount Sion chapel. His memoranda record visits, in the saddle as always, in 1778, 1780, 1782 and 1784, in the autumn or winter, and 'not without difficulty: part of the road being scarcely passable through the abundance of rain.' The swell visitors would have departed, but the people heard him with rapt attention. He stayed frequently with the Boones at Mount Ephraim House, who appear to have been enthusiasts for all causes of reform, in church and state.

In the crowds and the fervour we get another glimpse of the common people of Tunbridge Wells, and the country folk from the highways and hedges of the neighbourhood. The Methodists indeed appealed to all, and made a point of setting up their stand in the fashionable places as elsewhere. An aristocrat born, well-received by the king and queen, the Countess of Huntingdon could rally high society to her meetings wherever she held them: they came – like Nash and Chesterfield – and they were moved; but few were chosen. Upon the ordinary people however, in Tunbridge Wells as up and down the country, Methodism, though in no sense radical at that time, had a direct impact that the long, erudite sermons of the establishment could not hope, nor indeed tried, to make. At the same time, Methodism took the breath away from the small Nonconformist groups which had been modestly planted here. It can be no mere coincidence that the Independents, the Baptists, and the Presbyterians, whose chapel seems to have been taken over by the Methodists, fell into decline in the last years of the century.

There were also a crop of religious eccentrics, whose stories are given by Sprange: Thomas Dunmall the Prophet, who lived on the Common and told Lord Chesterfield that he had been with Jonah in the whale; William Whiston, a distinguished scholar and royal chaplain, who lectured the Company with some highly individual views and millennial prophesies; William Huntingdon SS (Sinner Saved: no connection with the Countess), converted coalheaver and revivalist preacher, who married a wealthy widow and died in retirement at Somerville Cottage on Mount Ephraim in 1812; and Mrs Boone, widow of a colonial governor, who kept open house not only for Wesley but for the poor and hungry, took up every religious cause while remaining an Anglican, and was wont to appear, says Amsinck, 'rouged

as for a dissipated court; clad in sackcloth, as for the conventicle.'

Meanwhile, the chapel of the Establishment, King Charles, jogged along, attended by its fashionable congregation as a matter of routine, and dependent on them for its support; until between about 1775–85, catching the change in the air, it shook itself up. The school rules and discipline were tightened, and more attention paid to need in admitting children: no family, as a rule, was to have more than two children there together – which seems to imply perhaps 25–50 families in need. Boys came in at six and girls at eight, both leaving at twelve after an examination in English and writing. The schoolmaster was still getting only £30 a year in 1776, but Okill at least was chapel clerk and lodging-house keeper as well. The charity sermons for chapel finances brought in about £50 a year; £80 in a good season. The rest came from sub-scriptions on the Walks – none, of course, would have thought of a single service charge for all the local amenities – which improved considerably after 1785, when a list was conspicuously displayed in the Upper Assembly Room. Hasted put the emolument in 1797 at £200–£250; not bad at all in those days. A new minister, Martin Benson, arrived (on Cumberland's recommendation, apparently) in 1786, and set a new and high standard of preaching – more 'energetic

The Springs, 1793. The spring itself is surrounded by a brick wall and wooden railing. A close look will reveal that the entrance into the enclosure is through two tall ball-capped columns.
(Tunbridge Wells Museum and Art Gallery)

and impressive' says John Britton, in which he was rarely surpassed: several of his sermons were printed. The ministry of the Word was still paramount: the congregation sat facing the pulpit, not the altar, the sexes apart. The first organ appeared, lent and played by one Friend at £5 a year – admittedly inadequate: there was a whip-round for him – and some good singing was heard. The Communion alms and the poor fund were regulated: none should be given more than 2s 6d and then only in great distress, or at lying-in. The surplus would be given out at Christmas, when the poor most needed bread and meat.

The holding trustees, a self-perpetuating body (when they remembered to do so) were made up almost exclusively of the aristocracy and gentry of the neighbourhood, led by the Earl of Abergavenny and later including Martin Yorke, Heron, and Captain Pannuwell;[3] with the bishop and a clergyman or two. They met from time to time, usually at the Sussex tavern when major repairs, or a new appointment, needed attention. Occasionally one of them would appear at the vestry meetings, and sign the accounts. Visitors still took part in these for some years. Nash's signature appears in the Minutes in 1743, and T Collet, presumably his successor, in 1761. Later on, the vestry became more local, but still genteel: Sir George Kelley and Cumberland often, tradesmen and lodging-house keepers occasionally. After about 1730, responsibility for the comfort of the Walks disappears, except for lighting and the upkeep of the bridge over the stream by the chapel.

Barrow's map of 1808 shows little change from Bowra's of 70 years before. Burr's four villages, the Walks, Mount Sion, Mount Ephraim-Culverden, and Mount Pleasant-London Road, had not yet grown together. The new residents on the Mounts seem either to have bought and enlarged existing houses, like Kelley, or to have rented them, like Cumberland. Lodging houses still predominated: Sprange's 1786 guide lists 83; 55 of them in the Mount Sion-Walks area, offering 418 chambers, many of them no doubt double, as well as 'garrets', and coach houses and stabling for 493 horses. Some families kept more than one house: the Frys had five, Mrs Shorey, Sir George Kelley's successor as lady of the manor, let three on Bishop's Down. From surviving lists of 1795, 96, and 97, printed by Sprange, it appears that 'fashionable' visitors and residents in the season may have amounted to 400 or so, with their attendant servants: about half the number in Nash's heyday. Royals like Ernest, Duke of Cumberland used to come. In 1793 the Upper Walk was at length repaved with flagstone and replanted with limes, at a cost of £700 raised by public subscription, and renamed the Parade. There were still, it appears, some fifty or more shops there; but according to Chalklin, rents showed a decline, especially of the public rooms in the freeholders' block: the balls, complained Tyson in a handbill, were not being supported by the leaders of the Company. The more sedate pursuits of music and reading were more popular. Recitals were advertised: Friend the chapel organist hired pianofortes, harpsichords, etc, and tuned them.[4] Sprange ran one of the two libraries on the Parade, as well as the post office and his printing business.

Sprange's bills and posters, of which the Museum has a collection, tell much of contemporary life at the Wells. Thus Dr Wallis, occulist, late of Leicester Square, gives a long list of his cures, with affidavit, and will give free advice to the poor, deaf, blind, or afflicted with internal or external disorders: they may attend with their overseers. Dr Campbell from Marlborough, army surgeon and Chelsea Pensioner, also advises gratis 'by the King's authority and licensed by Act of Parliament': he advertises pills, tablets, bottles, etc. There are advertisements of lost property and of petty thefts, with rewards offered: five guineas in 1796 by Lord Rodney, son of the famous admiral, after the robbery, from his lodgings in Mount Sion, of a tablecloth, boots, etc; 20 guineas by Sprange himself, who complains of frequent attacks on his property 'by some rancorous and wicked People', who maliciously damage his garden, shrubs and trees; Eridge Park similarly suffered. Another notice threatens prosecution at Quarter Sessions of persons allowing hogs to run at large in the streets – a subject appearing more than once. We find the following piece of Tunbridge Wells deference, Sprange's own, irresistible: did the recipients?

January 1796

Sir,

Having in pursuance of our Antient Custom been writing out my little Bills, and of which I am now making a formal delivery; will I hope plead for the presumption of having enclosed yours.

With the most grateful thanks for past favors, and a happy sensation from the reliance of what a delicate and persevering attention on my part, will prevail with you on the bestow of the future,

I beg to Subscribe myself
your very obliged, obedient servant . . .

As the century drew to a close, the winds of change blew a hurricane on the Continent. The Walks, like Jane Austen's Bath, probably felt little more than a breeze: the war with republican and Napoleonic France, says Trevelyan, 'was in the newspapers, but it scarcely entered the lives of the enjoying classes.' It was the poor who suffered, as it dragged on. But it meant more to Kent, which after all was nearest to the storm centre: Wordsworth's 'vanguard of liberty'.

Richard Cumberland.
(Tunbridge Wells Museum
and Art Gallery)

Through Sprange we hear of its impact on the town. Refugees arrive:
in 1793 there is an appeal on behalf of 23 emigré priests, who are said
to have been lodged in some cottages on Mount Ephraim, and later
received a small allowance from the government (Pelton, 1871).
M Signoret de Villiers, former cavalry captain and three times prisoner
of war, with a family to support, will give French readings in Miss
Sprange's rooms on the Walks; the Abbé Couture will teach French
and Latin. A camp for 7,000–8,000 men from 12 regiments was
pitched in Waterdown Forest in July 1793; Sprange printed a map of it.
They must have made an impact on a place of perhaps 1,000 people
before they moved on in August. Other troop movements went on from
time to time. There is a call for volunteers for the marine forces: ten
guineas and a crown bounty for each recruit, and a suggestive guinea for
the bringing-in of each able-bodied man; growing lads of 5′ 4″ and
under 20 years accepted. The Constable and Borsholder of Tonbridge
(so spelt) is to call up the local militia: a Tunbridge Wells troop is
mentioned. There is a diagram of sword exercises, and a doggerel poem
on the Kent Volunteers, by a trooper.

Sprange has notices also of national days of prayer and the order of
service: there was a day of thanksgiving for the fleet victories of Cape St
Vincent and Camperdown in 1797. The exploits of the brave old Duke
of York, who marched his men up the hill and marched them down
again, and was chased out of Flanders in 1799, were hardly cause for

rejoicing. But he was the king's son, well-known at the Wells, Ernest of Cumberland had been with him, and it was time to celebrate something. Diversions on Tunbridge Wells Common were given on 26 August by 'the Gentry Visitants to promote holyday happiness in honour of the brave Duke of York, and the officers and men employed in the expedition against the enemy who means no good to nobody.' Sponsored by the jokes of the gentry, they were perhaps the most appropriate comment on the exploits which were made the excuse for them. There was to be little further cause for rejoicing for some years.

In 1803, invasion became a serious threat, and there was a wave of volunteering. Richard Cumberland, who had once been an infantry captain, took command of a company of volunteer infantry, recruited, it is said, largely from the Tunbridge Ware factories. He was, he wrote in 1806, perhaps 'the most aged field officer of volunteers in the kingdom.' Lord Boyne commanded the Yeomanry. By that year, the invasion threat had passed, and the victory of Trafalgar had put repetition out of the question: Tunbridge Wells and all Kent must have joined earnestly in the national thanksgiving of October 1805. Seven years later, Wellington's victory at Salamanca gave cause for less restrained rejoicing. 'I had often heard,' wrote Mary Berry, 'of the beauty of an illumination at Tunbridge, but it very much surpassed my expectations.' Lady Wellington herself came in 1812, but not until a month after the celebrations. It appears from her journal that she had been here in 1809 and in 1810, taking the same house, apparently Douro House on Mount Ephraim. She made a sketch of herself in 1810, seated on a donkey, 'the saddle well back on the animal's crupper, to give the rider's liver a good shaking.' There is no evidence that Wellington himself came here: his spa was Cheltenham. The celebration of his final victory of 1815 was repeated on the Waterloo anniversary, it appears, until the middle of the century. Headed by a band, a troop of the inhabitants, home-guard volunteers and veterans no doubt among them, marched to the High Rocks, where they had dinner, speeches and songs, and plenty to drink, and returned somewhat less steadily later.

FOOTNOTES
1. Chalklin: Usually given as Kelly, but he signed himself Kelley in KCM Vestry book.
2. 'A brief narration of the work of Grace in raising and forming the Congregational Church of Christ at Tunbridge Wells, Kent', 1743; discovered in Mount Pleasant church.
3. He and Kelley made up the local justices' bench, sitting generally at the Gloucester tavern.
4. He was also a coal merchant.

CHAPTER EIGHT

NEW TOWN

*From a migrating colony, Tunbridge Wells has become a place of
considerable wealth, consequence, and respectability.*
Amsinck, *Tunbridge Wells and its neighbourhood*, 1810

*It presents to the eye a town of palaces – such is the imposing effect of
the view.*
A directory of 1822

While the French wars were still going on abroad, the population explo-
sion of modern times was beginning at home; and safe behind the naval
shield, Tunbridge Wells embarked upon a building boom. In the oldest
part, the Walks and Mount Sion, much improvement and refurbishing
of shops, inns, lodging houses and public places went on early in the
new century, and in the northern area, on land not subject to the
restrictions relating to the Common and Walks but now 'ripe for development', a new town rose.

On the Walks, two ladies already mentioned opened the new century and the general rebuilding with new or improved amenities. Sarah
Baker again rebuilt her theatre on the Lower Walk, and over the well
enclosure Elizabeth Shorey, Sir George Kelley's successor as Lord of
Rusthall Manor, built a new bath house. The late Georgian façade of
the theatre, c1802-4, may still be discerned behind the later stucco
facing and beneath the statue of Ceres added when it became the Corn
Exchange. Like King Charles chapel, the theatre straddled two counties,
the stage being in Sussex and the auditorium in Kent, the orchestra
being over the stream which divided them: an arrangement useful to
the actors, it is said, if pursued by the bailiffs. The Sussex Arms of
today, then the 'shades' of the hotel, was similarly placed, to the
advantage of the smuggling trade of the period. The new Bath House of
1803-5, supplanting the moribund 'folly' behind the Sussex and the
distant and dilapidated bath at Rusthall, is a classical, Roman revival

design by JT Groves. There were hot and cold baths of the mineral water, and over them, says Clifford's 1818 Guide, 'comfortable apartments, intended for invalids with small establishments who might wish to try a regular course of bathing.'

In the first thirty years of the century the Lower Walk, all Abervagenny property, was rebuilt in substantially its present form. The Royal Victoria and Sussex Hospital acquired its splendid coat-of-arms of the royal Duke of Kent and its present façade, the tenant, says Chalkin, spent £5,000 on the alterations. On the Parade, the buildings at the two ends, belonging to the lady of the manor, took on Regency fronts and their present general appearance; but the freeholders, lacking unity of command, showed less common enterprise. The lodging-houses and residences up Mount Sion also adopted the style which the road still bears, though there have been depredations.[1] Beyond the corner at the top, Marlborough House, a rebuilt lodging-house, is a complete specimen of the period. Howard Lodge and the terrace beyond, and Bedford Terrace opposite, are of this period, as are the three very nice houses nearby in Cumberland Walk,[2] the first two by the Amon Wilds of Brighton fame, whose motif, the ammonite capital, appears on the second one, and the third also with a seaside look.

In London Road, the Angel became the Kentish Royal Hotel, with a three-storey Regency front and a four-column porch. There were a White Bear and a Castle Tavern, but not in their present form. A little farther up, beyond the Wesleyan chapel, a group of late Georgian houses, including another bath house (Skinner's), occupied the site of the present General Post Office. Still farther up, and along Mount Ephraim and Bishop's Down, Regency façades may be picked out among much later – and a few earlier – buildings: especially near Culverden Row (now Culverden Street), which still has something of the air of a village centre. Farther along Mount Ephraim, Fenner and Nye had their Tunbridge Ware works at the Chalet – a nice little period place – converted, it appears, from the Baptists' chapel in 1824.

The northern developments began with the new century, and gathered momentum by the 1830s. Two noble families among others, the Herveys and the Grosvenors, sold their land there for building. Most of this consisted of terraces of small cottages for artisans, building workers, and other work-people for the new residential families. Much of it still remains in the areas west of Camden Road (Crown Field), and some around St Peter's (Windmill Field) and just west of Calverley Park Crescent (Pound Field), where the Bristol Arms and the name Hervey-town, like Grosvenor Road, commemorate the earlier owners.[3] The Grosvenor and Hanover/Rock Villa Road development was more genteel, in villas subject to strict covenants. The developers were fairly

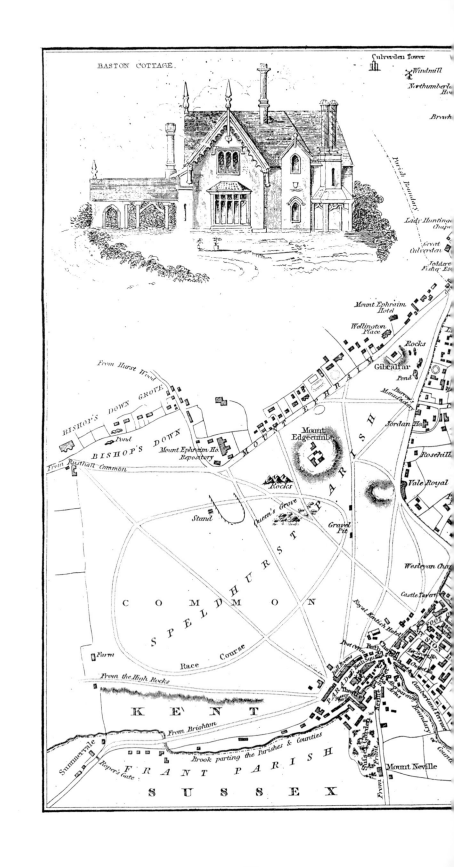

BASTON COTTAGE.

Culverden Tower
Windmill
Northumberl—
Ho—

Bru—

Parish Boundary

Lady Huntingc—
Chape—

Great
Culverden

Teddar—
Fisher Esq—

Mount Ephraim
Hotel

Wellington
Place

Rocks

From Hurst Wood

BISHOP'S DOWN GROVE

Gibraltar

Pond

Barrow's
Manufactory

Jordan Ho—

Rosehill—

MOUNT EPHRAIM PARISH

Mount
Edgecumb—

Pond

Vale Royal

From Rusthall Common

BISHOP'S DOWN

Mount Ephraim Ho.
Repository

Rocks

Queen's Grove

Stand

Gravel
Pit

Wesleyan Chap—

SPELDHURST PARISH

Castle Tavern

Royal Kentish Hotel

C O M M O N

FOOT

S P E L D H U R S T

Post Office

Race Course

Farm

From the High Rocks

CAR D— The Bath Square

Cumberland Terra—

Court—

Mount Neville

K E N T

From Brighton

Brook parting the Parishes & Counties

Summervale

Roper's Gate

F R A N T   P A R I S H

S U S S E X

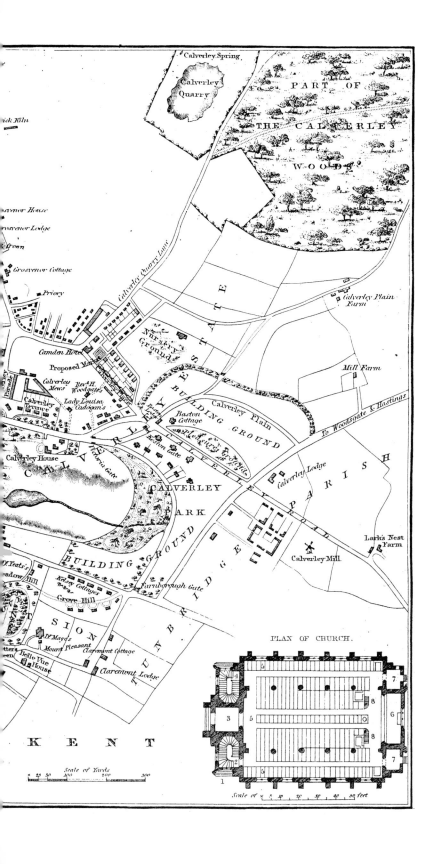

Calverley Spring

Calverley Quarry

PART OF

ick Kiln

THE CALVERLEY

WOODS

svenor House

rosvenor Lodge

Crown

Grosvenor Cottage

Calverley Plain Farm

Priory

Calverley Quarry Lane

Nursery Grounds

Camden Hotel

Proposed Mar

Mill Farm

Calverley Mews

Rev.ᵈ H. Woodgate

Calverley Plain

BUILDING GROUND

Lady Louisa Cadogan's

Baston Cottage

Calverley Terrace

Baston Gate

Pleasure Grounds

To Woodsgate & Hastings

Calverley House

Victoria Gate

C A L V E R L E Y   E S T A T E

CALVERLEY

Calverley Lodge

PARK

BUILDING GROUND

Lark's Nest Farm

Farnborough Gate

Calverley Mill

Mᵉ Yeat's Meadow Hill

Kelsey Cottages

Grove Hill

SION

Mᵉ Maye's Mount Pleasant

Claremont Cottage

Belle Vue House

Claremont Lodge

KENT

T U N B R I D G E   P A R I S H

PLAN OF CHURCH.

Scale of Yards
25 50 100 200 300

Scale of 10 20 30 40 50 feet

local people, from labourers with a cottage or two to professional and business men: some local family fortunes were founded or enhanced – JH Fry the retired butcher (Grosvenor), Stone the attorney and C Cripps the builder (Windmill Field, over 100 cottages, and Mount Calverley Lodge for himself), Langridge, son of a wheelwright (40 houses at the foot of Mount Pleasant) among them.

Upon this scene came a rich merchant and his architect, both London men, with a scheme for a new town, complete with all features and services, and a garden suburb. Of John Ward (1776-1855) not very much is known before his Tunbridge Wells venture; but he appears to have known, and to have had dealings with James Haliburton (1761-1837), a Lowland Scotsman who shortened his name to Burton before his tenth child, Decimus, was born in 1800, and had become by then one of the greatest of the builders of late 18th century London. In 1823, Ward bought Holwood Park, at Keston in Kent, earlier the home of the younger Pitt. He had the house completely rebuilt to the designs of the young Decimus, who had a flying start in architecture from his father, through the Royal Academy schools, George Maddox's office and then John Nash. He had already designed, under Nash's direction, Cornwall Terrace in Regent's Park, and had built the Colosseum, an amusement palace with a dome about as big as St Paul's; and at twenty-three was a flourishing architect with an office in the new Regent Street, engaged mainly upon public works in the Hyde Park area. His famous screen and triumphal arch at Hyde Park Corner, and the Athenaeum (1827-30), his principal building, were soon to follow.

The very successful Holwood rebuilding and the association with Ward proved to be the turning point in this brilliant young architect's career. It led to some twenty years' work at Tunbridge Wells, and to a very busy private practice, including a number of houses in the neighbourhood as well as more town layouts farther afield, though he still found time for such public works as Charing Cross Hospital, the Palm House at Kew, and others.[4] In 1825 John Ward acquired the Calverley estate, a large tract of farmland, nearly 900 acres running in a broad band eastward from the present Calverley Road to Woodsgate and across the Hastings road beyond. Northward, it extended to the quarry from which the building stone was to be taken, and southward to Calverley windmill.[5]

Like his contemporary Joseph Pitt, who was busy laying out Pittville at Cheltenham as a new resort, Ward proposed to develop the western part of his estate, about 56 acres, as a new residential town. Decimus Burton was to be the architect and planner, and his father

Previous page: Map showing the Calverley Estate, 1832. Baston Cottage, top left.
(Tunbridge Wells Museum and Art Gallery)

James, who lived at Mabledon near Tonbridge, was intended for the builder. Just then, however, James became interested in a similar scheme near Hastings, where he bought a valley in which he proceeded to create the new town of St Leonards on Sea. As a result, he had no time for Calverley, nor, it seems, money to put into the enterprise on which Ward may have been counting. The building contract went to Bramah and Sons of Pimlico, a firm founded by Joseph Bramah (1748-1814), celebrated for his locks, and a host of other inventions. They took the land on a building lease, laid it out to Burton's plan, and subleased the buildings which they erected according to his designs.

In his scheme, Burton made full use of the site, with its fine outlook over the south-west, and its existing roads and properties, notably Mount Pleasant House, then a plain standard Georgian building in extensive grounds. He was also clearly inspired in his Crescent and Park by the example of the old town, especially the Walks, the Common, the villas in their gardens. He had contributed five such villas to the Regent's Park scheme of his mentor Nash, 'that daring and highly picturesque conception of a garden city for the aristocracy', as Sir John Summerson has described it. Finally, Burton was a 'Greek Revivalist', in the movement which began in the 1760s. His Hyde Park lodges, his screen and Athenaeum showed its influence, and Holwood showed his special talent for applying the Grecian manner to a country mansion. He was not however dogmatic: Roman and Italianate forms appear also in his work, and he strayed at times into the Gothic. But in general he remained a faithful classicist to the end of his working days – by which time the Gothic Revival had come to prevail and Greek was quite demodé. An amiable, refined, quiet bachelor, Decimus was no campaigner. On this death in 1881, after twenty years or more in retirement, the *Builder* regretted that this had occurred within four days of that of the Gothic paragon GE Street, and had to remind readers who he was. Today (1974), the Greek Revival has received the appreciation due to it; but at the time of writing no Life of Decimus Burton, one of its most prolific and skilful exponents, has appeared in print.

The Calverley scheme falls into five parts: (1) the church of Holy Trinity and the Priory, chronologically first but not strictly part of the estate; (2) the shopping and business nucleus, in Calverley Road from its junction with Camden Road, with the Camden commercial hotel, the market-place, a five-part range of shops with lodgings over, and a row of cottages behind in Garden Street; (3) a more residential and perhaps professional quarter in the Terrace and Parade, with the Calverley Hotel; (4) leading to the Crescent, the northern Pantiles; and (5) the Park, the private garden suburb. More roads were planned, but not built up in the first scheme. All the buildings were constructed of

Tunbridge Wells sandstone quarried from the north part of the estate; milk-white when first put up, but soon to be discoloured by weathering to darker browns and greys, which do not throw up the lights and shadows of Burton's design details, and must have disappointed him. Another general feature was gardens; all the buildings, houses, shops, cottages, had them, many in front as well as behind. He made skilful use of the semi-detached pair, forming a block which was joined to the next, in the Parade and the Calverley Road group, by side porches with a single storey over, or shop fronts: a neat way of breaking the monotony of a continuous line and enhancing the dignity of each block. Burton achieved the same effect in the Terrace, where he also softened the façades with long verandahs and canopies – in contrast with the unbroken stretches of the Civic Centre which has replaced his Terrace and Parade.

The Calverley Hotel was the former Mount Pleasant House, or Lushington House as it had become; a lodging-house to which, in 1822, came the widowed Duchess of Kent on the first of five recorded visits to Tunbridge Wells, with her *major domo* Sir John Conroy, a small entourage, and her little daughter, the future Queen Victoria. The house seems to have been pretty thoroughly rebuilt by Burton, probably about 1840, with a long north front rather lacking in unity, and featureless except for a big white *porte-cochère*. The south front, with a long verandah, shared the picturesque outlook of Calverley Park, over and beyond its own large grounds. Inside, a large top-lit hall is surrounded by

Calverley Parade c1910. The war memorial was not added until 1923. Nos 5-6 housed, for a short time, the Municipal Telephone Exchange.

A Victorian view of the Calverley Hotel.

spacious rooms in Burton's classical style, giving the place, says Newman, 'the quality of eminent respectability so characteristic of its date.' A piece of the original wallpaper is preserved in a small bedroom facing north, said rather doubtfully, in view of such extensive rebuilding, to have been Princess Victoria's day nursery. The market, it seems, did not long flourish; in 1846 the market house and buildings became the town hall of the first local authority, and so remained for a century, until the modern civic centre was built.

The Crescent, then called the Promenade, was not in the original plan, but soon appeared (1830-5). It had 17 shops in its raised colonnade, their windows very like the 18th century ones on the Pantiles, and like it also, a circulating library in the centre, a vapour bath and shampooing at one end, and a band in the garden in front; and, one better, a fountain. The main building is not much enhanced today by its rather feeble central feature, which has lost the pediment that once surmounted it; but when the stone was freshly quarried, milk-white, the whole effect of the sweep of the crescent, the light and shade playing on it, the arcade brought forward from the building, with its white fascia and slender iron columns, set off by the garden in front, must have been brilliant on a bright day – as indeed it still can be. But there are now no shops: like the market, they did not flourish long; the lodging-house-keepers took over, the fountain and the band ceased in time to play; today the Crescent is private.

Calverley Park is Decimus Burton at his very best. Here is the fruit of his training and experience with Nash. There are 21 houses, built over a decade or so; all separate except one pair, all but three in the deep curve from Victoria Lodge at the Crescent end – a Roman arch above two Greek pavilions with Doric pilasters – to Farnborough Lodge at the other; this time a *cottage orné*, which has lost, alas, much of its *orné*. If not quite invisible to each other (as Nash wanted his villas to be), they are pretty well secluded by high hedges and some fine trees: some of the gardens are landscaped in miniature. The park land in front, falling steeply to the south, was judiciously treated by Burton – a good landscaper – so as to blend with the farther scenery, producing a setting more rural and 'romantic' than the contemporary park schemes at Cheltenham or Leamington. The architecture, although lacking the classical orders, is classical enough. Rather more Italianate, to the connoisseurs, than Grecian: solid, it is lightened by Burton's skilful play with deep eaves, cornices and ironwork in verandahs and canopies, and by distinctive features, carefully rationed, such as bow fronts, top storeys carried up to suggest towers, pediments; giving to the villas, none of them very big, a mansion appearance. Burton's success in adapting the classical style to a gracious 'country' house was repeated in his interior planning, features and decoration, producing elegance without over-emphasis or pretension.

There were two more lodges, by the east end of the Crescent: Keston, a very neat octagon, which is still there, and Baston, another *cottage orné*, which has gone. This appears to have been meant to guard another preserve, Calverley Park Gardens, in which Baston Cottage is said to have been built, in 1828, for Burton himself. If so, it was let by 1838, and Burton occupied a house in the Park (see Tithe Award). The Gardens were not developed, it seems, during Burton's active period here, which ran to the 1840s. In all, this activity appears to have produced some 90 housing units, some with shops, from cottages to villas, as well as the mews and stables, four lodges and two hotels, and the market-house: a new town for somewhere between 500 and 1,000 inhabitants, apart from hotel visitors and staff 'living out'.

The church of Holy Trinity was built before the rest; not merely for Calverley, but as the parish church of the new Tunbridge Wells. An excellent site was obtained – outside Ward's property – Lord Abergavenny and Martin Benson the King Charles minister led the subscription list, and the Church Building Commissioners, established by the Act of 1818 to provide new churches in the new and growing towns, made a grant. The Duchess of Kent, with Princess Victoria in attendance, laid the foundation stone on her birthday, 17 August 1827, and the building was consecrated in 1829, the minister being the Reverend HA Woodgate of the family of Woodgates of Somerhill. It was not until

Holy Trinity Church and the Priory, 1831. (Tunbridge Wells Museum and Art Gallery)

1 January 1833 (and some expressions of local impatience) that the new Parochial District was formed, out of the parish of Tonbridge. South-borough, with a church also by Burton, had preceded it in 1831. The first parochial incumbent was JN Pearson. The building cost £10,591 and held 1,427 seats, 811 free for the poor, mostly in high pews. In general, 'Commissioners' churches' had to be as big, and as cheap, as possible; the large majority were Gothic and in brick. This seems to have been regarded as cheaper than Classical, but not many architects succeeded in combining the Gothic mystique with the large preaching house that economy demanded: Burton was not among them. Building in stone, he produced a church certainly equal to its commanding position in the rising town; its size inescapable, its main features, the tower, the east end, windows, buttresses, bold and emphatic, not least the oversize corbel heads to the nave windows. But inside, his gothicism ran astray in a vast preaching house, where throughout its history, the Evangelical tradition prevailed. The columns of the arcade, carrying galleries on the way up, run very awkwardly into a flat ceiling. The shallow chancel, and its altar, were overshadowed even more than at King Charles by a three-decker pulpit placed centrally at the chancel steps. In later times they retreated to the normal position at one side, but a large eagle lectern took its place and still obscured the chancel.

Next to the church, Burton indulged in ecclesiastical Tudor, with a pair of large houses approached through an arched gateway and a court-yard, called the Priory. Perhaps he had a parsonage in mind; but it was not so used. Finally, in the prevailing Gothic for schools, Burton designed the Royal Victoria National School, off the Camden Road. In September 1834, the obliging Duchess of Kent laid the foundation stone, and gave £100 to the building fund. She had arrived with the Princess and her household from the Abergavennys at Eridge in August, escorted by a troop of yeomanry to Calverley House, where little girls strewed flowers in the way.

Calverley Park took a leading place in the history of garden-suburb planning, and set an example to the developers of Tunbridge Wells. By 1840, the two local magnates, the Earl of Abergavenny and the Marquess Camden, were emulating Ward and Burton in laying out Nevill and Camden Parks. The designs for the latter are indeed attributed by Colbran's guides to Burton, but there is no support for this. A small park of houses was also laid out in Grove Hill Road, opposite Farnborough Lodge, with austere classical gates at each end of its road, Birdcage Walk, which some think were Burton's work. Along the foot of Mount Sion lodging houses and shops were going up. The northern and southern settlements were drawing together; leaving however a large green gap on both sides of Mount Pleasant Road.

From a geographical expression, Tunbridge Wells was becoming a reality. The population of its hamlets has been estimated at the time of the first national census in 1801 (which worked in parishes and did not recognise the place as such) as about 1,000. During the ten years from 1813-22 the King Charles chapel's first separate register of baptisms recorded a total of 578 children; which seems, on the assumption that most local children were baptised there at that time, to indicate a population of 2,000 or so by 1822. The number of parental couples, about 350, suggests an influx of people rather than the outburst of fecundity which must have been general elsewhere.[6] By 1831 the census was able to record 5,929 inhabitants, 4,601 in Tunbridge parish (ie the northern and eastern region, including Mount Sion), 1,136 in Speldhurst (including the Walks, Mount Ephraim, Bishop's Down), and 192 in Frant: women outnumbered men by 3,254 to 2,675 – on account of domestic servants, no doubt. By 1841 the population was 8,302, of which, says Chalklin, two-fifths, 3,134, were in trade or occupation. Just over half of these were manual workers, and half again, about 800, were women servants: with 245 men servants, they made up a third of the working people, an eighth of the total population. Agricultural and general labourers were only 400 or so, the rest being gardeners, laundresses, ostlers, porters, coachmen, sempstresses and others; all ancillary to the leisured or professional people, as were, mostly, 319 employed in the clothing trade, and 20 surgeons and physicians. He contrasts Tonbridge, now far outstripped by its offspring, with 3,000 people, only 18 of them in clothing, five doctors, and but 60 of no occupation, mostly old people: Tunbridge Wells had 539, also elderly, but more wealthy: spinsters and widows, retired soldiers, professional and business people, and a sprinkling of noblemen. Tunbridge Ware, the only manufacturing industry, a special skill, employed but 23 people. The lodging house and hotels trade no doubt still employed far more: Clifford in 1822 lists 188 lodgings, with 658 best bedrooms and 638 for servants – considerably more than in the 1780s and 90s. Over half of them were in the old Walks area; R Delves ran several, in various places. In 1818 Clifford described the lodgings as for 'persons of condition', but by 1832 he found the cheaper lodgings 'equally numerous'. There were five substantial hotels: the Royal Victoria and Sussex, Royal Kentish, the Mount Ephraim (1834, formerly the Hare and Hounds inn), Castle, and Calverley (1840) and the Swan and Camden commercial hotels.

At the Royal Sussex and the Royal Kentish stopped and started the coaches running between the Wells and London, Hastings and Rye, Brighton, Maidstone and the Medway towns; increasing in number with the rise in population and traffic from four a day to London according to Sprange in 1817, to eight (four from each hotel) given in the *Tunbridge Wells Visitor* in 1833. For more private travel the four-wheeled 'fly', the open carriage for local excursions and for still more local transport the sedan chair or the donkey could be hired. This animal is said to have been brought into fashion in 1801, at Tunbridge Wells, by Lady George Seymour; who must be the mother of donkey rides everywhere. We have observed the infant Victoria indulged in this recreation. 'The road surface,' reports Clifford in 1832, 'is now good, but the engineering of gradients and curves needs attention, and the turnpike tolls' – there were gates on all the five approaches to the town – 'have become irksome.'

The increase in coach traffic, and the steadiness of the catering trade, illustrate the continued importance of visitors: the first local journal, the weekly *Tunbridge Wells Visitor*, which came out on 7 September 1833, was addressed to them. Printed by Clifford for R Fry of the new circulating library on the Promenade, it combined literary features with local information, reports of notable arrivals, and, as time went on, local affairs. It ran till 1835, when hopes of developing it into a weekly newspaper failed. Two other journals, the *Phoenix* and the *Sphinx*, very briefly appeared in that year. Apart from these, the nearest provincial journals were at Brighton and Maidstone.

The *Visitor* and the guides still wrote up the waters in verse as well as prose. Thus Clifford in 1832 gives a doctor's analysis of the mineral content, advice on diet and drinking – not more than a pint or two a

The turnpike gate at Rusthall in the nineteenth century.

(Tunbridge Wells Museum and Art Gallery)

day now – and adds:

> These waters youth in age renew,
> Strength to the weak and sickly add;
> Give the pale cheek a rosy hue
> And cheerful spirits to the sad.

Comprehensive and thoroughly to be recommended: but certainly not *les eaux de scandale*. The season for visitors now extended from May to October, or even from March to November. Special occasions apart, public balls and card playing had declined by 1817 to once and twice a week respectively. Sprange called for some amusement, such as dancing in moderation, 'that should invite the invalids to be continuously in motion while they are at the Wells.' In response, Roberts the MC tried to revive the gay and fashionable life on the Walks, with public tea-drinking, dancing and concerts. There was indeed a great ball in 1820, when the royal Duke of Sussex, and a large company of sympathisers with his brother George IV's Queen Caroline of Brunswick celebrated the breakdown of her prosecution for adultery and of the King's attempt to divorce her. Undeterred by the official closure of proceedings by Roberts at midnight, and the seizure of the orchestra's fiddles – by the opposing faction or by those who thought that enough was enough – they improvised their own music and kept it up till morning.

The Assembly or Great Room was modernised by J Nash, a relative of the Beau himself, who held musical concerts there as well as dancing, and thoughtfully provided for billiards, as did the Sussex. He succeeded Sprange at the adjacent post office and library. Here the schoolboy Macaulay, most rapid of readers, spent many hours 'in the old corner looking out upon the heath, reading the old novels that lined the shelves.' So, it seems, did Thackeray, coming down for his summer holidays from Charterhouse in 1823, by coach from the Bolt-in-Tun in Fleet Street. 'How delightful they were,' he writes of the library books in *Tunbridge Toys*,[7] after another visit nearly forty years on, and is tempted to go and see whether they are still there; but is too bashful to go in and ask the young ladies at the counter for *Manfroni*, or *The One-handed Monk*. 'Absurd! I turn away abashed from the casement . . .' Here also came John Ruskin, too young, yet, to appreciate the library. 'Tunbridge Wells,' he recalled years later, 'was my Switzerland, and I used to be brought down here in the summer, a sufficiently active child, rejoicing in the hope of climbing sandstone cliffs of stupendous height (Wellington Rocks, presumably) above the Common.' But sometimes there were 'days of condemnation to the Pantiles and the band – under which calamities my only consolation used to be watching, at every turn in my walk, the welling forth of the spring over the orange rim of the basin' – and that iron stain on it.

Dowton, who in 1815 took over the theatre from his mother-in-law, also spent a lot of money on modernisation. Here Charles Kean appeared for four nights in September 1833, five months after the death of his father Edmund, who in his strolling-player days had earned 18s a week in 1806 from Mrs Baker there. The *Visitor* advertises Paganini 'himself' in November 1835. But the epoch of the Kentish theatre was before long to come to its end. Sloman, who succeeded Dowton, was playing to empty houses and forced to close in 1843. Outdoors, a correspondent to the *Visitor* in August 1843, noted on Rusthall Common the young swains plying their brawny muscles at cricket, and a party of young ladies at archery. The annual races, reorganised and better policed in 1834 after 'disgraceful scenes' in previous years, are declared respectable: Princess Victoria herself went next year.

As the traditional amusements withered, and the theatre began to wilt, more serious social and spiritual demands arose with the increase of population and the awakening of concern for its needs. On 21 June 1812 the Methodists, in the flood tide of Wesleyan fervour, opened their own chapel at the foot of London Road (the present Vale Road): the crowd was enough to fill the building three times over. Two years later the original Dissenting Chapel on Mount Sion was closed. In 1833, some ninety members of the Particular Baptists (those holding that only a limited number of the faith, 'the elect by grace', would be saved) were able to build a new chapel in Hanover Road, designed by Kewell, their pastor, in a plain neo-classical style like Decimus Burton's, and costing £1,265.

Five years later, and a few yards away, the Roman Catholics opened St Augustine's, by Joseph Ireland, also classical: the campanile by Elphick was added in 1889. Just above, at the Countess's Emmanuel ('Gothick') John Finlay was serving a forty-year pastorate, from 1809-1849. Meanwhile, the Congregationalists, reviving locally and nationally, went back to Mount Sion Chapel, and thoroughly restored it in 1830 at a cost of over £700, to seat 450 people. The Anglicans for their part, not long satisfied with their new parish church's 1,427 seats, now set about the building of a chapel-of-ease, Christ Church, by R Palmer Brown, which went on from 1836 to 1841. They produced a neo-Norman building in white brick with darker facings, a giant, overbearing three-bay porch supporting a square tower – a bold feature in the townscape from the top of Mount Pleasant – and leading to another big preaching house. It evidently was built to find room for the inhabitants of the lower town, now steadily increasing as the approaches to the Grove and the foot of Mount Sion were building up.

The erstwhile courtiers' chapel (King Charles the Martyr) was by now, it appears, another chapel-of-ease to Holy Trinity, whose parish boundary just included it. The trust deed of 1703 had declared the site to be in Tonbridge parish; but it seems that when the original building of 1678 was enlarged, the extension strayed into the corners of Speldhurst and Frant. Writing in 1797, Hasted, usually well-informed on such matters, put the pulpit in Speldhurst, the altar in Tonbridge, and the font in Frant, and added that the Rector of Speldhurst claimed the patronage, though he had not exercised it. He kept, it appears, a jealous eye on this peculiar chapel, part of it alleged to be in his parish, which included the Parade itself; and showed his displeasure, about this period, at its independent behaviour. Several stories have survived: how the altar – whose situation would be material – was deliberately moved by the chapel minister along the wall, out of Speldhurst and into Tonbridge parish; how the clergy and churchwardens of these parishes clashed outside, at a beating of bounds in 1817; how the Speldhurst Rector, W Gordon, marked the walls to claim his parish territory, and published a handbill demanding at least a joint jurisdiction with Tonbridge (no mention of Frant); and how a Speldhurst boy was pushed through a window of the chapel and pulled out through another, to exercise right of entry. On Benson's retirement in 1827, the Rector

*The Countess of Huntingdon's Emmanuel Church spire once graced Mount Ephraim.
Notice the water trough and street light at the junction with Grosvenor Road.*
(From a postcard c1910)

asserted his claim to a voice in the new appointment. He probably had
a case; but the trustees ignored him, and appointed WL Pope, Scholar
and Fellow of Worcester College, Oxford, and a man of mark. He
removed the wall marks; but in 1926 they were inserted in the brick-
work, for historical interest. The chapel had by then become a parish
church with its own boundaries.

Towards meeting educational demands, the Church of England,
which controlled public education, had found room by the 1830s for
100 boys and 110 girls in King Charles school, still held on the chapel
premises, and opened an infants' school for 160 in the newly-developed
Crown Field; and in 1834, Decimus Burton's Victoria school nearby.
The Visitor in 1834 called for more: there were 1,000 poor children 'in
this place', under 14. There were some 'penny (a week) schools', giving
'precarious and most inadequate education.' There were also private
establishments, notably Romanoff House Academy, a classical board-
ing school in the London Road, so named by its proprietor TR Allfree,
who had been tutor to the Tsarevitch of Russia, and spared no expense
in equipping it 'in a style of elegance for the health and comfort of the
pupils.' No Squeers on his staff. The more work-a-day J Knight, near the
Beehive in Grosvenor Road, taught the usual subjects and 'the Italian
method of book-keeping' at 5s a quarter. The demand for domestic
servants had led to the founding, about 1818, of an Industrial School
where 100 girls were taught the three Rs and trained for service.

The Poor Law Amendment Act, 1834, grouped parishes into

The Infirmary, 1842.   (Tunbridge Wells Museum and Art Gallery)

Unions, under Guardians of the Poor. Tunbridge Wells and South-borough formed a district in Tonbridge Union. A workhouse was built near Pembury (later the Infirmary and Pembury Hospital), for able-bodied paupers: the aged, infirm, and women went to Tonbridge, and children to a house at Rusthall. Here would be shelter, and work for those able to do it, in place of the outdoor relief which in recent years had pauperised and demoralised the needy. The conditions 'inside' must be such as to deter any who could work for the lowest wages out-side. Beyond this, the State of those days was not prepared to go: the field must be left to charity and good works. A number of voluntary societies arose in the new town: for lying-in relief (founded 1818); for providing clothes and bedding, and meeting distress (1826); visiting and provident societies; a Mendicity Society (1834) for giving a night's lodging to vagrants, with bread, cheese and small beer, in a house rented in the yard by the bath house; and in 1829 a Dispensary at the Foot of Mount Sion for free medicine and advice, and for promoting Jenner's new vaccination against the smallpox. By September 1835, now in larger premises, over 3,000 patients had been helped, and 1,372 vaccinated. All these activities were based in the older town, where the subscription books and treasurers lay in wait for inhabitant or visitor, as they had done in earlier days for other causes. In 1818 a savings bank was opened in King Charles vestry, Nash the Clerk keeping the books. Two banking houses, Beeching and Son at the Tonbridge and Tunbridge Wells Old Bank, Church Street (the house, Glynlea, is still there), and

Hurley, Molineux, Whitfield and Dicker at Lewes Old Bank, on the Parade, drew on London bankers.

In 1816 the local gentry, troubled by local vandalism and the failure of the constable and night watchmen of the three distant parishes to keep law and order in the growing town, formed an Association for Prosecuting Felons. The Justices, the real ruling class and virtually the only local government outside the boroughs, supported them. By the 1830s they were holding Petty Sessions twice a month at Stone's office on Mount Ephraim, and once a month at the Sussex Hotel, for Kent and Sussex cases respectively. By this time, the demand arose for an efficient local authority: Brighton, Hastings and other towns already had such. A local committee set up in 1832 noted particularly the need to enforce better drainage. It was the year of the Reform Bill, when reform was in the national air – and of the first of the epidemics of cholera, a disease borne by excrement, and no respecter of persons, which swept over and alarmed Western Europe. There was then no provision for public health. The cottages of Windmill Field and the Lew (St John's Road area) had no drainage at all. Slops and refuse 'were allowed to accumulate upon the roadside and in front of houses, not only to the discomfort of visitors but to the danger of public health.'

With main water supply there had been more progress. In 1814 Thomas Taylor, a local plumber, laid it to the Walks-Mount Sion area from a spring on land leased from the Earl of Abergavenny, free from the pervading iron. In 1826 the Tunbridge Wells Water Company was formed with 80 shareholders, which bought Taylor out and sank another shaft in Broadwater Down. John Ward, the Earl's counterpart to the north, also laid on water from Jack's Wood Spring to his estate. But attempts to raise money by public subscription for street lighting failed; and when in 1833 proposals for a gas supply were made, a public meeting of ratepayers and property owners called for a Bill to be prepared for Parliament, to set up an authority with powers and responsibilities for lighting, watching, and drainage, and to regulate carriages plying for hire, etc. A leading spirit in this was Aretas Akers (1799-1853), member of a rich and influential family which had settled in Kent from the West Indies, who had been forced by ill-health to retire young from a career at the Bar and came to Tunbridge Wells. There he soon became active in local affairs, as a magistrate, poor-law guardian, deputy lieutenant of Kent and chapel trustee.[8]

Some controversy followed the proposals of the committee. There were what the *Visitor* called 'personalities', and a 'fracas' in December 1833, with brickbats and the burning of an effigy – perhaps of John Ward, who threatened to oppose the Bill, as it stood, in Parliament. (He had been MP for Leominster in 1830 and was High Sheriff of

Princess Victoria returning from a morning ride. Note the Tunbridge Ware repository. The scene is at the end of what is now Church Road.

(Tunbridge Wells Museum and Art Gallery)

Kent.) He wanted to exclude his new town of Calverley, to which he was laying on water supplies, drainage, and lighting: Lord Abergavenny supported him. A compromise was reached: the Bill was redrafted in their favour, and introduced in 1835. It became law in July, as the Tunbridge Wells Improvement Act, for 'lighting, watching, cleansing, regulating, and otherwise improving the town of Tunbridge Wells in the counties of Kent and Sussex, and for regulating the supply of water and establishing a market within the said town'. Ward had the right to establish the market on his Calverley estate – and to the market tolls, etc, which were set out. He and the Earl could supply water and lay pipes outside their estates, and the new authority was not to turn their streets into public highways: the privacy of Calverley and Nevill Park, subject to lighting and watching, was secured. So were the men of property: all owners and occupiers of land not less than £50 a year – a substantial qualification – were to constitute the Improvement Commissioners, the town's new government: there was no provision for elections. Their powers were set out at length: they could levy a rate not exceeding, in general, 2s in the pound. The boundaries of their domain were fixed at roughly a mile round the parish church. The town of Tunbridge Wells had arrived.

In his *Visit to Tunbridge Wells* in 1823, John Evans found that 'unlike Margate, Ramsgate, or even Brighton, the company frequenting the Wells are of a select description', and he drops a number of aristocratic and 'highly respectable' names, from a duke and duchess to MPs. Such company failed to impress Cobbett, arriving in the same year on one of his 'Rural Rides'. He had no time for the place or its visitors, and escaped after one night's lodging. 'By making a great stir in rousing waiters and 'boots' and maids, and by leaving behind me the name of 'a d-----d noisy, troublesome fellow, I got clear of the Wells and out of the contagion of its Wen-engendered (he means London born or bred) inhabitants. But the town's chief exhibit, the visitor most prized on all counts, was Princess Victoria, recorded on at least five visits, in 1822,[9] 1826, 1827, 1834 and 1835. We have seen her, with her mamma, staying at Calverley, riding on a donkey, present at the laying of foundation stones, greeted with music and flowers. The inhabitants showed their appreciation by presenting her, on her seventh birthday in 1826, with a combined reading and writing stand and workbox in Tunbridge Ware, with rich trimmings. Colbran says that lots were drawn for the honour of designing it, won by Fenner. Parti-coloured woods from every part of the globe went into it.

The 1834 visit, when the royal party, took Boyne House on Mount Ephraim, was a busy one, with Victoria School's foundation stone to be laid, visits paid to neighbouring magnates, and prizes to be presented at the military tournament in the grounds of Bishop's Down Grove (formerly Sir George Kelley's, now DJ Robertson). The inhabitants this time decided to afford her – a Very Important Person, with William IV in declining health – 'a growing proof of their attachment and gratitude' by replanting the grove on the Common, by now much decayed, with which their forefathers had tried to propitiate Queen Anne. In the following February William Scoones, the lord of the manor's representative, attended by a large crowd which had marched up behind the town band, planted the first new tree – in pouring rain. After three days of planting by various local families – four Delves and four Stones among them – in lines of elms, limes, and sycamores, 550ft long, 200 people who had subscribed sat down to dinner at 3.30pm in the assembly rooms, Aretas Akers in the chair; tickets '5s with pail of wine.' No doubt the plantation was displayed to the royal family on their 1835 visit, when on 19 August they went to the annual races on the Common – 'very amusing', wrote Victoria in her journal: 'Amongst the number of beggars, itinerary musicians, actors, etc of all kinds, was a poorly dressed boy who recited with great feeling and talent portions of Scott's "Marmion" and some of Campbell's poems.' On the following Sunday she heard WL Pope preach a sermon – not so good, she thought, as some of his – at King Charles chapel. The royal party seem to have been assiduous in their public appearances, as well as in drinking the waters and visiting the shops on the Parade, patronising sales of work, and subscribing to good causes. Victoria evidently enjoyed it all. 'Many pleasant days were spent here,' she recalled long after in 1872, and the return to Kensington in October or November was generally a day of tears.'[10]

In 1837, two years after Tunbridge Wells had become a recognised town, this young lady whom its people had welcomed and taken pains, not unsuccessfully, to honour and make happy, became their Queen: the Victorian Age had begun. Before the end of her long reign, the new Victorian town of Tunbridge Wells reached its maturity. The foundations of the old one were still there – the healing waters; the scenery; the air, still as every guide-book proclaimed, pure and invigorating. But the second Tunbridge Wells arose upon new foundations: the railway; the ascendant middle-class; the cloth (as the clergy used to be called), predominantly Evangelical Protestant.

The Queen's Grove c1910.

The Queen's Grove, Tunbridge Wells.

FOOTNOTES

1. Notably the loss of Eden House, 1969, and Walmer and Bedford Houses, 1973; but NB the rebuilding of Nos 9 & 11, and the bank at the foot, an Adam-Regency essay of 1927.

2. Named after the author or the duke? In those days a country path beside the stream, commonly known as Patty or Paddy Moon Lane: she or he was, according to tradition, a dipper or possibly a lodging-house keeper.

3. The families' archives do not, at present, throw light on the origin of these two small estates.

4. In the neighbourhood he built, in various styles, or did major works to:–
   Mitchells, Langton, 1827: destroyed by fire 1837, and rebuilt by Dunk and Stevens (Colbran 1840 Guide). Now Holmewood School.
   Mabledon, Quarry Hill, Tonbridge, 1829-31: his father's house; bought by John Deacon the banker, 1830.
   Great Culverden, 1829-30, for Jeddere Fisher (builders, Cubitts); demolished for Kent and Sussex Hospital, 1934.
   Spring Grove, Pembury, 1829-30.
   The Grove, Penshurst, 1831-2.
   Burrswood Groombridge and Broomhill Southborough for Sir David Salomons 1831-8. Both much altered later.
   Bentham Mill, Southborough, 1832-3.
   Hollands, Langton, 1835-6.
   Bellevue, 1845, for Aretas Akers.
   From list of his works compiled by his pupils on his death, 1881.

5. Christopher Hussey derives Calverley from Culverden, the pigeons' wood; others relate it to a Sussex branch of the Yorkshire Calverleys, an ancient family, honoured with a baronetcy by Charles II. 18th century maps and other sources give the name, in various spellings, both to land and to property owners there. Sprange, 1786, for example, has Mr Calverley as a lodging-house keeper at the Culverden. Barrow does not mention.

6. There is a conspicuous absence of lodging-house keepers in the stated descriptions.

7. In Roundabout Papers, Cornhill Magazine, 1860.

8. Some of his letters, and a private magazine which he edited and circulated round the Akers family, are at KAO. See also Tonbridge School Historical Sketches, 1968.

9. Don Foreman, in Royal Visitors to Tunbridge Wells, points out that the Royal archives at Windsor make no reference to a visit in 1822. The local paper, The Maidstone Journal, makes no mention of such a visit.

10. The tradition that Victoria as princess or queen stayed at Eden House dies hard. The truth seems to be stated in Colbran's 1850 Guide; that the Duchess of Kent stayed there the year before and that Queen Victoria, on her visit to the town with Prince Albert, came to see her mother there.

CHAPTER NINE

RAILWAYS AND BUILDERS

Pre-eminently the watering place of the serious-minded.

Muirhead's *England* 1965

The 'Railway Age' may fairly be said to have begun with the opening of the Stockton and Darlington Railway, carrying the first passengers, in 1825. In 1836 the South Eastern Railway (SER) was incorporated, to build a line through Kent to Dover; and next year, the London and Brighton, which grew into the London, Brighton, and South Coast Railway (LB&SCR). These two companies were to give Tunbridge Wells its railway services. From a joint line to Redhill the SER struck straight across Kent, reaching Tonbridge in 1842, and Dover, 1844. Next year, a bill went through Parliament authorising a branch from Tonbridge to Tunbridge Wells and the ink was hardly dry on it when the railway line, pressed confidently ahead – with probably a wary eye on the designs of its rival in East Sussex – and arrived at Tunbridge Wells. Leaving the easy-graded main line in the Medway valley, just beyond Tonbridge to the east, the track took a reversing, back-handed curve[1] up into the sandstone escarpment, tunnelled under Somerhill, ran over the valley in Sir Edward Colebrook's estate on a handsome viaduct, and through the gap in the hills to a temporary terminus where the goods station is now. On 19 September a special train of 26 carriages, drawn by four locomotives, with brass band, brought together the top brass of railway and town: Major Stanhope Taylor, chairman of the Town Commissioners, and Sir David Salomons among them. There was a 'very elegant' dinner (*Maidstone Journal*); and 'the labourers of the line were subsequently regaled' for their sweat in this achievement. Thus refreshed, they pushed on, tunnelling through the strata of Hastings

Beds and clearing away Bell's brewery, to the present Central Station, which was opened in 1846, with the pleasing Early-Victorian-Italianate building which still graces the up-side: another was added on the down-side later, with a connecting bridge.

The town, whose more substantial citizens were among the country's chief subscribers in those boom years of 'railway mania', was well pleased. The new trains would be much quicker to and from London, even on the long haul of 46 miles via Redhill, than the coaches taking four hours or more on the 36 miles through Sevenoaks, and cheaper. Bradshaw's 1849 time-table gives five trains each way on weekdays and three on Sundays (all by changing at Tonbridge), timed to take two hours or so, except for a fast up train at 9am for the City swells, reaching London Bridge, then the terminus, in an hour and a half, and one down at 4.30, due in Tunbridge Wells at 5.55; both first class only. Only the early morning and evening trains catered for 1st, 2nd and 3rd classes; the 'Parliamentary' required by the Regulation of Railways Act 1844, carried the penny-a-mile travellers, on benches in trucks with a roof but sides open above seat level. The coaches, which in 1838 had been carrying 31,000 passengers, could not compete at the price, and fell into decline.

Meanwhile, the London and Brighton was reaching along the Sussex coast, and arrived in 1846 at James Burton's St Leonards, now a booming health resort, with Hastings, and Ashford – well inside the SER's

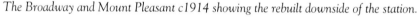

The Broadway and Mount Pleasant c1914 showing the rebuilt downside of the station.

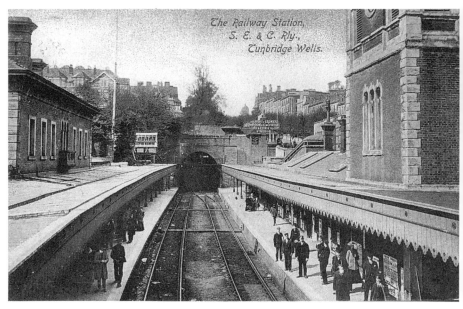

The Railway Station,
S. E. & C. Rly.,
Tunbridge Wells.

Central Station c1905, first built in 1846 and improved in the 1880s. The main changes were the covering of the platforms on both sides and the provision of a footbridge. In 1912 the whole of the downside was rebuilt and the clocktower replaced to the design of Sir R Blomfield.

chosen sphere – ahead. Blocking this with a line of its own, the SER then set out from Tunbridge Wells, through the successive ridges of the Weald, and reached Wadhurst in 1851 and Hastings next year. Unfortunately for posterity, the tunnelling was skimped and proved unequal to the reactions of the Hastings Beds to this disturbance. Re-lining carried out in the 1860s reduced the loading-gauge of the line, and therefore restricted the dimensions of the locomotives and rolling stock which could use it. This was to lead to difficulties in later years, as loads increased, for the designers of coaches and of engines capable of hauling them over an already difficult route; and was to obstruct electrification schemes. The LB&SCR arrived at Tunbridge Wells in 1866.

Railway empire-building went on throughout the century. Tunbridge Wells, on its own account and by its position on the way to the coast, became a strategic point and achieved five lines of communication: to central and west Sussex; to Brighton; to Eastbourne; and two shortened routes to London, through Sevenoaks (SER) and Oxted (LB&SCR). A link between the two companies' stations in the town, made in the 1860s, gave access to places on each railway. Most of this was 'the Brighton's' contribution, a network of country lines with delightful scenery but expensive engineering works, and not very lucrative traffic. Nearly all of these lines fell beneath the Beeching axe in the 1960s.

The townsmen generally approved the competititon. They strongly opposed railway amalgamation schemes in 1868 and 1878 as threatening a monopoly. In those days, also, their relations with the South Eastern were not altogether happy. The *Gazette* and the *Courier* have a tale of complaints by inhabitants and visitors, from the 1860s into the 1880s; chiefly about excessive fares, really disgraceful third-class carriages, and the lack of through bookings to places on other lines. In 1874 and 1881 the town's trading and improvement associations persuaded the Town Commissioners to draw up public memorials to the SER board, complaining of the complicated system of fares as inequitable and anomalous. There were in the 1870s, for example, six different SER fares to London, and the Tonbridge fares were so much cheaper that it paid to buy a ticket to that station and there re-book to London.

The South Eastern's attitude to fares, as its redoubtable chairman, Sir Edward Watkin, Bt, MP, made clear, was based not on mileage but on the cost of constructing the route and what it could get out of the travellers in return; not forgetting, of course, any competition there might be. There was, indeed, 'the Brighton', which had arrived at the present West station in 1866; but in the twenty years between the SER's short cut through Sevenoaks, reducing the distance from Charing Cross to 34½ miles, and 'the Brighton's' similar cut through Oxted, which reduced its mileage from 49½ via Three Bridges and Redhill to 37½, this company was scarcely a strong competitor for the London traffic. As Sir Edward saw it, Tunbridge Wells, a superior place, with plenty of

West Station, originally called the Brighton Station, was completed in 1866 and was the terminus of the London, Brighton & South Coast Railway. This view is c1905.

traffic, more of it first or second class than elsewhere, deserved a good service of trains, and could be expected to pay for it. He dealt with complaints at a shareholders' meeting in January 1874. 'I know there is a difference of opinion,' he said. 'A certain number of people want to bring in the *smaller* people (author's italics) – what Mr Gladstone at a meeting of the Metropolitan District Railway called "the democracy" – and the large landowners say, don't lower the fares or you will lower the character of the place: give more accommodation if you will, but don't lower the price . . . All the respectable inhabitants I think would not advocate our reducing the fares in money.' We may note that the Honourable JMO Byng, deputy chairman, lived at Great Culverden. The town's memorial, when it came, was turned down. The towns-people themselves were entirely opposed to cheap special arrangements and low fares which, as one of them put it at a public meeting in 1881, 'would bring down from London the tag-rag and bobtail they so often saw in the summer time at Hastings.' They themselves patronised rail-way excursions to the seaside and to the Crystal Palace.

On through bookings and connections, the two railways proved more vulnerable. In 1875 they were ordered by the Commissioners under the 1873 Railways Act to open the connecting line between their two stations to passenger traffic, and relieve the traveller from finding his own way, and re-booking. In the 1880s and 1890s, unpunctuality on all the southern lines was proverbial: *The Times* was very rude about it, but not much besides an occasional sarcasm appears in the local press.

In the 1880s a change for the better seems to have come over relations between the railways, the town, and each other, though grumblings are still detectable. An improvement in railway finances, and the good offices of Byng (who was to become Chairman of the SER in 1894) appear to have played a part. The fares were revised and simplified, and new bogie coaches appeared for the South Eastern third class, at a penny a mile fare – to the mixed feelings of Sir Edward, who held the view that comfortable thirds would attract passengers who could, and should, travel second or first class. In fact, third class takings by now far exceeded the others. The 1884 time-table shows 20 trains down from Charing Cross on weekdays, and 15 up; a few in less than an hour, including a short-lived express each way between Charing Cross and Eastbourne, calling only at Tunbridge Wells and using running powers over 'the Brighton's' Heathfield line. There was talk of a winter-garden like Eastbourne's, jointly financed by railway and town, and of a bridge at Upper Grosvenor Road, which was indeed built, after ten years, and opened in 1883. The SER station was extended and improved, with covered platforms on both sides and an overbridge.

Then, in 1888, 'the Brighton' steamed in on its new and shorter route from London through Oxted having taken over twenty years on the journey; longer than Homer's *Odyssey* and with considerably less persistence than his hero's. The Oxted route had been a football of the years of rivalry; often out of play. It seems to have been local landowners and Tunbridge Wells men (FG Molyneux prominent among them), who eventually prodded 'the Brighton', which had abandoned the infant line, into going on again – largely by putting up rival schemes for an Eastbourne connection. In the early 1880s they supported a link with the London, Chatham and Dover system. This did not suit either of the other companies, and 'the Brighton' took powers to resume works, over which it took another seven years. Putting on 13 trains to London, one taking 63 minutes and some others less than 74, 'the Brighton' offered the town, then about to become a borough, with an effective choice of routes, and the prospect of real competition. The rivals, however, very soon came to another agreement, and joined to present to the town a new, simplified but dearer schedule of freight charges. As the Town Clerk, WC Cripps commented at a protest meeting, the astute managers of the two companies had no intention of competing to the point of bankruptcy.

It would be hard to measure exactly how much influence the railway

This disused tunnel and signal gantry behind the Pantiles, seen from the coach park next to Sainsbury's, were part of the connecting line between the West and Central Stations.
(Charlie Bell 1992)

had upon the growth of the town. Its greatest proportionate rise in population, by eight times from about 1,000 in 1801 to 8,302 in 1841 – vastly greater than that of the country as a whole – owed nothing to the *iron* road. In the next forty years to 1881 the population multiplied nearly three times, reaching 24,309. The rate of increase then fell off slightly, as it did elsewhere at this time, producing 29,296 in 1891, just after the town had become a borough – with slightly enlarged boundaries – and 33,373 by 1901. This was impressive enough: much more than Tonbridge, an old established town, nearer to London and served equally well, or better, by road and rail, which had about 3,400 people in 1801 and 12,736 a century later. Elsewhere in Kent, Maidstone, the county town, with an adequate rail service, went up from 8,027 to 33,516 in the century; but Cranbrook and Tenterden, two very pleasant, distinguished Wealden towns with no direct rail services – indeed none at all for most of the century – began it with 2,561 and 2,370 respectively, and ended it with 3,949 and 3,243. The conclusion appears to be that Tunbridge Wells' natural advantages and already impressive growth attracted the railway to it, and this in turn encouraged more people to the prosperity, and so to the growth, of leisure and holiday towns, through the revolution they brought about in travel.

The following population figures for health resorts with comparable rail services may be interesting:

	1801	1851	1901
Tunbridge Wells	est. 1,000	10,587	33,373
Bath	32,200	54,240	49,839
Cheltenham	3,076	35,051	49,439
Leamington	315	15,724	22,889
Hastings	3,075	17,011	65,528
Eastbourne	1,668	5,795	43,344

In the first half-century (before the railways really got into their stride) the inland places, and in the second half the seaside resorts, made the going. The railways' share in this last was decisive. Between 1850 and 1875, travel is estimated to have multiplied by over seven times. The progress of Tunbridge Wells was not the most spectacular, but was more consistent than its inland rivals: in the last ten years of the century, Bath and Leamington declined in numbers; Tunbridge Wells went up 4,000 or so.

While the townspeople had no doubts about the benefits that railways could bring, much depended, here as elsewhere, upon the attitude of the principal landowners. John Ward and his family successors were the most likely to welcome the railway. He had bought the estate as a speculation; and Decimus Burton's layout plan covered many more acres than those he had built on. Still more would be ripe for development when demand, which appears to have hung fire in the first enterprise, should pick up again. They were in fact able to go ahead again in the 1840s, with a new builder. This was William Willicombe, a self-made man, in an age and a trade, noted for such. Born in 1800, he came in 1829 to Tunbridge Wells from Bath, like Nash before him – and about as penniless as Nash had been when he first went to Bath. He became a workman with Bramah, and won the esteem of Ward and Burton. He may well have been responsible for the details of some of Burton's designs, and was given control of more and more works, until he took over Bramah's workshops when they went out of business. He appears as a builder in his own right in Colbran's first Guide of 1841.

He embarked upon building up the easterly part of the estate, with villas in their grounds along Calverley Park Gardens and Carlton Road, the smaller versions (much sought after, we are told) in Lansdowne Road, and the greater proportion of the grand mansions along the Pembury Road (then Calverley Fair Mile), and in Sandrock Road. Reaching outside the estate, he added to Camden Park and put up terraces in the High Street, in Mount Ephraim Road, and on the Parade; all in addition to the regular work of the building business of Willicombe and Oakley, and to various single houses, including a succession for himself.

Willicombe's work was in the contemporary classical, Victorian-Italianate style which succeeded Burton's: dignified and grandiose in the mansions, adapted and modified for the villas and terraces: growing more florid, heavy and debased as the 60s and 70s went by, but generally accepted as the proper form of respectable residence. His business ability and probity matched his energy: he abhorred debt, and never, wrote the *Gazette* in his obituary, started an enterprise which he was not sure he could finish. He served on the Local Board, from its beginning in 1835 to his death forty years later. A frank, friendly, upright man, he won general respect: the whole town seems to have turned out for his funeral procession from Ravensdale, his last house, to the town cemetery on 11 February 1875. Someone not ineptly called him the Cubitt of Tunbridge Wells. 'It may be truly said of him,' wrote the *Gazette*, 'that he found Tunbridge Wells a town of moderate pretensions, and leaves it a fashionable watering place of palatial residences, second to few in the kingdom.'

This, with some allowance for Victorian grandiloquence, was the pattern of the post-Burton Calverley building as it spread eastwards. The two big landowners on the periphery of the town, the Camdens in

Broadwater Down, quiet and leafy, c1910.

the east and the Abergavennys from south-east to the west, had similar
ideas, and proceeded, carefully and deliberately, to put them into
practice. The building of mansions and large villas in the Camden,
Nevill, and Hungershall parks went on, in no indecent haste, into the
1870s and 80s. In 1858 the *Gazette* noted that the growth of the town
had become one-sided, on the north and north-east, gave voice to the
hope that the Earl would restore the balance with another Calverley
Park in the south. A fitting response came, in due course, on Broadwater
Down, where from the 60s onwards, some forty-three houses arose, on
both sides of the tree-lined avenue, with RL Roumieu's Gothic church
of St Mark, 1864-6, paid for by the Earl, in the midst: its tall spire as
effective from a distance as Burton's Holy Trinity tower; but not more
rewarding inside. Frant Road's 30 villas arrived over the same period.
Linden Park and Montacute Road, nearer the town, followed in the
1880s-90s. Meanwhile the Camdens dropped out, after the death of the
third Marquess (1872), who was succeeded by a minor. In 1882 a large
part of the estate was sold. Away on the north-west, Bishop's Down
Park began to be developed about the middle of the century, and in
1890 Sir David Lionel Salomons, whose uncle had moved from Burrswood at Groombridge to Broomhill near Southborough in 1851 and
became a substantial landowner, began to lay out Hurstwood, hitherto
a rural walk open to the public.

This superior, genteel development of parks was to the mutual
benefit of the entrepreneurs and the railways. Apart from Lord Abergavenny getting a station at Eridge, their first-class carriages would

bring the residents and visitors; the second-class, perhaps the poor relations and senior staff; the thirds surely not . . . The servants would be recruited locally; the tradesmen and shopkeepers away down town would call for orders and delivery, by horse and cart or trap. An analysis of the 1851 census, made by a local study group under Dr HCF Lansberry, produces a picture very like that of 1841. Of the working population (about half the whole 10,587), eight in ten were concerned mostly with serving households and persons in one way or another, from tradesmen and craftsmen to building workers, railway porters and servants. The last, mostly women, accounted for 13.4% of the whole population; the largest group in the town, and more than twice the national figure in a period when domestic service was one of the chief – and for women the chief – occupation. As in other watering-places, women appreciably outnumbered the men throughout the century. Over 8% of the whole population were of independent means, no occupation, or retired.

Nearer the town centre, development was naturally more intensive. The succession of new churches and new parishes marked off by the Establishment gives some indication of the course of new building, which proceeded, broadly speaking, in a crescent from the north round to the east and south. In the north, the Lew, Queen's Road, Upper Grosvenor Road, and Woodbury Park – bought for development by the Conservative Land Society, with a new cemetery laid out when Trinity graveyard was full – became populous enough for St John's church to be built in 1858 by AD Gough. St John's was enlarged successively in 1864, 1871, and 1896, by the local architect EE Cronk; a new parish for it being cut out of Trinity in 1859. To the south of it, the cottage development of the Crown Field, the most intensive in the new town, spread back to the goods station and beyond. Across Camden Road the terraces became more genteel and cottages were succeeded by villas, increasing in substance as they spread eastwards, over Calverley land to Sandrock Road, past St James, built by Ewan Christian for a new parish in 1862. In 1888-9 St Barnabas, by JE and JP Cutts, greatest of the Gothic Revival churches in the town, rose above the close-built streets to serve the spiritual needs of the Camden Road area. To the south-east again, the continuing Windmill Field development called into being St Peter's; also by Cronk, with the first and only peal of bells in the town, 1874-5. Coming round to the older town, the builders filled up the High Street, spread up Grove Hill Road and the approaches to the Grove itself, and swept away Cumberland House and over the old bowling green.

In all this, residences, for richer, for poorer, appear to have predominated heavily for some time. In 1879 a local surveyor stated that for twenty years past, villas had been erected but until very recently,

Carolling, a photograph by H Peach Robinson taken on Rusthall Common.
(Tunbridge Wells Museum and Art Gallery)

few shops: building land in the town area could fetch as much as £10,000 an acre: Burton's houses on Calverley Parade and Terrace, once hard to let, now brought in rents from £60 to £150. By then however, the High Street was filling up with shops and business premises, and across the railway bridge Weekes and Paine, who had started as linen drapers in a converted cottage in 1854, had expanded to a large store, between two taverns, the Bridge and the Railway Bell.

Just beyond, the Great Hall, by HH Cronk 1870 in French Empire style, the two wings badly out of proportion with the centre, confronted the railway station. It was built by a locally formed company to supply the want of public rooms for entertainment since the losses in the old town, and included a restaurant and club rooms, and the studio of Robinson and Cherrill. Henry Peach Robinson (1830-91) was a painter turned photographer, who became one of the leaders in this new profession. His large pictures, each one telling a story, were the photographic versions of Victorian *genre* painting; the subjects mostly contemporary country scenes, the models dressed by him for their parts. In January 1975, two albums of his work sold at Christie's for £4,830. Another distinguished photographer, Thomas Sims (1826-1910) practised at 39 Grosvenor Road; and the famous photographer Julia Cameron herself lived for a time in the town.

Beyond the Great Hall, Charles Adie, a solicitor's book-keeper turned speculative builder, put up in the 1870s the tall terrace of good classical Victorian shops with lodgings over, which spread up the same side of Mount Pleasant and closed the hitherto green gap between the north and south settlements. At the top, HH Cronk in 1874 designed

Part of the Great Hall c1910.

Beeching's (now Lloyds) new bank; this time in Victorian Gothic. Above Trinity church and the Priory on the other side, York and Dudley Roads were built up from the 1860s with terrace residences and lodging-houses. Monson Colonnade, the terrace of shops under a balcony with separate residences above, was heralded in 1889 by a special supplement in the *Courier*. Meanwhile Adie, who had begun his local building career by taking a lease of a field on the south side of Calverley Road, was building shops along the frontage. E Waymark, 'drapers' suppliers', established on the corner the large store that in recent times became

Calverley Road with street market c1906.

Chiesmans.[2] Farther along on the other side, most of Burton's five-unit shopping block had become the frontage of George Smith's carriage works, one of the town's few manufactories – in the correct, craftsmen's sense of the word – established in 1845, and enlarged with extensive yards and sheds behind. Here, wheeled vehicles of all kinds were built, from two-horse driving 'breaks' to traps, and the Eridge Cart, designed for the Marquess of Abergavenny, a connoisseur in such matters: a sporting and station vehicle, light, graceful and durable.

On the Walks the Bath House had been given, by public subscription, a portico over the spring in 1847; but Mrs Shorey's enterprise had given way, before the 60s, to Grafton House, where John Luck sold transfer-ware porcelain, with his own mark, and views of the town on it. Beyond it, the back of the freeholders' properties had fallen into a miserable condition. Edwin Lee reports in 1849 'a low, antiquated and dilapidated-looking range of mostly wooden buildings';[3] the assembly room now very seldom used; not surprisingly, its presiding portrait of Beau Nash looking melancholy and in need of touching up. A report on the whole state of the freeholders' block in 1845 gave them some concern, but nothing radical seems to have been done until the late 1850s, when Willicombe took a lease of part of the assembly room area, cleared it, and erected in his customary Victorian classical style the three-bay block, now Nos 38-42. Gradually, the buildings on both sides were rebuilt: gables, straight or curved, appeared, giving a pleasing variety to the row. Nos 18-24, a pair of tall red-brick houses with white wooden rails and bay windows, and fine, big, soaring gables

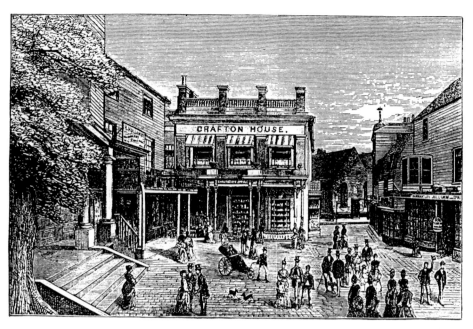

The Bath House 1879.

The Pump Room on the Pantiles, built in the late 1870s, set up to provide 'a place of resort for social intercourse, recreation and amusement', as well as to provide the facilities associated with a second spring.

bear the initials AN and the date 1884. The Swan seems to have had a Victorian face-lift. In the middle row, the buildings between the present wine merchants and the old fish market appear to have been rebuilt in mid-century or a little later. The Duke of York appeared in those days in classical style, with a date 1768 on it, and a pair of pillars supporting the upper storey on the walk. On No 41, the old Gloucester, Hughes the general grocer put up his family crest, carrying the date 1706, which still remains.

In the 1860s the place still wore, in some visitors' eyes, an air of departed glory. Thackeray saw there 'only a half-dozen of children and their nurses listening to the music (and) an old lady or two in a poke bonnet. The band, according to Miss E Hall on a visit in 1865[4] played execrably; probably outside the Musick Gallery, now moved back, on rollers, into line with the middle row. Known locally as the Dutch Oven, its lower storey was a boot-maker's shop – and so remained till 1974. People still drank at the spring, where the lord of the manor, Colonel Weller, renewed the basins in 1865. Miss Hall was 'amused at seeing the folks drink their glasses and then diligently scrub their teeth over with sage leaves to remove the marks of iron.'

At the end of the 1870s, a new effort was made to popularise the place. A Pump Room was built at the far end (like the Great Hall, by a company formed for the purpose), in emulation, it was said, of Bath and other spas. Architecturally it was not in their class; but it did contain a fountain, and besides the healing waters (from another spring), public and club rooms. The Parade became once again the Pantiles – or more often Ye Pantiles – in 1887, and next year the promenade west of the Musick Gallery was extended and built out over most of the old coach yard. The old talk of putting a bandstand there was resumed. 'Quite notable toilettes', reported the local 'Fashionable Visitor' in August, were to be seen any day between the select hours of eleven and one. But the Sussex Hotel had been closed in 1880, and succeeded by the Victoria Pantechnicon, a furniture repository, and by the Eye and Ear Hospital and Dispensary, which moved there in 1888. There were however, 37 shops, etc in 1889, catering for much the same trade and interests as in days departed; Booty the silk mercer (Nos 40 and 60-6); Pelton the bookseller (68); the Literary Society and a new companion, the Natural History and Scientific Society, founded by Dr G Abbott, surgeon to the Eye and Ear Hospital; the General Post Office with a Nash still in charge; Dusts had just arrived at No 1. Tunbridge Ware was still being made by Hollamby at 23, and Barton at 48.

Tunbridge Ware, the town's oldest industry, carried on by a small number of families, who made and broke partnerships, and inter-married – the Russells, Wises, Fenners, Nyes, Burrows, Bartons, Sharps, and

An advertisement from 1952. Little has changed externally in the last forty years.
(The Swan Hotel)

others – was indeed flourishing in the 19th century, in the new form of end-grain mosaic and marquetry which largely superseded the earlier inlaid work. In this process, probably invented, say the Pintos, by Burrows, about 1810-20, thin sticks of wood were assembled on end into blocks, designed according to patterns and charts as in tapestry work. They were then sawn through into very thin veneers, which were let into the surface of the article to be ornamented. There were a great variety of these, from watch cases and pen stands to all sorts of boxes, and chairs and tables. It was a highly skilled process: more than 100 different woods were used in it, and hundreds, sometimes many thousands of stick-heads, glued together and sawn on treadle saws, would go into the pictures, which had then to be polished or varnished. The designs ranged from simple geometric to floral compositions and highly finished landscapes. Prince Albert had a games table made for him. Barton and Nye, and Robert Russell won medals at the Great Exhibition in 1851, and Barton went on till 1902, and became an alderman of the borough. Hollamby, active till the 1890s, appears to have had quite a big business. Several other makers were active at various periods, on the Parade and elsewhere – including Tonbridge and the south coast. Boyce, Brown and Kemp were still working in the Camden Road in the 1920s.

We should note here two other special local industries: mineral waters, made by Lyle and others; and Tunbridge Wells biscuits, made

THE SPA,

✥NEW HEALTH RESORT,✥

TUNBRIDGE WELLS.

THE HOUSE

Has an elevated, yet sheltered position, buil   on the sandstone. with southern aspect, overlooking the far-famed Common, and an extensive prospect of fine country ; and has been very materially added to, so as to render it

Capable of Receiving 150 Visitors.

The New Additions comprise—A lofty Dining Room, 60ft. by 35ft., Drawing Room, 57ft. by 33ft., Recreation Room, 39ft. by 19ft. ; all these rooms being 18ft. high. Billiard Room, 26ft. by 21ft., Reception Hall, Reading Room, Conservatory, numerous suites of Private Apartments, and a large number of spacious well-lighted Bedrooms.   The whole are connected by wide corridors, and heated by Hot Water.

Great Attention has been paid to Ventilation.

The Kitchen is on the upper floor of the New Wing, and all the Servants' Offices are quite separated from the Visitors' Rooms.

THE BATHS

Are on a very complete scale; comprising all the usual varieties to be found in similar Establishments, including Needle, Electric, and German, and also a well-ventilated Turkish Bath; and on moderate terms are placed at the disposal, also of the Nobility, Gentry, and Visitors to Tunbridge Wells. The Water used in the Establishment is pumped by Steam from a Well upon the Premises; Analysis shows it to be remarkably pure, and the supply is unlimited.

A STEAM LAUNDRY

Has been erected, and is now in full operation, and under efficient supervision.

THE STABLING

Is on an extensive scale, the establishment Four in-Hand Waggonettes, or other Vehicles, Mounts, &c., &c., frequently visiting the pleasant drives amidst the sylvan scenery of the far-famed Weald of Kent.

THE GROUNDS

Are 53 acres in extent, and embrace the most charming near and distant views; and situate as they are, between the Commons of Tunbridge Wells and Rusthall, cannot be surpassed in the South of England, and it need hardly be said that the air is peculiarly pure and invigorating.

The Resident Physician is Dr. PARDINGTON; and the staff includes experienced Bath Attendants and Medical Rubbers for those who wish to go through the treatment. While the Invalid will thus find all the appliances calculated to effect his restoration to health, those who are simply in search of a pleasant temporary abode in one of the most healthy districts of England, will meet with a thoroughly comfortable home on a large scale, fitted with every adjunct requisite for comfort, rest, and relaxation.

On application to the Manager permission may be obtained to view the Grounds, Baths, and Public Rooms.

A magnificent Chalybeate Spring is on the estate.

TERMS :—From 10s. 6d. per day.

All Business Communications to be addressed to

THE MANAGER,

THE SPA,

TUNBRIDGE WELLS.

since 1862 by Romary of Church Road, and eaten by royalty and others the world over; the town's counterpart to Bath Olivers.

In London Road, near the Pantiles, the loss of the Sussex was offset by the rebuilding in 1878 of the Royal Kentish Hotel on a much larger scale, with a lift, speaking tubes, and an 'immense' kitchen. Its pleasing marble entrance porch with acanthus motif still shelters the hopeful bus traveller on inclement days. On Mount Ephraim, grandiose Victorian mansions, like Earl's Court (1866) and Bredbury (1867) arose to rival those in the Pembury Road. In 1875 the Wellington Hotel opened; and then, in 1878, with great éclat, including a special train from London for the very aristocratic and distinguished visitors, the Bishop's Down (Grove) Spa Hydropathic Sanatorium Company was opened . This was where the Queen had watched the Yeomanry tournament as a girl in 1834. With a large new wing and further additions, and 70-100 servants, the building would provide 170 beds by 1884, and cater for over 25,000 visitors a year, many from overseas. There were 'handsome Turkish baths, and under Dr Pardington, the full range of hydropathy'. The building eventually became the Spa Hotel.

This, the Victorians' contribution to the water-cure, as sea bathing had been the Regency's and mineral water drinking the Stuarts', had come from Germany. By the 1840s, when the new railways were beginning to make sea bathing accessible to the many, the brine baths of Droitwich and the cold douches and wet blankets of Malvern and Matlock were attracting the fashionable sufferer, always in search of the new and different; and big hydro-hotels arose and filled up. In Tunbridge Wells, apart from Mrs Shorey's venture and a plan in the 1840s for a new German spa at Grosvenor House, there were a few private baths; but nothing on the scale of Bishop's Down Spa – 'a health resort in itself', claimed its proprietors, with its own amusements and amenities, including a 'bijou theatre'. This new enterprise, and the Pump Room, revealed the now residential town's efforts to remain in, or get back into the spa business. There were still in 1889 some 110 lodging-houses, of various grades, but they had left Mount Sion and the springs for the 19th century town, especially Calverley Promenade (the Crescent) where they had succeeded the shops. Many, perhaps most of them would have been residential rather than for visitors, and some for the lower classes. There was at one time at the end of Newcomen Road a 'model lodging-house' erected, in the 1840s, as part of Lord Shaftesbury's campaign for the improvement of often appalling conditions in such places, which led to the Act of 1851 requiring lodging-houses to be inspected.

Previous page: The Hydropathic Centre, now the Spa Hotel. From a guide of 1884.

For the visitor, the guide-books paraded the attractions: the 'general balminess' (Colbran) of the air, impregnated with the aroma of broom and gorse, and of the iron mingling with the atmosphere; the delightful scenery, the local excursions to the High Rocks and the country seats of the mighty. And the amusements? Pelton, 1874, has the familiar concerts, lectures, readings; the ball, once a year now, for all the best people; also recent 'sensations' from London, and 'popular enter-tainment of the amusing-modern type'. Outdoors, there was hunting with a choice of packs, fishing, shooting, archery, croquet, and annual athletic and swimming sports; not least cricket on the Upper Ground on the Common. Here Kent played a game or two, in most seasons from the 1840s to the 1880s. The early giants – Felix Wanostrocht, Alfred Mynn, Fuller Pilch, were followed by Ivo Bligh, the Hearnes, Lord Harris and the Penns; and of course, WG and EM Grace. In 1882, an England XI, including the Graces, Shrewsbury, Townsend and Maurice Read, bowled out the Australians after tea, on the last day, and on a sticky wicket, for 49 runs in 55 minutes (Parnham, 7 for 25), but the match was drawn. Soon after that, however, Kent deserted the town: Lord Harris does not seem to have liked the pitch. In 1862 the Blue Mantles were founded by local gentry and visitors. Linden Park club dates from 1876. Tennis, under its first name of Sphairistike, arrived in 1874, and golf in 1889. Football seems to have begun about the same time. In blossom time, the Horticultural Society (founded in 1836: the oldest in the country?) displayed the competing produce of the abundant gardens. In June, the farmers of the south-east, from 1862, brought their animals to the Agricultural Show; in 1881, the Bath and West held theirs here, the Prince of Wales came, and the town was illuminated. In November, the Bonfire Boys annually kept the Fifth with elaborate pageantry, bands, blazes, and burnings, in which Guy Fawkes and the Pope were accompanied at times by more topical effigies.

Altogether, a pleasant round; but hardly amounting to regular, continuous attractions. Pelton had to admit that 'the place cannot be called gay in the sense in which the epithet is applicable to Brighton or Scarborough'. The local press was more critical. The pioneer weekly, the *Gazette* (Colbran, 1853) was followed, after the repeal of the paper duty in 1861, by the *Journal* (Liberal) and the *Weekly Express*, as well as some more ephemeral efforts. These were joined by the *Kent and Sussex Courier* (Conservative; Edwardes, 1872) and the *Kent and Sussex Advertiser* (Liberal, Clements, 1881). *The Kent and Sussex Illustrated Fashionable Visitor, Court Guide, Arrival List, etc*, a *Courier* publication, reviving earlier ventures in snob appeal, had a short career in 1875 and in 1888-90. They gave a good deal of space to national news; but also reported what was going on in the town, with residents', visitors', and in varying degrees their own views thereon, and on what ought to be done, about amusements and amenities as well as more serious affairs.

The *Gazette* in the 1850s and 60s was calling for a new public hall, pump room, improvements to the Common and the Grove including paths, seats, and attention to the trees, and a promenade beside the road along Mount Ephraim – not altogether in vain; but years before the event. Two pressure groups, the Tradesmen's Association (1857/8) and the Association for Promoting the Interests of the Town (1874; later the Improvement Association), took up these causes, and the railway matters already described. 'The place still does not seem to be half-awake,' wrote Alpha, a resident, to the *Gazette* in 1855. 'It reminds me strongly of the enchanted castle in the fairy tale.' But 'this town was never intended,' declared a defender in 1860, 'and is now less than ever adapted, for the frivolous and the gay' (shades of Lady Muskerry and the water poets), but for 'the valetudinarian, the retired, the contemplative though cheerful admirer of nature, the benevolent and the devout, and long may it preserve this character.' The Holiday Correspondent of the *Daily Telegraph*, on a visit in 1879, was impressed. 'Pony carriages with invalids, the broughams of medical men, ladies and gentlemen on horseback, barouches bearing ineffable dowagers, lastly a grand landau with two splendid white horses and servants in grand liveries, the equipage containing, it was whispered, a Duchess. These were signs unmistakable that we were entering the precincts of Tunbridge Wells the Fashionable, the Cheerful, the Salubrious.' Mount Ephraim he classed as 'among the most typically respectable localities in England. The good things of life are enjoyed there in a placid, undemonstrative and equable manner. Life beats in no feverish throbbings on Mount Ephraim.'

FOOTNOTES

1. This was done to ease the gradient; it meant that branch line trains had to set back. In 1857 a direct curve was built. The old trackway is still visible on the right of the line approaching Tonbridge.

2. Later the Army and Navy Stores before being rebuilt in the same style in 1989, this time being used for smaller shops with offices above.

3. *Baths and Watering Places of England*, 1849.

4. AR Mills, *Two Victorian Ladies*; Muller, 1969.

CHAPTER TEN

THE MODERN JERUSALEM

Tunbridge Wells was a kind of sacred city . . They looked upon it from without as a kind of modern Jerusalem.
The Archbishop of Canterbury, in luncheon address at opening of
St Barnabas Church, 1888 (Courier)

From the *Daily Telegraph* correspondent's picture (see last chapter), one essential figure is lacking: the parson, the guardian of the moral tone of the place. We have already noted the creation of new parishes. The temples of the Archbishop's modern Jerusalem were arising on all sides: in 1889 there were a score and more, nine of them Anglican, without counting mission halls or small meeting rooms, but including new buildings or rebuildings at Rusthall, St Paul (1849-50, cruciform sandstone Gothic, with a central tower and some surprising lancet windows, by HJ and NE Stevens); Mount Pleasant Congregational church (1847, its grand Roman portico added in 1866); Emmanuel (1865-7, Gothic Revival by Wimble and Taylor, with a needle spire); Vale Road Wesleyan Methodist church (Gothic, 1873), Rehoboth Strict Baptist (1851, classical, off Chapel Place) and Calverley Road Baptist Tabernacle (1884, Gothic, by Lander and Bedells). They were served by a number of earnest, active, impressive clergymen and ministers, often of good family, their talents and their own or their relatives' private means devoted to their calling. Their influence, during long ministries, strongly Evangelical for the most part, dominated the town's affairs.

Outstanding among them all was Edward Hoare, Vicar of Trinity 1853-94, Rural Dean, and honorary Canon of Canterbury, in which diocese West Kent was included at this time. He was born in 1812 of distinguished Quaker stock on both sides – his father one of the Hoare

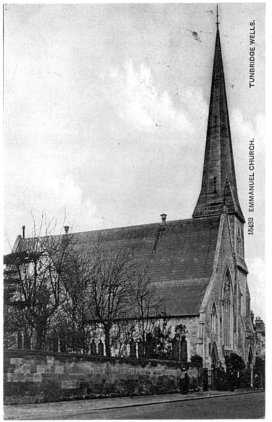

Above: St John's Road c1906 showing St John's Church, the Canon Hoare Memorial, Kelsey's Brewery and, extreme left, WC Holland, florist.

Left: Emmanuel Church, Mount Ephraim, demolished in 1974.

family bankers, his mother a sister of Elizabeth Fry – but his parents brought him up as an Anglican, and, after a distinguished career at Cambridge and earnest searching of heart, he joined the ministry, and came to Trinity Church from Ramsgate. Tall, handsome, athletic (though his health was not good), he filled his church to overflowing, and may indeed he numbered among the town's attractions. It is said that people came to live here in order to hear his sermons. These, long but lucid, were delivered with strong voice, clear style and deep conviction from the three-decker pulpit which he liked because it brought him up to the gallery level, while the flat ceiling made a good sounding-board. They were reported *in extenso*, in the local press, over the years. At every important function, from public meeting or dinner to funeral, he was there to preside or to give an address. As vicar of the mother-parish and later as rural dean, and with the strong support of his patron John Deacon of Mabledon, he made it his mission to uphold and to extend Protestant Evangelical Christianity through the churches, the schools, the homes of the town. With Ward, Burton and Willicombe, he stands among the makers of the Victorian town. The *Church Times* (High-Church) called him the Protestant pontiff of Tunbridge Wells. He was indeed one of the leading Protestants of his day, his voice heard – with full local echo in the press – at the Islington meetings over half a century, at Church Congresses, diocesan conferences, Church Mission-ary Society and Church Association meetings . . . It was heard also about good causes in the parish and in the town's affairs, from poverty and unemployment to local government. He took no seat on the local board (nor did his Anglican colleagues, apart from Sir Henry Thomp-son) but his influence through the Ministry of the Word was all the greater: as great, it may be said, over the morals of the town as Beau Nash's had been over its manners. Each of these two very different men had his message, each attracted the fashionable and the respectable, each expected and depended upon this.

Less prominent in the news, but no less active and beloved, was WL Pope, minister of King Charles, 1829-1879. Like Hoare, who would have made a considerable bishop, he more than once refused prefer-ment. Pioneer in education, friend of children and of the poor, treasurer for some years of the infirmary and curator of the Grove, he contrived to get many things done while generally avoiding controversy, and won everyone's respect and affection; not least his fellow clergymen's, of all denominations. When he died in 1879, 'We never recollect a funeral', wrote the *Gazette* of a town that seems to have made the most of such occasions, 'exciting equal interest in this district.' So great was the crowd that the mourners could hardly reach the graveside. When he came to King Charles, Mount Sion was a separate village. By the end of his nearly fifty years' ministry it had become part of a large town; but its oldest religious building was still merely a chapel-of-ease. After alterations by Ewan Christian, including a new, re-orientated chancel, the building was consecrated as a church in 1887, and two years later a District was assigned to it, including the Pantiles, a stretch of the Common, and very little else. To this day the 'eclectic' congregation comes from farther afield.

We may also mention here TW Franklin, the real founder of Christ Church and minister there, 1835-57; the Congregationalist J Radford Thomson, who wrote Pelton's guidebooks and later became a professor at Hackney College, 1863-82; and Thomas Edwards of Salem Baptist chapel, who composed his own book of 483 hymns – 'Waters in the Wilderness' – and was a popular preacher on the Common, 1866-93. We shall meet others later.

The weight of the town's support to its clerical pastors and mentors may still be seen in the size and accommodation of the churches – even King Charles when a chapel could seat 800 – which the faithful of all denominations built, enlarged, rebuilt, which they filled every week, and maintained, as going concerns, with their vicars and curates, ministers or pastors, very largely by their own contributions. There were no ancient endowments in this new town, even for the established church; but the latter could levy Church Rates on the parishioners of all denominations for the upkeep of the church fabric, until 1868, when after mounting protests (and some refusals on principle in Tunbridge Wells and elsewhere) this right was abolished. Generous donors would subscribe to projects: Jones-Gibb, who had retired to Bredbury on a fortune made in the East, paid for the spire of St Peter's and the organ at Trinity, among many other things in the town. Pew rents – Gibb had 'sittings' in several churches of more than one denomination – collections, and offerings at festival times would make up the needed income: finance in Hoare's day was much the same as in Nash's.

Nearer home, in Frant Forest and parish, by Hawkenbury, was a cluster of shacks called Tutty's Village; apparently after James Tutty of Brenchley, who was martyred with four others at Canterbury, near the end of Mary's reign in 1558.[1] A God-forsaken place, its people 'living in a state of heathendom and sin, and none cared for their souls,' until in 1836, 'two pious females' of the Congregational community at Tunbridge Wells, venturing where the Frant clergy feared to tread, started a Sunday school nearby, in the house of one Baker. The school flourished, a chapel was built in 1839 for £200, and in 1844 a day school was started where dedicated women taught for a penny a week per child, plus 5s basic salary. Eventually, in 1889, after devoted service by the deacon William Damper – 'the Bishop of Tutty's Village', as Pope called him – the present Congregational church of Hawkenbury was built. By this time the Anglicans of St Peter's had become interested, and put up their mission church.

There was a mission field even nearer home. 'We cannot flatter ourselves,' said Canon Hoare in 1860, after taking a sample from 200 families in his parish, 'into the hope that there are less than 142 persons out of every 407 whose habit is to live without the public worship of God.' This meant that 65% of the adult population of the town went to church – a remarkable proportion compared with today's, and indeed with the 47.54% of the 1851 census for the whole country; but he was concerned about the 35% who did not. Hoare himself, and his parish staff of curates and lay helpers, were zealous enough. They ran, we are told, five Sunday Schools, Bible classes, sewing evenings, night schools for working men, parish rooms in the poorer parts of the parish, temperance lectures, a clothing club, coal club, penny bank, a free registry for servants . . . But the most prominent, and controversial, activity in the field, right in the Camden Road area itself, was to come from the extreme wings of the Christian movement; the Salvation Army on the one side and the High Church, Ritualist St Barnabas on the other.

In 1865 William Booth, a Methodist minister, started the Salvationist movement in the East End of London: like Wesley before him, he sought out the neglected and least promising members of society. Now, seven years later, his wife Catherine arrived in Tunbridge Wells in a Mission Week organised by the Wesleyan Methodists; almost a century after Selina, Countess of Huntingdon had received her call to the town. Ten years or so later, 'the new Salvation Army' was operating from a succession of temporary headquarters; a mission chapel, the Calverley Road baths, a hayloft, a warehouse. Then in 1885, thanks to two more 'pious females' the aptly named Misses Wells, who were here on a visit, they secured the old gasworks site in Varney Street, 'a disreputable area surrounded by beer shops, lodging-houses and small tenements of questionable character.' Just the place for the Army's campaigners, all working men themselves: only one, it is said, had a banking account. Next year, General Booth presided at the foundation of the new citadel, and Mrs Booth opened it. The Army was not the first to infiltrate into the area. Others were already nearby: the Primitive Methodists in Camden Road (1857), the Congregationalists in Albion Road (1873), and in Commercial Road (1877) the Church of Christ, founded for 'reviving the faith, life and spirit of New Testament Christianity.' The Salvation Army however, brought a new militancy. The Puritan respectability of the town was affronted at the disturbance of the Sabbath calm by street parades with drum and brass, and people, including working people who liked a snooze on their one day off, wrote

Brick and stone interior of St Barnabas Church c1910.

angry letters to the press. The rougher element reacted by rowdy inter-
ruptions of the evening meetings and rioting at the Sunday processions.
A 'skeleton army' turned out to drown the band with discordant noise:
flags were torn down, uniforms torn off, instruments broken; and
youths appeared next day, some of them several times, before the magistrates. As in other towns where the same sort of thing was going on,
the latter would support the Army in its hall – where 400 people would
come to evening meetings – but not in the street. Eventually, a
compromise was reached in the bye-laws of the new borough, which
allowed meetings on the Common, and laid down a minimum distance
from the nearest houses. Elsewhere, notably at Eastbourne, disturbances went on, and more stringent bye-laws incurred General Booth's
wrath.

The story of St Barnabas begins with the appointment of CR Pearson
as Vicar of the new St James Parish in 1862. The son of JN Pearson of
Trinity, he had a strictly Evangelical upbringing and was thoroughly
acceptable to Canon Hoare; but before long he developed disturbing
'deviations'. The Ritualist controversy then raging in the Church of
England descended from the earlier High Church or Tractarian movement. This had emphasized the Catholic against the Protestant aspect
of the Church, including the mediatory position of the priest, and led
to the revival of Catholic ceremonial. Beginning with the wearing of
surplices by the clergy at Morning Prayer, the practice, and the argument, spread to choir robes, the holy table (wood) or the altar (stone),

to candles and crosses, chancel screens, genuflections, incense . . . To the Protestant Evangelical all this meant Popery; a word still very emotive to many, not least in Tunbridge Wells, where the Protestant Alliance and the Reformation Association flourished. At St James parish meetings Pearson – whose actual innovations would raise few eyebrows today – faced vocal opposition, led by one of the church-wardens, WF Browell, JP and town councillor. Meanwhile, in 1870, a mission church of St Stephen had been built in Stanley Road, by and in charge of HA Hitchcock. Lately curate of Mayfield, he was an example of the 'slum parson' which the High Church movement was producing. He wanted to bring in the men he saw on a Sunday in their working-clothes, 'standing about, evidently without any intention of going to any place of worship.' He filled his church; but he proved too hot and advanced for the gentler Pearson and his Archbishop, who revoked his licence.

The venture led however to the creation of a new parish to serve the Camden Road district. Pearson and Hitchcock were patrons and HS Iredell, who had arrived in 1876, was the first incumbent. In 1888 St Barnabas was consecrated, on the same site, to replace St Stephen's, which although enlarged had proved too small. Pearson had before this left St James (1881), which reverted to the Evangelical tradition.

The fine church (Cutts brothers) cost, without the 183ft campanile which would have made it more prominent on its not very conspicuous site, £18,000, a good deal of which had still to be raised when Arch-bishop Benson consecrated the church. The initial stipend was £150; enough for a celibate priest to live on, but not comparable with the Rural Dean's £900. Canon Hoare was conspicuously absent from the ceremony. His eyesight was failing, and his doctors, he explained, had advised him to rest . . .

The Archbishop, after his reference to the modern Jerusalem, appealed for the unity and peace appropriate to the celestial city. The leading citizen, Stone-Wigg (who had entertained the Archbishop in Hoare's default), was more worldly: this fine new church would be good for the town's prosperity. If this was the best he felt he could say, the *Courier*'s enlargement of it is too good a Victorian piece to miss. The British *paterfamilias*, when deciding on his family's summer holiday, always had to take account of his womenfolk. 'One of the essential points on which the feminine mind requires to be satisfied is the nature of the ecclesiastical accommodation to be provided in the place . . . Woe to the town which does not possess a church or chapel of the particular complexion which meets with my lady's approval.' The Archbishop's appeal for peace was at once countered by Clayton, a barrister of Bishop's Down, in a pamphlet criticising him for not observing several illegal ornaments and practices in the church; and a controversy broke out in letters to the press, and in pulpits such as JW Weston's (St John's, 1858-91) and on the Roman side Canon Searle's (St Augustine's, 1867-99). This continued, on and off, into the new century. Meanwhile, St Barnabas was well attended. Like the Salvation Army at the other extreme, its services offered something different from the Evangelical orthodoxy.

The churches, building new schools and extending old ones – every parish had day and Sunday schools, and some of the denominations had theirs – retained their hold on public education throughout the century. The town in 1890 boasted that it had no need for any School Board to be set up under the Act of 1870: the National Schools of the Church of England were cheaper to run, and received the benefit of a grant and inspection. How many children were still left outside was not stated. WL Pope had his King Charles schools removed from the chapel to a new building at the back, set up a girls' and infants' school at General Murray's old house on Mount Sion, and with the teachers he chose (notably Diggens the headmaster), made them a model to the town. Among numerous private schools, run or visited by clergymen, Rose Hill preparatory, in the London Road, had as pupil in the 60s Robert Baden-Powell, future hero of Mafeking and Chief Scout, who used to walk from Speldhurst, the home of his uncle and aunt – a sister of WL Pope. Hamilton House girls' school was founded in 1860, and a middle-grade school for girls was established in 1882 by George Jones of Emmanuel (1849-88), another active educationist parson, with the aid of a large donation from Jones-Gibb, at Vale Towers, the home of the former Romanoff school.

The need for a middle-grade school for boys, teaching commercial subjects to the sons of the business and tradesmen, rather than purely classical subjects as in the Public Schools, fired a long controversy with Tonbridge. In 1538 Sir Andrew Judd, a local boy who became master of the Skinners' Company, founded a Grammar School there, for the education of poor boys of the parish. By the middle of the 19th century, the company had built upon this foundation a flourishing public school. Then in 1869, after complaints from many parts of the country that ancient endowments like Judd's were being misused for the education of boys whose parents were not needy and did not live in the place, the Endowed Schools Act was passed, 'to promote greater efficiency in putting liberal education within the reach of all classes.' The Skinners' Company offered a scheme which would include a middle-grade school, at Tonbridge 'or some adjacent locality.' This, said Tunbridge Wells Local Board, should mean *their* town, by now much the most populous part of Judd's parish; they had the boys, and could raise the money needed for their contribution: Tonbridge already had the public school. War broke out between the towns, with the Skinners' Company hold-ing the prize (and hoping to keep control) and the Charity Commis-sioners considering where it should go – with an inclination towards Tunbridge Wells. After years of public meetings, arguments, and unacceptable proposals, both towns were rewarded. In 1887 the Skinners' School, a red-brick Tudor building by EH Burnell, opened in St John's Road; a year later the Judd Commercial School (now Judd Grammar School) opened at Tonbridge.

A very different grade of school was started in 1851 by Thomas Jay, one of 150 missioners of the Town Mission and Ragged Schools Society. He began in an old cottage near the gas works, where he had found (by his own account of 1869), 'in one room a man and his wife and seven or eight children and a baby being rocked to sleep in a fish basket. The ceiling was ornamented with red herrings and in the corner were heaps of rotten old rags ready to be sent to the marine stores.' Two years later, another lady-bountiful in our history, of Mount Sion, put down £50. Others subscribed, and a little building was opened in Golding Street, near the centre of the Salvation Army's later operations. Preaching, teaching, and working there and among the hop-pickers of neighbour-ing hamlets, Jay could report in 1869 an average school attendance of 70 boys with excellent teachers, some of them 'ladies of breeding'. Some 60 boys had gone into the Royal Navy, others had been assisted to emigrate to Australia, and ex-pupils who had made good returned to gladden his heart. He worked also among the prostitutes of the town, and with the help of John Ridgeway of Christ Church (1857-71) and his wife, had sent 100 women to refuges in London, and found them jobs in service. Much of his work was what would later fall upon probation officers and other welfare workers. Many of his boys and girls were rescued from the magistrates, whose sentences could be severe: one boy got fourteen days in Maidstone Gaol for sleeping rough in someone's outhouse.

The Modern Jerusalem was not immune from the drink and crime which disfigured other towns and challenged Victorian respectability. The notebooks of Police Constable Barfoot, preserved in the town museum, illuminate the night beat of a policeman in the 1860s; looking in at various pubs, dealing with disorders there; picking up the occa-sional drunks from the pavement; and appearing in court. Habitual drunkards like Harriet Lawrence – 'a confirmed Bacchanalian' (1862), and G Waghorn, a fly-driver (1881) were continually before the magistrates. Drink undoubtedly aggravated the disturbances of Salva-tion Army meetings; but it does not appear to have been the serious problem that London and the industrial towns had to face. The town overwhelmingly supported Sunday Closing, according to a poll in 1881, when the subject was before Parliament. In 1881 there were 112 pubs and beerhouses, and 44 convictions for drunkenness; the slightly larger Maidstone had 159, and 111 convictions.

Serious crime is not conspicuous, until 1888 when two young men, one of them working at the Baltic Sawmills, shot and killed the time-keeper – 'a masters' man' – one night. The crime went unsolved until the Salvation Army captain revealed that they had confessed to him after an evangelist meeting. He had told them that they must confess to the authorities before they could be right with God, and after consulting his superiors, went to the police. The town, horrified but clearly fascinated, was treated by the *Courier* to special editions, with *verbatim* reports, of each day of the trial at Maidstone, and of the scene in the gaol and the hangman's 'arrangements' on the morning of the execution, which took place in spite of a plea by Canon Hoare for a reprieve, on 2 January 1889.

Jay's and other missionary enterprises were a part of the Evangelical Victorians' attempts to deal with the problem, endemic in the growing towns, of poverty and distress, which could afflict even middle-class, respectable Tunbridge Wells, without factories or dockyards, its meanest housing far superior to the back-to-back slums of the industrial towns. Its working class, as noted earlier (Chapter 6) consisted mainly of what may be called 'attendant' labour in house, stables or shop. The most modest household aspiring to be middle-class had at least one resident servant – a status symbol; her living conditions, like those of the shop workers, very dependent upon her employer and ranging from squalid to comfortable. There was always the risk of dismissal. There were also the home or workshop based trades, the dressmakers, laundresses, repairers, upholsterers, joiners . . . some of them notoriously 'sweated labour'. Hours of work for all would be long, and in Tunbridge Wells, shopkeepers were in no haste to reduce them: 'a sufferer' wrote to the *Courier* in 1875 of hours often from 7am to 9pm, and no early-closing day, though all other towns had one. Behind his anonymity, he called upon customers to boycott shopkeepers who would not grant this reduction in working hours.

Beside these attendant workers there were a good number of labourers and skilled men in the important building trade, including brick works, notably at High Brooms, where Adie had the Steam Brickworks and Pottery until 1879 when his creditors sold it off. The High Brooms Brick and Tile Company, makers of high grade bricks, ran from 1885 to 1968. These men were liable to be thrown out of work and into distress during hard winters and in bad times, when building was interrupted. As a country town, Tunbridge Wells had still an agricultural interest

200

POSTAL AND TELEGRAPHIC SERVICE.

Mr. W. NASH, Postmaster.

HEAD OFFICE, ROYAL PARADE.

To TUNBRIDGE WELLS and LONDON.

TUNBRIDGE WELLS :—Letters posted at the General Office before 9.45 a.m., 2.50 p.m., 10.0 p.m.
Delivery commenced in the City about 2.0 p.m., 6.0 p.m., 7.0 next morn.
LONDON :—Letters posted at the General Office before 6.0 p.m., 8.0 a.m., 3.0 p.m.
Delivery commenced in Tunb. Wells about 7.0 next morning. 10.40 a.m., 5.40 p.m

IN TUNBRIDGE WELLS.—Letters posted at the General Office Parade up to 10.30 a.m., are delivered by mid-day delivery. Those posted before 5.30 p.m., are delivered in the evening.
THE BOXES OF THE BRANCH OFFICES CLOSE AS FOLLOWS:—

WEEK DAYS.	a.m.	p.m.	p.m.	p.m.	p.m.	SUNDAYS.	p.m.
*CALVERLEY ROAD	9 10	1 45	6 15	7 45	9 0	7 45 p.m.	9 0
FRANT ROAD	9 10	2 15	7 0	7 40	9 0	10 0 a.m.	9 0
HIGH STREET..................	9 15	2 5	6 35	7 50	9 0	7 50 p.m.	9 0
*MOUNT EPHRAIM	9 15	2 5	5 30	7 45	9 0	7 45 p.m.	9 0
LEW	8 55	1 30	5 45	7 30	9 0	7 30 p.m.	9 0
CAMDEN ROAD	9 0	1 30	6 0	7 40	9 0	7 40 p.m.	9 0

MONEY ORDERS issued and paid, and SAVINGS BANKS open at Head Office, Parade, and at Frant Road, the High Street, Calverley, Mt. Ephraim, and Lew Offices, daily from 9 a.m. till 6 p.m.; on Saturdays till 8 p.m.

* *The Offices marked with an (*) receive Telegraphic Messages, as also do both the Railway Stations.*

THE PILLAR LETTER BOXES CLOSE AS FOLLOWS:—

WEEK DAYS.	a.m.	p.m.	p.m.	p.m.	p.m.	SUNDAYS.	p.m.
BEULAH ROAD	8 45	1 35	6 10	7 30	9 0	7 30 p.m	9 0
BISHOP'S DOWN...............	8 15	2 5	4 50	7 50	9 0	7 50 a.m.	9 0
BROADWATER DOWN......	9 20	2 15	6 40	7 40	9 0	11 15 a.m.	9 0
St. MARK'S CHURCH	9 25	2 20	6 25	7 45	9 0	11 20 a.m.	9 0
CAMDEN PARK	8 30	1 55	6 30	7 50	9 0	7 50 a.m.	9 0
CHURCH ROAD	9 20	2 10	5 30	7 50	9 0	11 40 a.m.	9 0
GROSVENOR ROAD	9 10	2 0	5 25	7 50	9 0	7 45 p.m.	9 0
HUNGERSHALL PARK......	8 45	1 0	4 45	7 55	9 0	8 40 a.m.	9 0
HURST WOOD LANE	8 0	12 0	5 25	6 45	9 0	8 0 a.m.	9 0
PEMBURY ROAD	8 45	1 0	7 30	8 40	...	7 30 p.m.	...
QUEEN'S ROAD	8 40	1 40	5 50	7 0	8 50	7 40 p.m.	...
S.E.R STATION	9 10	2 0	6 35	7 50	9 0	7 50 p.m.	9 0
L.B. & S.C.R. STATION	8 45	2 20	...	7 15	9 0	8 45 a.m.	9 0
RUSTHALL COMMON	...	1 50	...	7 35	...	10 35 a.m.	...
UPPER GROSVENOR RD...	8 45	1 50	5 20	7 15	8 45	7 50 p.m.	...

Letters for Ashford, Brighton, Canterbury, Deal, Dover, Eastbourne, Folkestone, Hastings, Lewes, Maidstone, Margate, Ramsgate, and St. Leonards, must be Posted before 9.15 p.m.

Direct Mails to Hastings up to 4.30 p.m. delivered same evening.
The position of each Post Office and Pillar Letter Box is marked thus ● on the Map of the Town.

The above are correct at the time of Publication of this Guide, but are liable to alteration.

LOCAL BOARD OFFICERS.

(Offices :—Town Hall, Calverley Road.)

Clerk.—Mr. T. LEWIS.   Collector.—Mr. STEVENSON.
Surveyor.—Mr. BRENTNALL.   Inspector of Police.—Mr. J. J. EMBERY.

Postal and Telegraphic information from a guide of 1879. Note that letters posted in the General Office before 10.30am would be delivered in the town by mid-day delivery, and those posted by 4.30pm to Hastings would be delivered the same evening.

with its Corn Exchange, agricultural shows, and farmers' clubs. In the 1880s a general depression afflicted all. A meeting of leading residents heard in January 1886 that 'the mechanics of the town (presumably the skilled craftsmen) had had very little to do . . . for the last two or three years, building having been almost at a standstill, and agriculturalists had suffered from the general distress consequent on bad seasons.' Between 600 and 1,000, mostly building labourers, were reckoned to be out of work.

To the Victorian, with his philosophy of the Lord helping those who helped themselves, of hard work and thrift, of self-restraint in drink and sex, of cleanliness coming next to godliness, poverty and distress, like crime, were an affront. There was a widespread failure to understand that low wages made thrift unreal and poverty inescapable – to some thirty per cent of the population – and a tendency to think of those who lacked the middle-class virtues as somehow fallen from grace rather than as victims of a rapidly changing and unequally adjusted society. There was, after all, the workhouse. At the end of our period, in 1890, there were 546 inmates in Tonbridge Union; about 1% of the population. The local workhouse at Pembury was said to be a model of its kind, with central heating. At Christmas 1889, the inmates got through 650 lbs of beef, 109 plum puddings, and half a pint of beer each, with oranges, tobacco and snuff and put on their own entertainment – more decorously, it seems, than on an earlier occasion in 1858, when 318 panes of glass were broken and 'ribald and improper songs were sung' (*Gazette*).

The more thoughtful saw that the workhouse – a penal settlement in the eyes of the poor – was not enough. Not yet ready for national schemes, they tried local good works and preventive treatment, 'prudential charity', setting up institutions to encourage thrift and mutual help. We have seen that Tunbridge Wells played its part here: in 1858 there were 58 institutions, religious, social, cultural, listed in the guides. Penny banks, savings banks, loan societies we have noticed. The numerous Friendly Societies came together, about 1862, and celebrated with an annual Amalgamation Day festival, virtually a public holiday, with band and pageantry. In 1878 their hall, the exuberant Gothic building in Camden Road with the amusing elephants supporting its porch, was opened by Princess Louise Marchioness of Lorne, who lived at Dornden. The adult education movement sponsored by Victorian pioneers like George Birkbeck to make good some of the shortcomings of the day schools, produced a Mechanics' Institution, which moved in 1872 from Belgrave Road to new premises in Dudley Road, with lecture and reading rooms and a good library. There were classes for girls, from a 'working' class at a penny a week at the Ragged School to the Industrial School and schools of cookery and domestic economy. In 1888 a movement led by two doctors, Pope and George Abbott, started the more comprehensive Technical Institute, in Walmer House on Mount Sion. JAR (later Sir John) Marriott, adult-educationist, was giving Oxford University extension lectures.

For the sick and ailing of the labouring population, the Dispensary of the 1830s moved up to Grosvenor Road in 1842 and had grown by 1884 into the General Hospital, in premises continually being enlarged and extended, with a separate children's ward and about 50 beds: supported, as all such institutions were, by voluntary contributions. Subscriptions and donations – the Jones-Gibbs handsomely to the fore – were augmented by church collections (£652 in 1884) and a Hospital Saturday Fund. A letter from a governor or other subscriber would secure admission or treatment. Until 1877, when it became too onerous (and open to abuse), the hospital surgeons and physicians used to visit as well. Epidemics of cholera in 1854 and smallpox in 1863 severely strained the out-patient department and dispensary. A homoeopathic dispensary, started in Hanover Road in 1863, was looking for larger premises in 1890; and in 1888 the Eye and Ear Dispensary, opened in Vale Road ten years before, moved to part of the old Royal Sussex Hotel and became a hospital, under Abbott. The lying-in and clothing societies still found plenty of work for the ladies bountiful.

To all these constructive and remedial ventures, the well-to-do and leading citizens of the day contributed their patronage, and their services in committee and management. The relief of actual distress called for more immediate help. The Union Guardians, despite the 1834 Act, were giving out-relief (to 1,251 in the first week of 1890) and night's lodgings (16,112 in 1885) to vagrants. The reconstituted Mendicity Society in 1885 received 3,644 applicants, including 866 local inhabitants not eligible for out-relief. To the winter problem of unemployment and consequent distress, the town's reaction took the form of soup kitchens and jobs of digging and stonebreaking. Most of the churches ran soup kitchens in their schoolrooms, opened in January. Tickets for the Mechanics' Institute kitchen could be bought in December 1860 for 2s 6d a dozen at Colbran's; WL Pope had one for invalids; bread, beef and coal at 6d for five cwt were dispensed at Trinity Vicarage; free suppers were laid on by benefactors at the Ragged School. The Salvation Army at the end of the period ran very well organised schemes of meals and jobs of work. By the middle of the century, the Town Commissioners were being pressed to put men to work on local improvement projects, such as planting trees on the Common, improving the cricket grounds there, making up an esplanade on Mount Ephraim, dear to the heart of John Colbran of the *Gazette*, and forming a lake for the children,

Brighton Lake on the Eridge Road c1910.

dear to the heart of WL Pope. This project, raised a a public meeting in 1858, was carried out and passed into local folklore as 'Pope's puddle': now the Brighton Lake. Most of the other works were also done, sooner or later, with 'unemployed labour' and under official supervision; but not with public money: a voluntary fund was raised.

All this was charity, as the *Gazette*, while critical of methods, proudly acknowledged in 1858. 'Perhaps there is no town in England in which so much is done with a view to elevate its labouring population, socially and morally, as in Tunbridge Wells': more money was raised there, it claimed, for charitable purposes, proportionately to the population, than anywhere else in the United Kingdom. The writer might perhaps have added that his town had an easier problem than most, and could better afford to deal with it. The townsmen were indeed continually exercised about it. In the bad year 1886, the leading citizens were calling publicly for the usual help, but also for discrimination. Doles they had no use for: works were the answer. Opening purses, they quickly raised £1,500. But the unemployed, or some of them, were by now vocal, and impatient with charity: reform was in the air again in the 1880s. The Social Democratic Federation had been formed in 1881, the Fabian Society in 1883. Tunbridge Wells, strongly Conservative in politics though with an active Liberal minority, heard about Socialism. The Social Democrats, led by Willis Harris, put on a procession of workless, and a small deputation of workmen, all about to be put out of work, went in December to the Local Board. They wanted the

Commissioners to borrow money against the rates, for financing relief and public works. 'By this here Blue-Book in my hand' said one, 'you have power to borrow "for urgent necessity", and if starving is not an urgent necessity, I don't know what is.' (*Courier*). They reckoned that 4,000 men, women and children were going hungry.

Some on the Board were sympathetic, but the main establishment was not yet ready for such ideas. They tended to divide the poor into two groups. There were the quiet and deserving who should be given meals. Mountain, the new minister of Emmanuel, called for centrally organised penny dinners. The deserving should be found temporary work and encouraged, perhaps, to emigrate to the colonies. Then there were the idle beggars who infested the town every winter – 'rag-and-bone men picking up where they could' and sponging on everybody; and able-bodied but wrong-headed, ungrateful men who would refuse charity and work – such as breaking stones for roadmaking, even at 1s 9d a cubic yard against the Highway Board's 1s for flints and 1s 3d for Kentish ragstone.

The town's local government and public affairs were run throughout this period by a combination of gentry, senior tradesmen, and a professional man or two. The justices remained exclusively of the nobility and gentry. The earlier examples of Sir George Kelley and JS Pannuwell, of Aretas Akers and RW Blencowe were followed by a succession of aristocratic and middle-class men of ample, independent means and public spirit, imbued by those principles of 'Evangelical Victorianism, secularised as respectability' (GM Young, *Victorian England*) which held society together. An outstanding representative, and a lay counterpart of Canon Hoare, was the Honourable FG Molyneux (1805-86), son of the second Earl Sefton. After a career in the foreign service, he came to Tunbridge Wells 'for a few weeks only' and lingered on, at Gibraltar Cottage, until he rebuilt Earl's Court on Mount Ephraim in the 1860s, and spent the rest of his life there. His name crops up, generally as chairman or contributor, in every good cause, public occasion or meeting, especially to do with schools, infirmary, friendly societies . . . He used to give hot suppers in the winter, at the Ragged School, to poor children, and to hand out sweets to them on the Common, and money to needy ones he met in the street. 'I owe far more to Tunbridge Wells,' he said at a presentation to him in 1875 (the proceeds of which went to hospital works) 'than Tunbridge Wells owes to me.' He was a prominent Liberal, sat on the justices' bench, and presided over the Town Commissioners during an active period, from 1862-78.

The monthly meetings of the Commissioners, or Local Board as they came to be called, are fully reported in the newspapers. They discussed the usual things, important and trivial, that take up local government's time. Their constitution was certainly not democratic – nobody's was, in the modern sense, in those days – but they were as amenable as most authorities at least to ratepayers' opinion, expressed not only through local pressure groups but also in quite frequent public meetings on points at issue, well-attended by members of the board and house-holders, and often leading to a poll, a referendum of ratepayers, whose majority view would be accepted, at least for the time, as settling the matter. More than once the board's decisions were thus reversed.

Like every other growing community in times of change, they were concerned always with problems of water supply, gas, drainage, street works: not much appears about housing, and, as noted, they left educa-tion to the churches. Water supply gave continual trouble, as it has since; ironically, if the word be allowed, in a place so rich in mineral springs: the iron was not good for pipes, nor, as the doctors had conceded in the spa days, for all stomachs. In 1865 the board obtained powers to build a reservoir at Pembury, and bought out the two private com-panies. Ten years later, they wanted to go in for a bigger scheme, but a poll of ratepayers turned it down as too expensive. Water shortages followed, especially in the dry summers of the 1880s, when street water-ing – a necessary and considerable item – and domestic supplies had to be curtailed. The ratepayers were duly admonished by the board, but something had to be done, and an extension of Pembury reservoir was put in hand. This, dogged by disputes with contractors – in which the board came off badly – was eventually completed in 1886. It cost £30,000 but was hailed as adequate for thirty years to come. A sewage

Gibraltar Cottage on the Common c1910, one of the early factories for Tunbridge Ware.

scheme was authorised in 1868, and two sewage farms, north and south, laid out; but not until Dr Webber, a recent arrival, had severely attacked the existing health provisions. His criticisms reached the London press in 1864, and caused consternation in the town, fearful of losing its reputation and its visitors. A mob smashed the windows of his house on Mount Sion, and special constables had to be sworn in to stop the rioting.

The 1835 constitution, putting local government in the hands of all £50 freeholders and lessees, set up a self-perpetuating oligarchy; by no means exceptional for that time, but hardly adequate for a town of 8,000 or more, as Tunbridge Wells became in 1841. It lasted unchanged, however, till 1860; though the Commissioners gained more scope and powers, eg in the Town Improvement Act of 1846, which tightened procedure, re-defined the boundaries, and did away with turnpike trusts within these. By 1860 the number of persons eligible to be Commissioners was between 200 and 300, but it was difficult to get a quorum of seven for meetings, except when some contentious matter brought out the 'backwoodsmen'. The Reverend Sir Henry Thompson, Bt, Rector of Frant (1844-68) and brother-in-law of Lord Abergavenny, who was a ratepayer in the town and served on its board, pointed to the adoptive clauses of the Local Government Act, 1858, but to little effect until with William Delves (Lord Abergavenny's estate steward and for 44 years on the board) he forced the issue by holding public meetings. By a close vote, the elective clauses were adopted (1860: confirmed by Act 1864). The number of commissioners was fixed at 24; one third to be elected annually. From 1864 the rateable qualification was reduced to £30 for a vote, but not an equal vote. The higher the rateable value, the more the votes, rising to six for property valued at £250 or more. The most substantial owners and occupiers, those with the largest stake in the locality, who paid most of its finances and were likely to take most part in its affairs, would thus exert the greatest weight: the classic aristocratic principle, generally accepted, in one form or another, at that time. Voting was not by ballot: the voter received a paper from the town hall, put his initials against the candidates of his choice, and returned it – or failed to do so, as many did, or spoiled their papers.

Sir Henry had wanted to go farther, and pleaded with much skill, tact, and good humour the case for incorporation as a borough; but he was twenty years before his time. Not till 1881, when the population had passed 24,000, was this question reopened; this time by the Tradesmen's Association. Eight years of noisy meetings, pamphlets, petitions and counter-petitions followed. The promoters set up an association, with BS Wilmott as chairman and Dilnott Stokes secretary, to campaign for popular control, with equal voting, by ballot, for all ratepayers, in

Reading the Charter at the Old Town Hall, Calverley Road, January 1889.
(Tunbridge Wells Museum and Art Gallery)

separate wards. Under the existing system there were no voting divisions, and the poorer areas tended to be unrepresented. The old guard, predominant on the board – but not confined to the gentry, who were in a minority – defended the system in principle and their past record in practice. Alterations were unnecessary; the town already had its police (from 1835, indeed) and lately its own justices; incorporation would cost money to secure; the rates would go up, and the party system would come in. In 1884 the reformers secured an official inquiry; but this went against them: the local band on the Pantiles, it is said, played the dead march from Mendelssohn's 'Saul' but followed with 'Not Dead Yet'. The reformers put up their own candidates at the annual elections, but could not break through the plural voting system. The press in general, the *Advertiser*[2] in particular, supported them. Even the Conservative *Courier* critically analysed the votes cast, and exclaimed in 1881 that the town was lamentably behind the fashionable towns in public spirit and local life. 'Caste of a most rigid and unbendable description holds sway, and that greatly to the detriment of the place.' The old guard however remained entrenched, until their position was turned, not by the local reformers but by national legislation.

In 1888 Stone-Wigg, chairman of the board and a leading opponent of reform, discovered that the new Local Government Act, establishing county councils, would mean the end of plural voting in any one district and the loss of half-grants towards the cost of the police in towns not incorporated, and would make it much more difficult for such towns to obtain new powers or status in future. The effect on the board was devastating. In a complete *volte face*, they hastened to petition for a charter. This time the official inspector made no difficulty, and the charter was delivered on 22 January 1889. A deputation went to fetch it, returning by special carriage, and the day was given over to junketing, with gunfire salutes, flags, bands, troops, processions, dressing-up, speeches, civic luncheon and dinner, bonfires and fireworks. Everyone turned out, everybody took part; the charter, held aloft by WC Cripps (Junior) the town clerk, was paraded in a gilded four-horse chariot. Armorial bearings were granted, with the motto 'Do well, doubt not' – which might have graced any local preparatory school: nobody, presumably, remembered or wanted Dr Walker's '*Fax Fonte Accensa*' of 300 years before.

Four wards, north, south, east and west, would in future elect six councillors each for three-year terms, and there would be eight aldermen elected by the council for six years. Stone-Wigg became the first mayor: he paid personally the legal costs of obtaining the charter and for his chain of office, and had recently paid for a new recreation ground by Grosvenor Bridge. The new burgesses numbered 4,594 – compared with the old aggregate of plural votes of about 8,000. The first council, with sixteen of the old board on it, contained the usual mixture of men of independent means, business and tradesmen, lawyers and architects or surveyors. The rates did go up, but the assessments were reduced. The total rateable value was £192,843, compared with £36,752 in 1848.

The growth of the general population, and of travel and leisure, brought a corresponding increase of distinguished people, among the others, to visit, to stay awhile, to return, to settle in the town as FG Molyneux had. The names of colonial administrators, public servants, soldiers, doctors, their widows, are numerous on the monuments in the churchyards of Trinity, Frant, Rusthall, and the town cemetery at Woodbury Park. A brief name-dropping must suffice here. Queen Victoria returned in 1849 to the scene of her childhood, with Prince Albert, to visit the dowager Queen Adelaide in the Calverley Hotel and, if Colbran is right, her mother at Eden House.[3] They brought with them another widowed queen, Marie Amélie of France, who had escaped to England from the 1848 Revolution, with her husband King Louis Philippe, under the guise of Mr and Mrs Smith.[4] Taken with the quiet gentility of the place, she came later to spend some years at Chancellor House, with her suite. Queen Victoria however did not return, except once to spend Boxing Day, 1876, with her daughter Princess Louise and her husband the Marquess of Lorne, at Dornden. The Prince of Wales's visit in 1881 has been mentioned: he used also to stay at Eridge. Other royal persons, and statemen, passed this way.

Macaulay, Thackeray, and Ruskin, the childhood visitors of earlier days, all came again later: Macaulay in July 1855, where he wrote to Mr Ellis from a house 'in a delightful situation – the heath is close to the door;' and revised his speeches for publication. Ruskin came the following year, to lecture on iron to a crowded assembly room at the Sussex. Recalling how he used to watch the water welling up in the Pantiles spring, and staining the basin, he moved into his subject with the remark which appears at the head of Chapter 3. Thackeray came in 1860 with his parents and his children, to stay at the house just below Mount Ephraim known today as Thackeray's House, where he wrote *Tunbridge Toys* from which we have earlier quoted (Chapter 8). The boys, he noted, still rode by on the hacks of Thomas Cramp, riding-master, as it used to be in the reign of George IV – the firm was to continue until the end of the century. On the Common, he surveys 'the beautiful purple hills beyond, twinkling with a thousand villas which have sprung up over this charming ground since first I saw it'. Among the many lecturers and preachers, besides the Booths, came CH Spurgeon, Moody of Moody and Sankey the American Revivalists, Annie Besant, and John Cummings (1802-81), Scottish church minister of Covent Garden, author of a hundred tracts and books, to deliver anti-papal lectures and keep bees (about which he wrote a classic) at his summer retreat, The Cottage, on the Common. F Brandram gave readings from Shakespeare; Patti and Sims Reeves came to sing; and JL Toole and George Grossmith to act in sketches. The town was not too serious-minded to enjoy the D'Oyly Carte company in Gilbert and Sullivan opera, though there was no adequate theatre. The Ben Greet Players visited the Spa. Sir Frank Benson, also to become famous with his touring Shakespeare company, was born at Eden House in December 1858.

The scenery does not appear to have specially interested any of the greater landscape artists of the Romantic period, but three members of a local family recorded it very pleasantly. The eldest, Joseph Josiah Dodd (1810-75?), produced in 1835 a volume of local watercolours which was presented to Princess Victoria on her visit that year; and with Thomas Wise illustrated Britton's book on the new town of 1832. He then went off to roam and paint, eventually ending his days, it appears, in Russia. Very different was his younger brother, Charles Tattershall Dodd (1815-78), who spent most of his life as drawing master of Tonbridge School and as one of the serious citizens of Tunbridge Wells, where he came to settle at Grosvenor Lodge and to be

The band pavilion, built in 1926 in Calverley Grounds, seated 1,200 under cover and another 1,200 outside. Destroyed by a firebomb in 1940.

the ardent secretary of the Temperance Society. He illustrated Colbran's 1839 guide, and frequently exhibited at the Royal Academy and elsewhere. His son, CT Dodd junior (1861-1951), travelled more widely but later followed his father to Tonbridge School (1904-27). He also exhibited regularly and helped to found the Royal Tunbridge Wells Art Club in the 1930s. The Town Hall and Museum have collections of the Dodds' local work. Horace and James Smith, authors of *Rejected Addresses*, lived at Mount Edgecumbe Cottage. Two famous engineers spent their later days here: Sir William Siemens, FRS, electrician and steel furnace inventor, who lived at Sherwood in the Pembury Road, where he generated electricity by steam and experimented with plants, from 1874 to his death in 1883; and his near neighbour Sir Morton Peto, Bt, maker of railways, who died at Blackhurst in 1889, aged 80. Neither of these took part in local affairs; nor did the celebrated Sir David Salomons Bt of Broomhill: his son who did, belongs to the next chapter.

FOOTNOTES

1. T. Timpson, *Church History*, 1859.

2. See its editor's (RHM Clements), *A Peep into the Past: The Jubilee of the Incorporation of Royal Tunbridge Wells*, 1938.

3. Don Foreman, in *Royal Visitors to Tunbridge Wells*, states that the Queen's mother, the Duchess of Kent, was not in town at the time.

4. Again Foreman claims that Marie Amélie and Louis Philippe were in town the day before and did not therefore accompany Victoria and Albert.

CHAPTER ELEVEN

ROYAL TUNBRIDGE WELLS

The town had grown in elegance, in beauty, and in wealth. He did not think any town in England could compare with it.

Alderman J Stone-Wigg, at a banquet in his honour, 1887

In that it is builded upon hills, Tunbridge Wells is like Rome, and in that its fashionable promenade is under the limes, like Berlin; but in other respects it is merely a provincial English inland pleasure town with a past.

EV Lucas, *Highways and Byways in Sussex*, 1904

The incorporation of the town coincided with a general opening-out of the scope and responsibilities of local government. It was an epoch of reform and of political activity, a new look at many institutions which appeared to need attention, and many new things which appeared possible to do and needing to be done.

In the town's concern with such matters it is possible to discern, if not too precisely, three phases. The first may be seen to run up to 1902, the year (incidentally) of the accession of King Edward VII. In this twelve years or so the town, influenced by some new men in Council with progressive views, but more, perhaps, by the pride of a new borough, adopts a forward policy: the town wakes up. In the second period, from the end of 1902 to about 1911, this proves too fast and a reaction sets in though efforts continue to keep the town awake; in 1909, the title, Royal Tunbridge Wells, recognises the long connection with royalty, its civic pride, and its Edwardian social tone. After this, the third period seems rather an anti-climax, with national political questions overshadowing local ones: the local electors become apathetic.

We have noticed earlier some signs among liberal-minded citizens and among the traders and hoteliers, of dissatisfaction with the town's complacency. In the closing years of the century this became more vocal. In 1890 the town's hoteliers combined to call on the Council for more amusements and amenities. The attractions of the continental spas and watering-places, patronised by Edward the prince and future king, were becoming well-known among the followers of fashion. Resorts at home could not compete, wrote the publicist George R Sims, simply because they were too dull, especially in winter. As for the Wells, the illustrated society journal *The King*, remembering how its former notorious gaiety had been dis-creetly forgotten in the Victorian epoch, remarked that 'if one were asked to draw a comparison between Tunbridge Wells and a continental resort, it might be said that whereas the latter offers every facility for passing this life agreeably, Tunbridge Wells has offered equal facilities for agreeably passing the next.' This itself appeared to be long in coming: people never died here, declared the *Courier* later, except of *ennui*.

The new Council began, sensibly, by using powers sought by their predecessors and just obtained in the Improvement Act, 1890. They funded their debt and raised capital by the issue of £126,000 Corporation Stock – one of the first of the new boroughs, apparently to do so. They also took over the Grove, and a major share in managing the Common. The four Grove trustees, set up by the gift of 1703, had not been conspicuously interested in the place. Then in 1863, WL Pope was appointed curator by two functioning trustees, the Earl of Abergavenny and Hussey of Scotney Castle, and set about clearing away dead and dying trees and planting new ones, and tidying-up the footpaths.[1]

The Common, 'aptly described,' said Scoones, one of the manor stewards, 'as being of the same importance to Tunbridge Wells as the sea is to Hastings and Brighton', had become a place not only for grazing, walks, cricket, circuses, open-air meetings, bonfires, and the burning of gorse on festive occasions, but also for driving vehicles all over the place, the digging of marl and turf, hanging out clothes, beating carpets, tipping rubbish, and other unauthorised doings. There were complaints and disputes over rights, involving the lord of the manor, the freeholders and the local authority (eg the enclosure of St Helena cottage) and demands for trees to be planted and shelters provided. A new Rusthall Manor Act of 1863 had required a register to be kept of all freeholders and persons claiming rights there, and empowered the lord and freeholders to make bye-laws; but this had not proved effective. The Queen's Grove of 1835 had not grown very well; more trees were needed there and elsewhere. Some concerted planting, by voluntary contributors (Molyneux, Stone-Wigg, and others) and, it appears, by labour recruited from the unemployed, was done in 1869, and a 'Charter Group' was planted in 1889. Commemorative planting, and gifts by the Marquess of Abergavenny and others, have changed the face of the Common from bare heath to wooded landscape.

The periodical water crisis soon arose. The confident predictions about the works of 1886 were already proved false by 1893, when a consulting engineer (Mansergh) had to be called in. He criticised the whole Pembury-Blackhurst-Tangiers collection system as fundamentally inadequate, and much preferred the original alternative of collecting, in the Groombridge area, water from Ashdown Forest. Mindful of past rebuffs from the rate-payers, the Council staged a public meeting; and found them, predictably, both critical of the present situation and horrified at the expense of the Ashdown proposals. Rumours reached the London press, and put off potential visitors. Was it true, wrote a retired major-general, that the reservoir had burst, and polluted the water? At this point, a private company, the Mid Kent, offered to supply water from artesian wells. Had there been a Ratepayers' League then, they would have seen in this the solution; but the Council, inspired by Councillor Putland, decided to try a deep bore themselves, at Pembury; and to the universal relief, it proved successful. A filter plant was put in, more wells were sunk in the years following, and the situation was saved – for the time.

In 1894 the Council had, or received, another inspiration; to go outside their membership and call in as mayor for the year from November 1894-5 the city man, engineer, electrician, photographer and Jewish baronet Sir David Lionel Salomons (1851-1925). His uncle Sir David (1797-1873), of Burrswood and Broomhill, came of a rich mercantile and commercial family, which had come to England in the early 18th century. He was the first Jew to become – the legal obstacles being successively and not without difficulty cleared away for him – JP, High Sheriff and deputy Lieutenant of Kent, Alderman of the City of London, MP, and Lord Mayor of London: he became a baronet in 1869. His nephew followed him in the baronetcy, and was chairman of the County of London Electricity Company, member of the council of the Institution of Electrical Engineers, director of the SER and master of the Cutlers' Company. Continuing also his uncle's alterations to Broomhill, he added a water-tower with a celestial telescope on top, a huge wing of workshops built mostly of brick and stone from the estate, and there constructed a theatre for experiments, and the largest electro-magnet and electric organ then known. His household had electric light, telephones, irons, sewing machines, long before anyone else. His astonishing and monumental stable-block, overshadowing the house, came to contain the 'horseless carriages, of which he was a pioneer, as well as 'the perfect machine for transport – I mean, of course, the horse.'

The stables at Broomhill,
once home of Sir David
Salomons.
(Charlie Bell 1990)

Clearly a man of outstanding energy and achievement, and not one to do things by halves, the new Mayor set about galvanising and advertising the town. Three hundred guests, including the Lord Mayor and sheriffs of London and many distinguished people, sat down to his inaugural banquet at the Great Hall.[2] Then, under his electrifying influence, the Council embarked upon municipal trading. In 1890, a private electricity company, the South of England, was already canvassing the area, but the Council were unwilling to grant a monopoly, and the company withdrew. Some, including Col TJ Holland of Mount Ephraim House, saw no great need yet for town electricity. The Council were persuaded otherwise, and set up a *public* monopoly. They raised a loan, built a power station by Grosvenor Bridge, and in Salomons' mayoralty had the mains laid in the central area of the town, and in London Road and the Pantiles. In October he and his wife inaugurated the system by driving in procession – and in one of the new-fangled horseless carriages – from the power station to a well-publicised electricity exhibition, which overflowed the Town Hall in Calverley Road.

The streets were decorated and the coloured lights in Mount Pleasant were 'entrancing'. At sixpence a unit the price of the new light rivalled that of gas, and by 1897 the profits enabled the rates to be reduced by a penny. So much for Colonel Holland; but he was biding his time.

A few days after the electricity show, Sir David on 15 October 1895 crowned his mayoralty with another exhibition, of horseless carriages – the first motor show in England, and at Tunbridge Wells! Undeterred by the Act of 1865, which limited the speed of road locomotives (steam traction engines at that time) to 4mph – 2mph in towns – and required them to be in charge of three men, one of them going in front with a red flag and a trumpet, Salomons had the show in the Agricultural Show-ground (part of the present Showfields Estate). Before a galaxy of distinguished persons and a vast crowd, many brought in by excursion trains, Sir David's Peugeot, said to be capable of 15mph, the Honourable Evelyn Ellis' Panhard-Levassor, a motor victoria, a De Dion et Bouton barouche, and three tricycles, all French (as most new motors were) ran a chequered career round the field. The Volunteer Steam Fire Brigade

The Winter Garden and Aquarium that never was, in the Crystal Palace manner.
(Tunbridge Wells Museum and Art Gallery)

put on a competition between their engine and a Daimler petrol tender. Then, quite illegally (but had not the borough its own police?) the show finished off with a real run to the railway station, through the crowds and in a shower of rain. The London daily papers reported fully. The local *Courier* – which had become out of humour with this spectacular mayor – thought the show less attractive than other shows could be, but had no doubts that the new motors had come to stay. Refusing a further term, Sir David then retired, though not into obscurity. It was during this *annus mirabilis* (*pace* the *Courier*) also that the tree-planting above mentioned took place on the Common, the Nevill Cricket, Football, and Athletic Company was formed to make a new ground, and the Council bought from the Calverley Estate the land on which the Technical Institute, the indoor swimming baths, and, years later, the present Civic Centre were to be built.

Sir David began 1897, the year of Queen Victoria's Diamond Jubilee, by promising to give Southborough a theatre – the Victoria Hall. Tunbridge Wells was debating how it should celebrate – better

than in 1887, hoped the *Courier*. They were not wanting in new proposals, and some old ones were brought out and groomed. The public library, a runner scratched in 1889, was now it seemed, accepted – in principle at least, for the town decided, also in 1895, to adopt the permissive Act – though there were years to wait yet. The winter garden project turned up again: on the Calverley Grounds, or by Warwick Park, with rustic walks and fountains – as Benge Burr had suggested long ago – leading to a fine glass pavilion like Bournemouth's? Or a theatre? The Great Hall was clearly inadequate; no leading companies now came. Through the efforts of the Improvement Association, a company was formed in June 1897 and a site fixed upon above Monson Road for 'Her Majesty's Opera House' – a title preferred to that of theatre, which Canon Hoare, it was said, would not have approved. He had in fact died, aged 87 and blind, but still at work, three years before; to the deep grief of the whole town. In the jubilee year a memorial to him, in the form of a Gothic cross with a plaque-portrait, by John Oldrid Scott, was unveiled at the entrance to the new Culverden Park.

The winter garden, the fountain, the Calverley grounds ideas went back into the files. The object finally chosen for public commemoration of the 1897 Jubilee was the building of a children's wing and enlargement of the General Hospital, then in Grosvenor/Goods Station Roads. Sir David Salomons came in again with £1,000, and later, one of the new X-Ray units; but he cast serious doubts on the whole financing and management of the institution; with good reason, as an independent report confirmed, and it was not until 1904 that the new buildings, by Percy Adams (part of them still standing) were opened. In the same year the Homoeopathic Hospital, in which two Quaker doctors, F Nield and his daughter Edith took a leading part, moved to a new building by CH Strange in Church Road.

The Opera House was opened in 1902; a decorative, green-domed Edwardian building by JP Briggs, occupying a large block at the top of Mount Pleasant, with bank, shops and offices outside and a theatre within. A flourish of leading artistes and companies began its career. Paderewski came (not his first, or last visit), and in due course and among others Clara Butt, Melba, Martin Harvey, Mrs Patrick Campbell, Julia Neilson and Fred Terry; mostly on 'flying matinees', followed in the evenings with Benson's Shakespeare company and others on tour, playing such popular favourites as *Floradora*, the *Chocolate Soldier*, the *Merry Widow*. The Great Hall still offered one-man shows by such as Backhaus, Mischa Elman and Albert Chevalier.

Meanwhile, the Nevill athletic ground was opened in 1898 and Kent County Cricket Club found it good enough in 1901 for a resumed annual cricket week, in June. This and the succeeding Agricultural

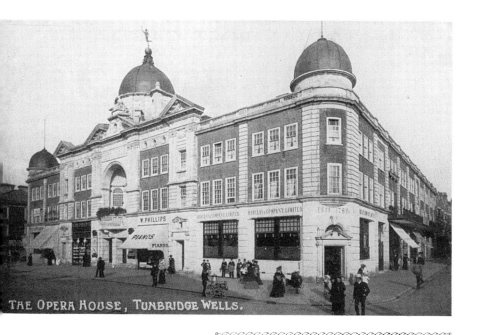

THE OPERA HOUSE, TUNBRIDGE WELLS.

Above: The Opera House c1910. So called to avoid offending the sensibilities of the town by calling it a theatre. The statue on the dome is long gone.

Right: An advertisement for the Opera House from a guide of 1928.

The

OPERA HOUSE

ROYAL TUNBRIDGE WELLS

General Manager - - Mr. W. GRIFFITHS

The Fashionable Resort for Residents and Visitors.

Situated in the Centre of the Town.

Visited by all the

Principal West End Companies

For times of Performances, see local announcements.

Bookings for 1928 include—

Sir Frank Benson's Co.; The Acquittal (with Godfrey Tearle); Potiphar's Wife; Quest; Sunny; The Wrecker; Up with the Lark; Lady Luck; The Terror; Thark; The Silent House; The Constant Nymph; Desert Song; The Co-Optimists "A" Co.; Yellow Sands; etc., etc.

High - Class LOUNGE
(Fully Licensed)

BOX OFFICE — ('Phone T. W. 456).
OPEN DAILY — 10.30 a.m. to 4 p.m.

NOTE—All Omnibus Services stop at the Front Entrance to the Theatre.

show made a gala occasion. The town would not run, as some on the Tradesmen's Association wanted, to a carnival and battle of flowers; but there were decorations, the Opera House put on something special, and Alan MacKinnon, with a high-class amateur company, emulated the Canterbury 'Old Stagers' on the last night of cricket week. The first *Official Guide* came out in 1902, and JRF Lutwidge – three times mayor, man of good family and culture, one of the last, by now, of the wealthy, paternal citizens of the town – put on a firework display to celebrate King Edward's coronation.

When incorporation was being discussed, its opponents feared that it would be followed by the intrusion of party politics. This proved to be so, but in a moderate form – as it has remained Conservative, but included Liberal members. In addition, though not until 1896-7 a handful of Social-Democrats and Fabians secured seats for a time, mostly for the working-class East Ward. David Geer, a paperhanger, seems to have been the first, followed by F Lawson Dodd, dentist brother of C Tattershall Dodd, and HC Lander, an architect and Fabian. Another Labour Councillor, W Bournes, became the first working-man to become a JP (1904).

The climax, and the downfall, of the forward policy came with the telephone undertaking of 1900-02. A private company, the National Telephone Company, had bought out an earlier one and operated a small system from 1896. Its progress did not satisfy the Tradesmen's Association, two of whose members, RA Robinson (later to become Sir Ralph Robinson, chairman of the London County Council) and Alfred Nicholson, both pharmacists, got on to the Council in 1898 and 1899 respectively, and pressed for action under the Telegraph Act 1899. This statute handed over to the Post Office all the trunk lines in the country, and empowered the Postmaster General to grant licences to municipalities for setting up their own systems. Urged on by the two chemists, the Council in 1900 refused permission to the NTC for new mains (and won a lawsuit on the point), and instead obtained a licence for a municipal undertaking. Next year, they had the Lord Mayor of London down to open the first municipal telephone system in England, with already 500 subscribers to the NTC's 600, spread well beyond the borough boundaries and into the surrounding countryside. The central exchange was in one of Decimus Burton's houses on Calverley Parade, now corporation property. There were to be 48 more, covering an area of no less than 180 square miles of Kent and Sussex.

That Tunbridge Wells, of all places, should become a pioneer in so ambitious an undertaking almost takes the breath away. Clearly, the two chemists had great persuasive powers, but also the support of enough councillors to secure a majority.

War broke out between the rival telephone undertakings. There clearly could not be room for both – the Council would not even allow the NTC to be connected to the police or fire-stations – and one must prevail. When, in 1902, the Council applied for a further loan of £15,000 for the next stage in their scheme, Colonel Holland, hotly supported by Matthew Edwardes of the *Courier* (and not too scrupulously; his journal was full of angry but anonymous letters), sponsored the opposition at the Local Government Board inquiry, and founded a Ratepayers' League to contest municipal trading. The Council maintained their case, ably put by Cripps the Town Clerk, but their engineer, AR Bennett, was roughly treated by Holland's counsel. At this point, the NTC was inspired, by someone, to put in a take-over bid. The mayor (Lutwidge) and a majority of the Council, frightened by now at the financial implications of what they had taken on, decided to beg the Postmaster General (Austen Chamberlain) for permission to accept the offer, and to hand over the public system they had so proudly inaugurated less than two years before. The case became national news: an influential deputation urged the PMG to stand firm by government policy. As, however, the Council no longer wanted a loan, and he was not prepared to step in himself, he had little choice but to agree. The good news was too much for Edwardes, who collapsed and died on receiving it: EH Strange, Alderman and Liberal, member of the family which had lived so long in the town, had died also, of the strain of the affair, it was said. In a few years' time, the PMG of another, Liberal, government was, indeed, to have the last word, when the licence of the National company ran out in 1912 and the telephone system was taken over by the state.

Meanwhile, municipal trading at Tunbridge Wells was decisively checked. The Ratepayers' League, securing agreement with their policy from Council candidates, or putting in their own men, mostly from the upper 'private belt' of the town, made or restrained the pace. In 1904, while the gas company was fighting back with its new incandescent lighting, the League members tried to turn the Council flank again, with a take-over bid from a private electricity company; but though by the end of that year the *Courier* could claim that they had reached a working majority on the Council, electricity stayed public; and greatly extended its scope in later years.

One thing the Council realised they must continue was to advertise the town. In 1904 an Attractions Committee went to seek co-operation from the SE&CR. To the town's disappointment, the second station (the present High Brooms) had been given to Southborough in 1893; but in 1898 a Pullman express (first class only) had been put on at 9.05am up and 3.44pm down. Then in 1899 the South Eastern and the

The Mayor at the opening of the newly-widened Mount Pleasant bridge at Central Station, 16 May 1907.

London, Chatham and Dover Railways had at last reached a working amalgamation under a joint committee and a new chairman, Cosmo (later Sir Cosmo) Bonsor. The mayor (EE Robb, an accountant) laid some ambitious proposals before him. 'We have at last recognised,' he said, 'that the glory of Tunbridge Wells as a health resort has to some extent departed, and, if we are to take our place in the front rank, and compete with such places as Harrogate and Bournemouth, we have got to do something.

The Council contemplated spending 'large sums of money' on instal-ling modern electric curative baths which would be among the most up-to-date in Europe, with the latest radiant heat (King Edward liked it). Besides the baths came the old familiar schemes: a Kursaal – the Germans' equivalent of the winter garden – with orchestra, public gardens, bandstands and so forth, and for water drinkers on the Pantiles, where 25,000 glasses were still downed yearly, another establishment, something better than 'the little insignificant well – open to any dog.' Why go to Carlsbad when the water was here? And if the Council would widen the Mount Pleasant railway bridge (long desired), would the SE&CR put up a new station building there, more worthy of the town (also long desired)? Cosmo Bonsor replied co-operatively. The bridge was indeed widened three years later (architect, Councillor H Elwig), and eventually, in 1912 the new station building on the down side, by Sir R Blomfield, an imposing affair on a very narrow site,

For many years, the High Rocks tourist attraction had its own halt on the Brighton line.

with clock turret, was opened. The Brighton, not to be left out, opened a halt in 1907 at High Rocks, which then had a lake, variously used for fishing, boating, and skating.

Like Prospero's cloud-capped towers and gorgeous palaces, the Council's ambitious schemes, once again, faded away; leaving only, it appears, a grant of £500, later raised for a short time to £1,000, for hiring bands, and an enlargement of the Pump Room by Elwig to form a hall to hold up to 1,000, which was blandly passed off by the *Courier* in 1912 as a substitute for a winter garden. The old town band had depended on subscriptions and collections. It was good enough, says CH Strange (*Jubilee of Incorporation*, 1939) to have once secured an engagement for a world tour on the SS Ceylon, after which it came to be called the Ceylon Band; but it dwindled away. The new bands came from the continent – the Bayreuth, the Blue Viennese, the Blue Hungarian – and from the British military, and played, at various times, in the Grove, Calverley grounds, the Grosvenor Recreation garden, and on the Common, as well as in the new bandstand, opened at last on the Pantiles; an Edwardian gabled affair by Featherstone. Roller skating becoming popular again, a new rink was opened in 1909 by a private company at Culverden Down, the former ground of the Rangers, a professional football club. The town's amateur team played at the Nevill ground. A Borough Advertising Association, formed in 1908, did some more aggressive advertising of the town – on a very small budget.

The High Street 1906. The building marked Nevill Bakery did not receive its glass 'conservatory' on the first floor until the 1920s, when the owner, John Brown, acquired an old orangery from Hever Castle.

The best advertisement, probably, came from Buckingham Palace, to which the mayor (HM Caley, an architect) wrote, of the long connection of the town with royalty. King Edward VII was by that time more familiar with Biarritz; but he knew Eridge well, and with his excellent memory no doubt recalled his visit to the Agricultural Show in 1881. On 16 April 1909, the announcement was published that HM the King had been 'graciously pleased to accede to the application of the burgesses of Tunbridge Wells, by resolution of the Town Council, that the borough be authorised to style itself a Royal Spa' – a title held only by Leamington, which had more enterprisingly secured it from Queen Victoria in 1838. There was no celebration: the rates, as rates do, had reached a record, at 6s 4d in the pound for the year.

During this time, unemployment and distress in the winter, and in the bad years for trade and agriculture, continued to trouble the town's conscience. The soup kitchens, the annual fund-raising, the mayoral appeals to find jobs went on. The Baptists fed 200 men one night and 200 women the next, in 1907. Gradually, more systematic methods evolved. The coincidence of Charles Booth's '*Life and Labour of the People of London*' (1889) with his namesake the General's '*In Darkest England, and the Way Out*' (1890), stirred the public, not least in Tunbridge Wells, where the relative smallness of the problem pointed, perhaps, the contrast between riches and poverty. The Nonconformist clergy, led by Mountain, called in the Salvation Army from London to describe at a public meeting their organisation of work-for-food depots, with a register of local employers wanting men, and newspapers offering jobs, and writing materials for applications. A scheme was started on these lines, with good response, in January 1891, and repeated later: in 1902 a register was opened at the Town Hall. The socialist and social-reform groups called for £1,000 to be allocated from the rates to useful works, and in 1904 for a national system: the beginning of this came next year, when registers were made compulsory. In February 1909 about 100 unemployed, with a contingent from Birmingham, marched to the workhouse, and tried to see the Guardians. People still wrote about loafers and questioned the need for relief, but the Corporation register contained 472 married and 127 single men, and a record sub-scription fund of £874 was spent on wages, plant and relief tickets. Later in the year, Labour Exchanges were set up throughout the country, and in 1911 the contributory unemployment fund, part of Lloyd George's famous National Insurance Act, met the relief problem.

The public conscience had also been troubled, since the 1880s or before, by bad housing: in Tunbridge Wells mainly by the overcrowding which Jay had encountered in the East Ward, and by out-of-date sanitation. In 1897 a crowded public meeting, with the local clergy, Dr Abbott, and the Socialist councillors prominent, prodded the Council into setting up a Housing Committee. This discovered that about 80 houses were unfit and 24 more were overcrowded and considered plans for a housing estate of cottages with small gardens. Land was chosen and tenders obtained; but the scheme was then lost in disagreements and delays, and in 1902 was caught and killed in the Council's new policy of retrenchment. The bad houses were dealt with piecemeal.

The passing of Canon Hoare coincided with national signs of decline in the Evangelical dominance of the Victorian age. In the town, no voice as stirring as his was now to be heard – or so fully reported – from the pulpit. AT Scott of St James (1866-1925), Rural Dean and later Archdeacon of Tonbridge, succeeded him as the leading Anglican divine. The big Protestant and Temperance meetings went on. In 1912 the aged General Booth received a civic welcome to a full Opera House, while crowds waited outside. On his death later in the year, a public memorial service was held. If not so many went to church these days, they were enough to call for two new parishes in the north; St Matthew, High Brooms in 1902, and St Luke's, formed in 1911 out of St John's and St James', with a church (1910) by EE Cronk. The Friends' Meeting House arose in Grosvenor Park in 1894. Most remarkable of the new churches, for the circumstances in which it came to be built, was St John's Free Church, by Caley, opened only a few yards away from Emmanuel, whose minister, James Mountain, had left it for his new spiritual home, on being converted to adult baptism. He raised a building fund, and took many of his former congregation with him.

If the clergy still kept the town's conscience, this, and their own, were more disturbed by ideas of social reform and more secular attitudes. These showed up in a nationwide division about education. We left the Church of England in charge of primary education in the town, with its own form of religious instruction, and satisfied that it could keep out the Board schools. The cost, however, laid a considerable burden on Church people in a town where the church had no endowments to speak of, and the whole cost of running the establishment – churches, schools, personnel – fell upon the congregation, apart from state grants to the schools, which the recipients never found excessive. The great Act of 1902 recognised (among many other things) that the voluntary schools were still very much needed, and provided for them to share in the rates in the same way as the state schools, as well as increasing the grant from central sources. This roused the resentment and the fears of the Non-conformists, who had few schools of their own, and (like the freethinkers in this), looked to the state schools. The gist of their objections (there were many complications) was against payment of rates for education including religious instruction of which the objectors did not approve. A campaign of resistance was mounted.

In Tunbridge Wells, there was practically no alternative choice of school: the Anglicans by 1913 had 19, the Roman Catholics one, and the rest three, apart from Sunday Schools. James Mountain, whose conscience was clearly troublesome, declared he would go to prison rather than pay the rate, and won some supporters. They were not imprisoned, but had to suffer the distraint and sale of their goods to meet their default: the sales being by auction, sympathisers bought in the goods. The argument went on also in the borough's elementary education committee. In 1913 the Non-conformists demanded a state school; not, they said, for sectarian reasons, but because the existing schools were not adequate for the growing population: they claimed, at the same time, that 40% of the children were not 'C of E'. The Anglicans replied that this would mean four such schools, one in each ward. The committee, under AT Scott as chairman, turned it down; the Baptist member, Dr Usher, dissenting.

While the borough remained, alone in Kent it was said, without municipal control of elementary education, higher education had come under the county council, working through another local committee. It took over the middle-grade school for girls at Vale Tower, and moved it to Southfield, near the Skinners' school (1909-12), where it later became the Girls' Grammar School. The independent Girls' High

The Technical Institute by HT Hare, opened in 1902, now the Adult Education Centre.

School moved in 1900 to Camden Park, leaving Fairlawn, Mount Sion, to the Eye and Ear Hospital. The flourishing Technical Institute, after an interlude at 42 Calverley Road, moved in 1902 to a new building with an attractive façade, not seen to best advantage in Monson Road, by HT Hare. It cost £12,000, which Colonel Holland (now a county councillor and later alderman) demonstrated could be raised, thanks to central and county funds available, without a charge on the rates. Lord Avebury declared it open, and 800 students were enrolled for full-time courses. Next year, to the town's disappointment, the county took it over.

Apart from things already mentioned, our third period, from 1909 to 1914 has not much to offer except the local activities of the women's suffrage movement, part of the political questions which were agitating the country by then. In Tunbridge Wells, as elsewhere, there were two 'suffragette' wings, the non-militant, of which Sarah Grand, a very popular novelist of those days who lived at 10 Grove Hill, was a leading figure; and the militants, mostly young women of the middle and upper classes who enlivened the town. Sylvia Pankhurst's visit in 1912 was followed by an outbreak of throwing lighted matches into postboxes. In 1913 Miss Olive Walton and Miss Davidson hid beneath the Opera

House stage and burst upon the performance with posters and cries of 'Votes for Women!' In April the pavilion of the Nevill ground was burnt out. An indignation meeting, at which Sir Arthur Conan Doyle spoke among others, declared its disgust, roughly handled Olive Walton and other venturesome young women, and started a subscription for another pavilion – the present one, designed by CH Strange, architect and councillor. As for the corporation, the rates came down, outstanding loans were paid off, and in 1913 none of eight council vacancies was contested.

Meanwhile the town went on growing, if not so fast. In 1894 the Liptraps Estate and the outlying north sewage farm, and in 1900 Rusthall New Town, were taken in. By 1911 the population reached 35,697, with still that preponderance of females which characterised the watering places and residential towns: 21,147 to 14,550 males. The contribution of what may broadly be called Edwardian architecture shows up in red brick, in contrast to the Victorian sandstone, yellow stock-brick and stonework, and the Regency stucco. It produced three notable public buildings in the Opera House, the Technical Institute, and the Tunbridge Wells and Counties Club, 1909 by Cecil Burns in bold neo-Georgian, just above the not very noteworthy General Post Office, moved from the Pantiles in 1895. St Luke's was neo-Gothic. For the sought-after visitors, new hotels arose. FG Molyneux's Earl's Court, with three big storeys built on top and a new wing added, towered up on Mount Ephraim and offered 100 bedrooms, at moderate prices, from 1904; and a large private hotel opened in Molyneux Park, close by. The Bridge, tall and turreted, adjoined Weekes'; the Castle had an Edwardian face-lift, with attic gables and tile hanging.

For residents, the main house building consisted of filling-in near the centre – High Street, Lonsdale Gardens, the north side of Lime Hill Road, etc – and building up roads laid out in the Culverden-Molyneux Park area and part of the Liptraps estate in the north, and in the Abergavenny estate in the south, including the Montacute Road area, Madeira Park, and up Warwick Park to the Nevill ground. In this estate (Councillor) Beale, and sons, built large red-brick houses, sprouting gables, turrets, balconies, black and white timbering, tile-hanging, in Edwardian profusion: they look their best amid the gardens rising up Madeira Park.

As the *Courier* divined in 1895, the new motors had come to stay. Earlier complaints of the nuisance of noisy, smoky, frightening steam traction-engines on the road were succeeded by letters about dangerous driving (eg down Grosvenor Road) and reports of accidents, with demands for stricter speed limits for motor vehicles. The 4 mph limit imposed in traction-engine days was raised, by the public efforts of

Mount Pleasant c1910 before the right-hand side was built upon.

Salomons and others, in 1896, and the maximum became 20 mph: police traps were set. The too familiar scene of later times was being rehearsed. Private motoring was still a luxury, for the rich, the former 'carriage people' throughout the period, except that doctors began to have them. Coach-builders became motor works: Rock, Hawkins and Thorpe (Thorpe was mayor 1904-5), and Stevensons and Tunbridges were advertising their chassis at Olympia show stands in 1912.

About 1906, motor buses which began to resemble the London General Omnibus Company's famous 'Old Bill' of World War I appeared here. A writer to the *Courier* in 1969 recalled that the first one had a habit of running away, and had to be replaced by horses. By 1909 however the Autocar Company was running a motor service, which reached as far as Hadlow in 1912: three Leyland buses were bought, and a 38-seater coach for pleasure trips. Their offices were in the Opera building. A motorcycle club was active. For the invalid, paved roads had made possible the wheeled bath chair, drawn by a donkey or pushed by human effort. In July 1912 the first aeroplane was reported over the town, on its way to Eastbourne: it returned by road, with propeller trouble, and stopped at Stevensons' in London Road, while the aviator lunched at the Grand Hotel.

Among distinguished residents at this time were CM Doughty (1843-1928) author of the classic '*Arabia Deserta*', who settled for some years in 1887 with his family at No 2 Beulah Road; Mary Anderson, a famous *Juliet*, at 17 Ferndale; and in 1899 the boy Frank Kendon (1893-

1959), later a minor poet. His recollections of town life, seen from his 'musical uncle's' dairy in Calverley Road, where china swans graced the window, 'their wings up and their backs full of eggs, and clear jars of honey in the comb, and model milk churns' appeared in *The Small Years*, 1930. In the evenings Uncle took him for walks in a town as impressively quiet as Lady Jerningham in her day and Joseph Hone in ours found it. In 1900 died William Nash, last of the line of Nashs at the Pantiles post office. The portrait of his famous ancestor passed to the Corporation, which had it restored in 1966-7 by the National Portrait Gallery. Dr Roy Strong declared it to be the work, not of Hudson as believed, but William Hoare.

The South African war, that traumatic experience for the British Empire, and the death of two monarchs, occurred in our period. The town, whose volunteers and rifle range had long flourished, saw off thirty of them to the war, and welcomed all but one of them back, it seems, in state. It was not too sober to break out in spontaneous jubilation, as everyone did, on the night of 18 May 1900, when the news arrived, about ten o'clock, of the relief of Mafeking, defended by its erstwhile schoolboy Sir Robert Baden-Powell. Soon afterwards, when Pretoria fell, a mob attacked the Dodds' house in Grosvenor Road – Lawson Dodd at least was a 'pro-Boer' – smashed the windows, and got out of hand: the town clerk had to come up with the Riot Act in his pocket. Haldane's Territorial and Reserve Forces Act of 1907 transformed the Volunteers into yeomanry, cyclists, and two infantry companies under Colonel Simpson. With their mobilisation, and the outbreak of the first world war in 1914, we close our chapter – and an epoch.

FOOTNOTES

1. See his pamphlet, A Word about the Grove 1868.

2. Many rose again hungry, it appears, for the occasion was too much for the caterers, who had to cook and serve from a tent in January.

CHAPTER TWELVE

THE TWENTIETH CENTURY

Tunbridge Wells is Tunbridge Wells, and there is really nothing like it upon our planet.   HG Wells, *Christina Albertas's Father*, 1933

The facts of life never seem to have impinged very much on this town . . . It's always 1884 in Tunbridge Wells, never 1984.
                    Joseph Hone, BBC broadcast, *The Listener*, 23 December 1971

In the world of comedy, Tunbridge Wells is at the other end of the scale from Wigan Pier.   *The Financial Times*, 21 August 1973

The world in turmoil

Alan Savidge found writing the town's contemporary history rather less easy than that of the previous 300 years. The pace of change was rapid and difficult to encompass: '. . . the picture becomes bigger, crowded with detail, increasingly difficult to focus. No time for a cool, detached, comprehensive review: only for an impression, even more of an impression than a general history must be . . .'

In his last chapter in the first edition of this book, Savidge marked out, in a personal statement, the impressions he had formed of the town in 'our own times'. He noted the loss of the borough's separate existence in 1974, when the Local Government Act 1972 changed boundaries and turned the area into a Borough Council whose influence stretched away 'from Speldhurst in the west to distant Cranbrook in the east, but not, *mirabile dictu*, to related Tonbridge in the north nor Frant in the south'.

He then took up the story where he had left it in 1914.

'Two world wars, 1914-18 and 1939-45 have come and gone. In the first war the town gave 776 of her sons and daughters, nursed the wounded in her hospitals, took refugees from Belgium as she had taken in émigrés from France a century before, and suffered the anxieties and heartbreaks of the warfare in Flanders and the stringencies of food rationing and shortages. A stray Zeppelin falling harmlessly in Calverley Grounds was the only direct impact of hostilities. This was very different from the second world war, when the town, after taking evacuee children from London, soon found itself in a forward defence area, on the path of potential invaders and of air raids upon the capital, and underneath the combat of the Battle of Britain and later the air defences against the flying bombs. In the circumstances, the loss and damage were remarkably light; the town owed much to its large open spaces, particularly the Home and North Farm sewage works, which appear to have had a special attraction for enemy missiles.

'Most of the damage was done in the critical summer and autumn of 1940, when 741 bombs of various kinds fell, and during the flying bomb raids of 1944. Altogether, 13 men and 2 women were killed, and 70 seriously injured; 13 houses were demolished, 98 severely damaged, and 2,596 suffered lesser damage. Air raid shelters were built, or formed in caves under St Helena and elsewhere, civil defence was organised for all, building and land were requisitioned for air defences, troops, government offices of all kinds; 166 names were added to the roll of honour of the previous war . . .' and here Savidge could bear it no more and left us pondering upon the impact of the loss and suffering, anxiety and tension of those times.

Development and growth

The town has continued to grow since 1911 when the population was 35,697. This remained largely static until it reached 38,397 in 1951, rising slowly to 39,869 in 1961. An influx of newcomers boosted the figure by 12% to 44,506 in 1971 and the population has now stabilised again, being 44,029 in 1991. The total population of the district stood at 99,598 in 1991. The town grew to meet the need and many new estates were built, which, as Savidge points out, are evidenced on the map, but less obvious is the housing provided by the conversions of large mansions, infill in spare sites and the replacement of large houses with more appropriate accommodation. Perhaps one of the most notable changes to the town has been the notion of town planning, both local and regional, which has put the development of the town into some kind of order, and has given the borough council a considerable say in how things are done.

Before and after the second world war, unofficial plans were drawn

A Comfortable House

makes a happy home, and Gas makes certain a comfortable house. GAS provides hot water for baths and for every other household need; ensures clean and simple cookery, and gives you radiant, cosy warmth to be enjoyed at once and varied or dispensed with at your will.

USE GAS and get help
:: without hindrance. ::

TUNBRIDGE WELLS GAS COMPANY.

Borough of Royal Tunbridge Wells.

CHEAP ELECTRICITY

LIGHTING
5ᴰ per Unit.

HEATING, COOKING & POWER
1ᴰ per Unit.

Prices of Current.

Within the Borough and Southborough.		In other Districts.
Lighting ..	5d. per unit.	5½d. per unit.
Heating and Power	1d. ..	1¼d. ..
Domestic Rate	¾d. ..	1d. ..
(plus fixed charges based on Rateable Value of premises or number of rooms).		
Extended Shop Window Lighting	1d. per unit.	1½d per unit.

For full particulars apply :—

R. N. TORPY, M.I.E.E., A.M.I. Mech. E.
Electricity Works, Stanley Road. 'Phone 565 & 936

Advertisements from the town's gas and electricity companies, 1928.

up, notably those in a pamphlet by members of the Rotary Club in 1936, edited by the architect CH Strange, and those produced in a report by the Civic Association for the Borough Council in 1945. This latter, impressive book, edited by Helen Spalding and including the work of architect Cecil Burns (1883–69), contained plans for an east-west bypass running in a 'U'-shape to the south of the town, linking Leigh with Pembury. It also looked at improving local roads; making a full two track rail connection between West and Central stations; provision of a central bus station; the reshaping of Calverley Grounds to include an amphitheatre; rebuilding of slum areas; and an ambitious plan for the Pantiles, to include a winter garden, repertory theatre and museum and art gallery. Sadly, despite the hard work put into the plan, little of it was taken up. Savidge takes up the story: 'Eventually, in 1966, the Council, in consultation with the County Council, produced a comprehensive scheme for the future treatment of the town centre, for public discussion – which it duly received.

'The Town and Country Planning Acts, 1947 and after, required the listing and grading of buildings of architectural or historic interest and gave them protection, if by no means complete, at least from forthright destruction or mutilation. The first Tunbridge Wells list was narrowly restricted, omitting even Calverley Crescent, but later revisions have considerably enlarged it and upgraded some of the buildings in it. The general conservation area was enlarged in 1974 and covers, roughly, the old town, and Burton's Calverley work, a greater area of the Common, Victorian roads such as Hungershall and Nevill parks, and Willicombe's work in Calverley Park Gardens, Lansdowne and Mount Ephraim roads.

'We saw the council turning away, in 1902, from their plan to build a cottage estate. By 1926 they had begun to move with the times, and built the first large estate at Rusthall. By 1974, 16 housing estates, large and small had been built, in three main areas: Powder Mill Lane, High Brooms and Sherwood; Ramslye and Showfields; and the Lower Green area of Rusthall.' The total of council homes was 2,782 in 1974, housing over 12,000 people with an estimated 3,200 families said to be on the waiting list.

In the last two decades of the twentieth century, housing continues to be a major issue. Despite the wealthy pretensions of the town, home-lessness is no stranger to it, and a survey by the charity Shelter in the late 1980s found the town to have a poor record in this regard. Since the 1980s, tenants of the council, by government policy, were allowed to purchase their properties at a discount under the Right to Buy scheme. A major change came in 1991 when, after a second referenda, residents voted to join the Tunbridge Wells Housing Association, (now the High Weald Housing Association) and all the council's properties were transferred to the new organisation in January 1992. There were 747 applicants on the housing waiting list at the time of

Powder Mill Lane and the new estate.

writing (a significant drop since 1974). Since 1974 the council has built 783 new homes within the Borough, the main estates being within the town. Private development has added 3,128 new dwellings dispersed throughout the Borough between 1981–93.

In August 1994 a Meridian television news item claimed that the town had over one hundred homeless people, (apart from those on the housing waiting list) most being single men whom the council had no obligation to house. The town has a reputation for charitable caring for the homeless, a reputation gained because of the night stop hostel which was enlarged in the early 1990s, and because of much activity by Christian organisations.

In his survey of new developments, Savidge noted the following: 'While cottages have arrived, others have departed, mainly from the Crown Field Estate, immediately behind the big chain-stores which have moved into the western end of Calverley Road, and on the borders with Goods Station Road; some of the space has become car parks. The 1965 town centre plan contemplated the removal of some 680 houses in that area, rebuilding another 855, and building 241 new ones. An instalment of this, involving clearance, was taken to a public enquiry in 1973 by the Civic Society (the lineal descendant of the old Improvement Association, the Civic Association of the 1930s, and the Fifty-nine Society of 1959), which considered that the little back-street terraces, still attractive and distinctive in their early Victorian styles, should as far as possible be preserved and renovated. In this, the Society was in line with changing views on merits and cost – to the environment as well as to the rates – of slum clearance compared with conservation.

'The private developer has been busy all round the town; from St James' Road through Ferndale to Hawkenbury, at Banner Farm running up to Forest Road and along Birling Road to Broadwater: in large estates and in the now fashionable 'closes' laid out in former private gardens and grounds. Between-wars Tudor has been succeeded by 1950s utility and now the neo-Georgian terrace.' This state of affairs has hardly changed although it is now supplemented by local and national developer 'country cottage' styles often named after villages in the region.

'The Town Plan also proposed to convert most of Camden Road into a residential street, and a private company put up a scheme in the 1960s for re-developing the Calverley Road end into a new shopping area. The conservationists did not welcome the loss of the market street of the town (which at the time had no street market), a bright, busy, friendly place for spare parts and gadgets, hobbies and cut prices, where everybody goes sooner or later.'

In the 1990s we know different, of course. Camden Road largely maintains the feel of a bazaar as described above, although the effects of

Top: Construction work proceeds. This picture is taken from behind the site of the old Drill Hall. The brick facades (left) were kept as part of Market Square.

Centre right: Building taking place seen from the new Meadow Road car park, 1990.

Centre left: The post-modernist lines of the Market Square and Camden Centre.

Left: The shopping centre is complete and the old Sandell Perkins building (once Haywards) has been demolished to make way for offices and a YMCA building, 1994.

(Charlie Bell)

the recent recession and a swingeing new business rate have meant a constant turnover of shops. As for the Calverley Road end, the land behind Calverley Road, and many of the houses mentioned above, have been replaced by a large shopping centre, Royal Victoria Place, along with some new community housing. The derelict houses in Belgrave Road have been replaced by a YMCA building and the old Haywards building in the triangle of land between there and Goods Station Road has been demolished to make way for offices.

Mr Savidge, were he ever to return for a visit, would not recognise much of this area: even the line of Victoria Road has been altered. The new shopping centre and its associated car park, meeting hall and palm house were officially opened on 21 October 1992 by the Princess of Wales, although the complex had been open for business since April 7 of that year. The immediate effect on the town was a spate of many empty shops, partly because many businesses moved into the Centre. The development was preceded in 1984 by the welcome pedestrianisation of the western end of Calverley Road which made shopping much more pleasant.

Royal Victoria Place, with its associated Meadow Road car park, must count as the biggest single building project to happen in the town in the 20th century. Its story is perhaps best told in figures. Covering 8.5 acres, the massive construction project employed over 2,000 personnel at the height of the work. It involved deep excavations, some of which went down 35 metres, coming within 2 metres of the top of the High Brooms–Tunbridge Wells railway tunnel.

The scale of the effect on the town can be judged by the fact that it contains 105 shopping outlets, 96 of which had filled by January 1994. The project created 1,700 new parking spaces in two new multi-storey car parks. An estimated 200,000 people a week visited the centre in 1994 with a target of 250,000 per week. At the heart of the centre is a food hall with obligatory glass-fronted lift and palm trees, nine metres high, transported from Florida and installed at a cost of £20,000. They must be maintained at a minimum temperature of 13°C.

The exterior of the shopping centre is a curious amalgam of styles with a mediterranean influence – pleasant in its own way but lacking in local 'feel'. The town is lucky that it held out for so long before allowing the development. One shudders to think what 1960s or 70s architects might have done. One only has to look at Union House, the development which replaced the Pump Room on the Pantiles, or the 1960s buildings in Church Road, or the telephone exchange in St John's Road, to see what might have happened.

Departures and arrivals

Alan Savidge noted the arrival of the motor car, road and air transport
and traffic; the commuter and the welfare state. 'The car, the van and
lorry, the TIR, zoom up in our picture, and with them, traffic lights,
Belisha beacons (1936), the roundabouts and one-way streets, the
traffic jams, the line of parked vehicles along – and increasingly on –
the pavement, the car parks . . . the revolution of the twentieth
century; the chief factor in the urban problem of today.

'Two notable arrivals are factories to the north of the town, and
office blocks within and around it. The 1945 Civic Association report
found room for light industry, to diversify the town's activities, and
North Farm, decently distant, was chosen for it. Some 58 acres were
laid out and 48 factories, workshops and warehouses have set up there
. . . (in the 1980s the site was partly redeveloped). There are also a
number of light industrial workshops in the town, but Romary, Lyle
and Tunbridge Ware makers have departed.' To Mr Savidge's list of
arrivals, we might add the multi-storey car park, sports centre, shopping
mall, and the out of town retail park: large stores out of the town centre.
In the 1960s came the town's first multi-storey car park, adjacent to
the Town Hall and unsympathetically fronting the Decimus Burton
Calverley Crescent. The Torrington project by Central Station,
finished in the mid 1980s provided another multi-storey car park and
the town's first '80s-style large supermarket – Safeway, then the group's
largest store in the country. Then came the Sainsbury/Homebase
development at West Station in 1990 and 92, the old station building
being restored and turned into a restaurant.

Further large retail warehouses sprang up in the 1980s in an unlikely
place – the industrial estate on North Farm. At first the council
appeared reluctant to allow such a development, and there was a
famous battle with the management of the Texas DIY group over
whether or not the company's bright blue and red livery was suitable for
the Tunbridge Wells environment. This was a piece of priggishness
which did little to diminish the town's reputation for being 'disgusted'
about everything. Soon, however, the council had a change of heart
and allowed a whole series of further retail warehouses to grace
Longfield Road and the new Kingstanding Retail Park adjacent to it.
This was all made possible by the building of a short piece of road which
at last connected the town via Longfield Road with the A21 south of
Tonbridge and thus opened up a new access to the area.

The development of the retail parks, and the vast scale of the Royal
Victoria Place shopping mall, mark a new era for the town, showing as
they do the council's strategy for making the town a significant regional

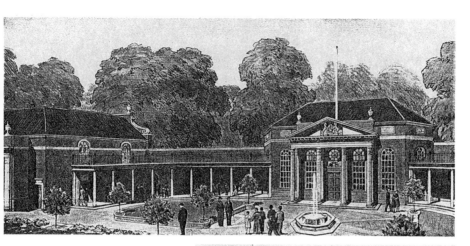

Above: On the site of the Corn Exchange and Assembly Rooms, the Civic Association in their plan of 1945 proposed a social and cultural centre. The building on the left would have been a museum and art gallery and the one on the right was to be a repertory theatre.

Right: The 1945 Civic Association plan for the Pantiles envisaged a Winter Garden on the site of the Pump Room.

(Courier Printing & Publishing Co Ltd)

retail centre, comparable with Bromley to the north, Maidstone to the east and Brighton to the south.

In tandem with this growth came the long awaited refurbishment of the Pantiles. In 1975 Savidge looked at the Walks with a weary, if not jaundiced eye: 'As in Victorian and indeed Georgian days, (the Pantiles) has had its ups and downs, structural and otherwise: Union House for the old Pump Room, new bandstand (1973) for old, a garden where Nos 30–36 were pulled down . . . in 1939. The 1945 (Civic Association) committee took a poor view of the whole place, no doubt showing the effects of five years of war without repairs and decoration, but in their opinion sadly and stupidly neglected over a century by a

The Pantiles Garden, mourned by many when it was built upon in the 1980s.

town ignorant of its history and values. Their proposals . . . amounted to a transformation: the rebuilding, in a more urbane and imposing Queen Anne or Georgian style, of several houses above the colonnade; a large circular glass winter garden in place of the Pump Room; the opening up of the Lower Walk to make a formal garden, the old Sussex Assembly Room revived as a concert hall, the old theatre, later the Corn Exchange, converted to an art gallery and museum, and a new repertory theatre at the western end.'

In the mid-1970s, nothing had been done to revive the area. 'Meanwhile antiques and old furniture stores have arrived in considerable numbers adding to the air of times past the faint smell of the museum piece . . . Other spas and towns have their promenades, their shopping arcades, but none quite like this.

'The more the pity that the main approach, from Nevill Street, should have presented for some years the dreary spectacle of Dust's former stores, empty, boarded up, its early nineteenth century buildings visibly decaying and ready to fall down.'

Eventually, on the back of the 1980s boom, a developer was found who could afford the major restoration work, and the Pantiles, in a concerted effort by all concerned, was put to rights. The Corn Exchange became an up-market shopping mall; the Assembly Rooms house *A Day at the Wells* heritage centre, the Fishmarket, now restored to its former glory, is the Tourist Information Centre, and new paint glistens on old buildings. The old uneven paving on the Upper Walk was replaced and new trees planted to restore the limes which were badly damaged by the

1987 hurricane. Amidst great controversy, the garden at 30–36 was redeveloped and the missing tooth was sympathetically replaced by a building which reflected its own times as well as the past.

Restored to their former glory, the Pantiles are now marketed internationally to the discerning tourist. The town seeks to attract limited numbers of high spending tourists. There is still some way to go on this: a recent survey showed that the average day-tripper spent £1.50 in the town, hardly the price of a pint of beer.

Despite a slight air of a theme park, the Pantiles now feels much more as residents remember it. Savidge's lyrical evocation of the Pantiles on a good day in the 1970s still holds true: 'on a fine day, the buildings, all done up, gleam white in the sunshine; the children try the waters and the teenagers quaff the beer outside the Duke of York; the band plays once more; the players put on Shakespeare from the bandstand; Morris Men dance; Punch and Judy squabble; the June art exhibition splashes the screened railings with colour, and a Carnival weekend fills the place with strollers in gay costumes of times past; bunting, sightseers, photographers and Beau Nash himself.' In the 1990s this is still an accurate picture, but we might add that even on a bad day in the summer we can meet and chat with Bell Causey, eat al fresco, buy quality kitchen ware, visit the multi-media *Day at the Wells*, marvel at the fancy prices in the exclusive shops, and buy the odd antique or piece of refined antique furniture. On a Sunday one could also join the market in Sussex Mews courtyard, and at any time of the year one can stop to ponder on the beauty of the town's (if not the country's) first pedestrian precinct. Visitors might even come across the annual sedan chair races.

Among other arrivals to the town since 1914 Savidge noted 'in no indecent haste, the public library and museum. In 1916 the Corporation was persuaded to rent a shop in Crescent Road for an educational museum. This moved to Abbotsford in Upper Grosvenor Road and then to Mount Ephraim, where Dr JCM Given became honorary curator. In 1921 the surviving trustees of the Mechanic's Institute in Dudley Road offered its library to the Corporation. The new Civic Centre, built in the 1930s was planned to extend to a library, museum and art gallery, but these, delayed by the war and requisitioning, did not become available until 1952. (The design of the Civic Centre was by Messrs Thomas and Prestwick. It replaced a Decimus Burton terrace, one house of which, for many years, housed the town's telephone exchange.) Meanwhile, the quest for a winter garden led to a pavilion for concerts and dancing in Calverley Grounds (1926), which was destroyed by a fire bomb in 1940. The 1945 Civic Association committee drew up an attractive scheme for this site, which remains on paper.

'Arrived are several more public recreation and sports grounds, some the gifts of past mayors, adding to the town's intricate green pattern and catering for the young as well as the old. The 1945 committee remarked that youth had been left to make its own amusement, with not enough encouragement to find the best. The criticism is still made: the problem of adequate outlet for youthful exuberance exercises the town, as it does others.' The town closed its Monson Road baths and opened a new swimming pool in St John's Road in 1974. Later a sports centre was added, initially called the Sports and 'Y' Centre because of its attempt to make it a centre for young people. A most encouraging development has been the successful opening of The Forum in 1992 in the Fonthill Pavilion on the Common (once containing public toilets and later a brass rubbing centre). The venue is open most nights and offers a range of music including rock and jazz. It has become established as one of the premiere venues for this kind of entertainment in the South East.

Of departures, there have been many. Savidge noted the demise of the Victorian-Edwardian family; the mansion or villa and grounds they filled; the army of servants; and the churches, and the schools they kept going. 'Gradually, by the aftermath of the second war, the big houses became empty, creating a vacuum – and a serious loss of of rate-income to the Corporation – for many years. This has been filled by the residential hotel; the nursing home; the public charitable institution; by conversion into flats; by demolition and new building in the grounds.' Of the once numerous hotels, many now house the elderly, some are converted into flats; some, like the Earl's Court on Mount Ephraim have become offices.

'Nowhere,' he says, 'has change gone deeper than those "millionaire's miles", Pembury Road and Broadwater Down; nor yet more discreetly. The tall trees still line the latter, the cedars and exotics spread over the wide grounds of the former. The high rhododendron hedges and shrubberies hide from the passer-by the mansion now converted into flats or the space where it was until the other day . . . Ten of Broadwater Down's 44 houses of the great days have gone, as have Grovehurst in Pembury Road, home once of jam and mustard kings, Henry Reid's and BH Collin's Dunorlan, Lutwidge's Shandon, St George's School and its Victorian interior woodwork, despite protest; but Concord House, once Ferncliffe, has been listed and spared. Sandown Court, once the mansion of Sir Robert Gower (solicitor son of a former alderman, mayor 1917-19 and an MP) is now a secondary school (later rechristened as a community college). Sir William Siemens' Italianate Sherwood became in the 1930s Sherwood Park Spa, the centre of the last attempt to return to the water treatment business. A guide book of 1935 reported

Some more Tunbridge Wells notables

Born here were HW Fowler (1858-1933), famous lexicographer of the King's English; Arthur Waley (1889-1966), equally famous as translator of Chinese poetry into English; Sir Tyrone Guthrie (1900-71), stage director, pioneer of the radio play, the open stage, and new theatre-building ventures. Quietly – very quietly in some cases – retired here were Frank Pape (c1930-54), illustrator of many books in the Bodley Head Classics; Ethel Irving (1869-1964), Edwardian actress in the grand manner, who abruptly left stage and society on her husband's death, and spent the last 30 years of her life here, a recluse, under an assumed name; Pauline Chase, a celebrated *Peter Pan*, who also ended her days here; HW Betteridge (1892-1972) naturalist and for some years art master at Skinners' and St George's, a worthy successor to the Dodds. Better known were Rupert Gunnis (1899-1965) of Hungershall Park, writer, national authority on church sculpture, chairman of the local bench, alderman, sponsor of art exhibitions; Air Chief Marshal Lord Dowding (1882-1970), Commander-in-Chief, Fighter Command, in the Battle of Britain, 1940, who spent his retirement at Calverley Park: buried in Westminster Abbey; and, latest in the evangelical line of Wesley, the Countess of Huntingdon, and Edwards, probably the most familiar of all our list to the town and one of its numerous eccentrics, John Collimbel (1880-1972), 'Gospel John'. He came from Nottingham to Frant as an agricultural labourer in the first war, stayed, and spent his days until well into his eighties parading the top of Mount Pleasant with sandwich-boards carrying good tidings, and more often, warnings of the wrath to come. Richard Cobb grew up here and left us his legacy in *Still Life*.

the discovery of a new spring there, 'with qualities unique to this country,' but similar to the waters of 'Nauheim, the famous German heart centre. Every type of spa treatment is already available . . . arrangements are in hand to bottle new water for sale throughout the country.' The second world war intervened; the place was taken over by Kent County Council as a maternity and nurse's home.'

Siemens' house still stands in 1994 and is owned by the health authority. The buildings opposite Trinity church are long gone, replaced by rather insensitive 1960–70 offices.

'In the same discreet way as in Pembury Road and Broadwater Down, and with fewer losses, the parks, gardens and roads of Victorian-Edwardian dignity have changed with the times . . . Calverley, the model park, remains almost intact, and so does the crescent hard by, although some of the houses are divided, the Park lake and the Crescent fountain long ago filled in: secluded from noise, private, guarded by resident dragons, no thoroughfare for motors. The other works of Decimus Burton have fared less well at the hands of time and the developer. Baston House and Lodge have long vanished. Of his Terrace and Parade and their pleasant gardens in front and mews at the back,

there remain only a pair of houses next to the Police Station, now
offices, minus their nice canopies . . . The old Town Hall, originally
his market house of 1833 in Calverley Road, lingered on as the School
of Art and Crafts till 1959, when in poor shape, it was demolished for
Sainsbury's and a neo-Georgian office court. (Sainsbury's moved out in
1990 to their new superstore at West Station.) The five-part composi-
tion of shops and dwellings further along the road, where Smiths had
their carriage works, survives, its unity much impaired by additions and
unsympathetic shop fronts. Behind them, the first of Burton's row of
stone cottages has recently succumbed to decay and to commercial
interests. The little gothic schoolmaster's house, in poor shape,
remains of his Royal Victoria School. His Culverden House was cleared
away in 1928 for the new hospital by Cecil Burns, opened in 1934.'

Savidge spoke with regret about the changes he saw in the town:
'There is no doubting the office invasion; the old villas converted, the
new blocks much more assertive. The glass mass of the government's
Land Registry at Hawkenbury, a kind of official Crystal Palace (by RP
Mills, 1963), glances in the sunlight at the roof sign, RELIANCE
(since removed), across the town in the converted Earl's Court Hotel.
In London Road, the brutal Merevale House, also governmental, with
another behind and above it; the blocks already mentioned in Church
Road; another rising above Mount Pleasant: the telephone exchange at
the Culverden, the monolithic, oversize PPP building: all square, hard;
accountants' architecture as Betjeman has called it.'

Savidge chronicled the loss of churches in a secular age. The once
pious town had plenty to lose. 'A number of outposts, in Albion Road,
in St John's Road, have been abandoned. St Augustine's gave way to
Tesco's supermarket in 1969; the Christian Scientists retreated in 1959
to Linden Park Road from their church in St John's, built only in 1931
to a highly original design by Cecil Burns – still there but altered
beyond recognition when taken over as offices. (In 1994 they house the
national headquarters of the Freight Transport Association.) The
Countess of Huntingdon's Emmanuel, whose spire set off the Culverden
scene, and made an attractive counterpoint in the northern townscape
to St Mark's on the southern hills, disappeared in 1974 to make way for
car parking at the hospital; the stout Kentish ragstone resisting the
breakers to the last.'

There is much relief in the gloom. Trinity church, the town's first
parish church and another Burton design, stood 'closed and silent,
dilapidated and desolate, awaiting its fate,' when Savidge published his
book in 1975. In May 1975, the Church Commissioners had prepared a
draft scheme for demolition. 'If no other use can be found for it,'
bemoaned Savidge, 'the church which overflowed Sunday after Sunday,

Cecil Burn's unusual Christian Science Church in St John's Road awaiting conversion to offices.

and rang to Canon Hoare's resonant voice while the carriages waited outside, whose tower has so long dominated the skyline from the Common – if a little uncertainly since two square office blocks were allowed to rise up close by – will disappear.'

To the relief of many in the town, Trinity was saved from this fate by a band of volunteers who set about restoring the building and turning it into an arts centre. The battle was long and progress slow, but by summer 1982, enough headway had been made to stage the first two-week season. Now Trinity Theatre and Arts Centre thrives, still largely run by volunteers, open 50 weeks of the year and offering bar and catering facilities as well as a wide range of theatre, dance, music and exhibitions. Conversely, Christ Church in the High Street is now (1994) in a state of disrepair and, although the subject of a development plan which will keep worship on the site, appears to have no firm future. King Charles the Martyr, recently redecorated internally, continues to thrive and is one of the architectural gems of the town.

Savidge included the Great Hall and the Opera House as losses, because they had departed from their original functions. 'There was period in the 1920s when John Christie took on the lease of the Opera House and gave it new life with London plays, Gilbert and Sullivan, orchestral concerts, and talked of a festival of opera – Wagner and

Mozart mainly; but to the loss of the town, he took his ideas and his wealth off to Glyndebourne's more glamorous glades. Tunbridge Wells has not followed Edinburgh, Bath, Brighton, Cheltenham, Aldeburgh and others.' Twenty years later, we see the development of an opera and music season at Broomhill, the one time house of Sir David Salomons. The most unusual science theatre there has proved admirable for this purpose and the enterprise looks set for a bright future, at last putting Tunbridge Wells on the map of musical venues.

'In their turn, the movies have arrived and retreated. Camden Road had two cinemas, there was the Kosmos (1914) in Calverley Road, and in 1934 the Ritz . . . went up at the top of Mount Pleasant: in its modified form of three 'houses' it survives as the Classic (MGM as from 1993),' and the only cinema in the town.

Despite Savidge's tendency towards regret for what has happened to the town, there is much to be thankful for in Royal Tunbridge Wells. Much of its remains intact and, on the whole, the town has managed to grow and develop without losing its human scale and feel. New developments, such as Royal Victoria Place have tried to adapt to the town and blend in. Many of the town's buildings have been sensitively restored, at least on the outside, and such buildings as the Great Hall (rebuilt 1984) and the old motor works at the top of Grosvenor Road bear witness to a different trend in town development.

Newer buildings, such as the Private Patients Plan building in Vale Road, opposite the old Post Office, are less strident than the litany of disasters chronicled earlier. The Civic Society has much to be thanked for in this respect. Their annual awards of plaudits and brickbats to recent architectural developments has undoubtedly brought about a wider appreciation of the specialness of the town.

An aspect of heritage about which the Civic Society can do nothing is the sad decline of the large family business, and of stores which were unique to the town. Names such as Waymarks (department store), Weekes (department store), Haywards the ironmongers, Goulden & Curry the much loved bookshop in the High Street; these and many others will soon become misty in the town's collective memory.

Transport

As elsewhere, the car and the lorry have transformed life in the town forever. Public transport struggles to compete but is a shadow of its former self. 'The internal competition of the two railways ended after the first war, when they became part of the Southern Railway, which in turn became the Southern Region of British Rail after the second,' and which is now known as Network South East the operating name of the

South Eastern Train Company: a new venture set up to speed the move towards rail privatisation – the circle is completed. The report in 1963 of Dr Richard (later Lord) Beeching caused consternation in the town, but the damage was not as bad as it might have been. 'At their most drastic, the sum of the various rationalisation schemes would have amounted to putting back the railway clock almost to its beginning in 1845; dealing with passenger services at a new station near to the original one, instead of the Central; scrapping the direct Hastings line to the south and almost the whole of the Brighton network beyond Eridge in the west. All this aroused strong opposition from the organised commuters and other travellers of the area, and threats to the Central Station and the Hastings line were withdrawn, but the once-prized links with Brighton and Eastbourne have been cut, and traffic from the West (LBSC) Station reduced to a branch service between Eridge and Tonbridge.'

The Hastings line was fully electrified in 1986 and given a new lease of life, as the '1066 line': there are still 34 trains every weekday to London, but the link with Eridge has been severed and that line is now in the hands of the Tunbridge Wells and Eridge Preservation Society, affectionately known as TWERPS, which intends to reopen a commuter service during the week and tourist specials at weekends. The new venture is to be called The Spa Valley Railway. Progress has, however, been slow. The line still awaits a running licence but has an aim to be operational for passengers by Easter 1995.

'The story of the bus system is similar. The Autocar and Redcar companies competed for the local services beween the wars, their rivalry leading in the late 1920s to a war of fares: in March 1928 you could have gone to Tonbridge for a penny. The Victor ran an eastern service. Then, in 1935, the Maidstone and District Motor Services took over, and 'rationalised' many of the village services. After the second war came the private car invasion, the rise in operating costs, staff shortages, forcing the company, like the railway, to cut country services further, to abandon some of them, to increase fares; leading to complaints and falling traffic.' Since the deregulation of bus services in 1986, the situation has been fluid, with over nine private operators coming on the scene. A 'war' between Maidstone and District and the large newcomer Shearings, ended in the former buying out the latter's bus service in December 1991. New ideas to the town have been the smaller minibus-type services, and a flirting with the idea of park-and-ride schemes which so far have had little public success or support. Plans to run park-and-ride from Langton and Pembury have met with local opposition.

Being a large town, Royal Tunbridge Wells gets it fair share of traffic congestion at peak times, but several improvement schemes keep traffic flowing reasonably well at other times. The centre of town is partly helped by London Road acting as by-pass, but this merely channels traffic into the bottlenecks at the top of Grosvenor Road and in Southborough. The east-west axis still cuts through the town causing hold-ups at several places. Currently there are no plans to provide the town with a bypass and one must assume that traffic congestion will get worse with time.

Education

'In primary education,' Savidge informs us, 'the holding action of church and Council, which lasted right up to the second world war, with 18 church primary schools, by then generally fallen out of date and inadequate, gave way to the 1944 Education Act. The Anglicans accepted 'controlled' status. The private secondary schools – St George's, Hamilton House, the Girl's High School – have all gone.' The town is served by a range of secondary schools and offers a variety of comprehensive, community college and single sex grammar schools. Two schools disappeared in the 1980s due to falling numbers: Huntleys Secondary for Boys in Culverden Down and Ridgeway in Southborough. In the latest change to the education system, schools have been given the opportunity to become grant maintained, being independent of the local authority, and several have taken up this option. The old system of Grammar, Technical High and Secondary School, introduced after the 1944 Act, has now gone.

'The idea in some minds that Tunbridge Wells should be just the place for one of the new universities came to nothing: the impact of the modern student on the watering-place of the serious-minded would have been interesting. The West Kent College of Further Education has spread itself, from two former mansions in Broadwater Down to the former motor works of Rock Hawkins and Thorpe at the top of Grosvenor Road, and along St John's, where some one-storey workshops by Elie Mayorca, in which might be called the 'exposition manner (1958-9), do duty until the whole complex moves to a new centre at Tonbridge.'

Since Savidge wrote those lines the college has moved from the motor works although it keeps its toe-hold in St John's. With it has gone any pretensions that the town may have had to become a centre for further or higher education. However, the town still has much to do with learning, containing as it does a thriving Adult Education Centre in the old Technical Institute in Monson Road; part of the nationally recognised Kent Adult Education Service; and playing host every summer to hundreds of foreign students who flock to the town to improve their English and get away from their parents.

West Kent College in St John's Road. Behind is the glass front of the Grammar School for Boys, once the Technical High School for Boys – known locally as the 'Tech'.

(Charlie Bell 1994)

Water supply

Surprisingly, for a town that made its reputation upon water, water shortages continued to haunt the town for many years. Savidge noted the preoccupations of the time: 'Water supply has remained on the agenda. The 1945 committee, noting the recurrent crises, commented that while the official guides boasted of the purity of the water, the townspeople had been repeatedly inhibited from drinking it or using it. They found the existing spring and boreholes, augmented in 1927 by a new borehole at Saint's Hill near Penshurst with a pipeline to Rusthall, still basically inadequate; and recommended that the town should look, not to the southern heights of Ashdown Forest, but to the northern chalk and greensand of the Sevenoaks area; hoping also that the local jigsaw of water authorities' areas would one day be simplified. Eventually, after further shortages in dry summers, the municipal undertaking was sold in 1973 to Sevenoaks and Tonbridge Water Company, which became the West Kent Water Company, but new resources did not flow in time to prevent another serious crisis in the summer of 1973.'

The situation has eased over time, although a series of several very dry winters in the late 1980s and early 1990s caused serious worries about the supply of water to the town and region. The new privatised water company, South East Water – an amalgamation of West Kent Water, Mid-Sussex Water and Eastbourne Water – has maximised the benefits of the pooling of resources and the provision of new supplies.

New boreholes at Matfield, Eridge and Saints Hill, combined with extra pipelines and a larger reservoir at Langton Green (1988) have all contributed to ensuring water supplies in the town into the 21st century. The new works at Saints Hill, Penshurst, is of interest in that it is the first biological water treatment facility in the country. It was officially opened by local MP Sir Patrick Mayhew in 1993. The success of the new measures is demonstrated by the fact that Tunbridge Wells has had no hosepipe ban since 1990 to the time of writing, despite other areas in the surrounding region occasionally suffering this fate.

Shocks to the system

On the 16th October 1987, a fierce hurricane hit the whole of the south east of England. By dawn, much of the face of the area had been completely altered. Millions of trees were flattened and there was much damage to property. 29,000 homes were without power in the Tunbridge Wells area, nearly all roads were blocked, and British Telecom drafted in 400 engineers from all over the country to repair faults at the rate of 4,000 a day. The army was called in to help clear power line routes and roads. 300 trees fell onto the Tonbridge–Hastings railway line. In the town centre, a high crane, being used on the Meadow road car park, crashed to the ground. The row of lime trees on the Pantiles was blown over onto the buildings opposite on the Upper Walk. The Grove sustained much tree damage.

The Common suffered badly with many trees uprooted and broken. This disaster brought about a positive development. The conservators and other interested parties appointed a warden and set about developing a conservation plan for this unique area. The plan is thoughtful and wide ranging. It aims to restore some areas to their pre-hurricane state, but also sets out to recreate some of the original (and much earlier) vistas; manage separate areas in different and appropriate ways; restore some heather areas; reinstate acid grassland; restore and maintain ponds; and manage areas of woodland and scrub. The Commons can never be restored to their original state of open heathland, partly because grazing is no longer possible and partly because people have got used to the trees, but the conservation plan is a positive move to keep the Common as an attractive and varied asset to the town.

A major political surprise came in the 1994 local elections when, for the first time since anyone can remember, the Conservatives lost overall control. The idea of a 'hung' council was quite alien to the town. The complexion of the council after May 1994 was 24 Conservative, 20 Liberal Democrat, 3 Labour and 1 independent, with the Conservative mayor having a casting vote. This political shift is in itself an indication of the changes which have taken place in the complexion of the town since 1974.

Town 2000

The image of the genteel upper to middle class town, unaffected by the world, and keen only to preserve its bourgeois complacency has been inappropriate for a long time. There is still a lot of money in the town and a strong strand of middle class life struggling to preserve itself. In 1994 British Telecom announced that it was finding it hard to fill the Telephone Book for the area because so many peopled wished to be ex-directory. A spokesman for the company is alleged to have ascribed this to 'snobbishness' but it is just as likely that people wished to protect themselves from the unwanted attentions of nuisance calls, double-glazing representatives and the conductors of surveys; all of which have become a plague of life in Royal Tunbridge Wells, just as they have elsewhere.

In general, the town looks after itself well, and therefore the darker side of life goes unnoticed. In the past twenty years the residents of the town have had to come to terms with murder, armed robbery, muggings, homelessness, unemployment, drug abuse, rape and burglary. Their town is no different to any other in this respect. One of its mayors resigned from office after the discovery of some financial irregularities, something that was unthinkable in 1974 when Savidge wrote his book.

The site of Burton's old Town Hall. Beyond, several Burton buildings still survive.
(Charlie Bell 1994)

The history of the town has largely mirrored towns elsewhere. The introduction of the Community Charge to replace the ageing system of rates in 1990 caused problems of administration and collection. The unpopular measure, dubbed the Poll Tax by its detractors, caused a national campaign of non-payment and civil disobedience which eventually led to its being replaced by the Council Tax in April 1993. The system was linked to people, not addresses, and it proved impossible to trace all those eligible for the tax. Others simply could not afford to pay, and the town witnessed at least one undignified spectacle of a pensioner being imprisoned for non-payment. The collection rate under the old system was over 98% but under the Community Charge it lay between 91-97% over the three years it was in force.

The town is more outward-looking than it has been for a long time. It pays more careful attention to its advertising and promotion both nationally and abroad. In an attempt to raise its profile the town has entered the Flowers in Bloom competition since 1990 and has received a fourth place and two second places. It came first in the 1993 Transmanche in Bloom competition. Royal Tunbridge Wells has also become interested in cycle racing, a little ironically as it provides no facilities for ordinary cyclists, and has hosted a stage of the 1993 Milk Race and a stage of the British leg of the Tour de France in 1994, which entered Kent on 'Le Shuttle' through the newly opened Channel Tunnel.

Savidge felt that the town was not likely to be 'progressive', and in the sense of major innovation he was probably right, although there is a sense that the town has been brought fully into the twentieth century, albeit retaining a sense of caution about anything new. In 1975, he brought us back to Benge Burr's *rus in urbe*, and described Tunbridge Wells as 'still essentially a country town'. In a sense we know what he means. The town still feels less urban than Maidstone, Brighton or Bromley.

'Even among watering-places, where green amenity is to be expected, Tunbridge Wells appears to have more, at its very heart, than any except Harrogate, which also seems to have been built in the midst of common and parkland. In this, and in its still delightful private gardens; its tree-lined streets with their habit of running up and down and taking inviting curves; its small stones or spalls paving paths in the old town; in those red paving bricks – also, alas, on the departure list like the brickworks at High Brooms (closed in 1968) that made them, a pleasure to the eye if . . . a stumbling block to the feet – in all this lies its charm.'

The town bustles now, and has become a truly regional centre for commerce. And yet, it is still a pleasant place to walk in, and there are now plenty of traffic-free areas in which to walk or shop, including the

Common, Calverley Park, the Pantiles, Chapel Place, Calverley Road and Royal Victoria Place shopping centre. In an odd way, the words of St John Colbran in his guide book of 1884 strike a curiously contemporary note, and perhaps serve to show us the perspective that we should apply to life in modern Tunbridge Wells: 'There is probably no town in the kingdom that has altered more in appearance during the last quarter of a century than Tunbridge Wells. It still, to a great extent, retains its rustic character, but the leading thoroughfares no longer boast of the splendid trees which used to excite the admiration of all, and what was formerly a scene of great sylvan beauty is now a busy commercial centre.' And perhaps, in this year of the opening of the new link between England and France, we should bear in mind another of Colbran's comments, which forces us to consider afresh the delights of the town in general and Decimus Burton's Calverley Hotel in particular: "If the Channel Tunnel, when completed, should fall into the hands of a French Invader, the Calverley Hotel would naturally be the headquarters of the Gallic Viceroy of perfidious Albion.'

Even allowing for different circumstances a hundred years later on, it does not seem too far-fetched that visitors to the town might feel that Royal Tunbridge Wells is still a suitable place to spend a day, a week, a month, a year or even a lifetime.

The leafy promenade of Calverley Road pedestrian precinct.   (Charlie Bell 1994)

A SHORT BIBLIOGRAPHY

A formidable mass of literature, from treatise to brochure, from newspaper advertisement to academic thesis, faces the student of Tunbridge Wells history. The excellent local Reference Library, recently reinforced by the Wigham-Richardson collection, alone carries some 300 or more books and booklets, some not published, which widely, as well as closely cover the subject: guides, directories, local church histories, natural and historical background and literary associations . . . The town museum also has a collection of MSS, bills and posters, school registers, pictures, etc. Much of the history of the town is available here. *A Local History Catalogue*, was published by the Reference Library in 1966: I have used this as a pretext to reduce the bibliography given here to reasonable proportions. I have also omitted most (though not all) works to which I have already made specific reference in the text or by footnote. The newspapers and other journals which I have consulted, cited, or quoted (chiefly the *Tunbridge Wells Visitor, Gazette, Kent and Sussex Courier, Archaeologia Cantiana, Sussex Archaeological Collections, Country Life*), and the documentary sources (Kent Archives Office, *Calendar of State Papers*. Historical Manuscripts Commission and Census reports are also indicated in the text or in footnotes, as are the records of King Charles church, and certain MSS. The minutes and other records of the Town Commissioners and the Corporation should also be mentioned.

I should here, too, record my debt to, and recommendations of such invaluable background material as GM Trevelyan's *History of England, British History in the Nineteenth Century*, and *English Social History*; Elie Halévy's *History of the English People*; the surveys of *Early Victorian England* edited by GM Young and his monograph on *Victorian England*; Geoffrey Best's *Mid-Victorian Britain*; and, among guides to a field of historical study new to me, the BBC broadcast series and book, *This was their World*, ed. A Rogers 1971, WG Hoskins' *Fieldwork in Local History*, and *The Study of Urban History*, ed. HJ Dyos, 1966.

P Amsinck, *Tunbridge Wells and its Neighbourhood*. 1810.
L & B Bailey, *History of the Nonconformist Churches of Tunbridge Wells*; MSS available at Reference Library. 1970.
Margaret Barton, *Tunbridge Wells*. Faber 1937.
Roger Beard, *From Royal Spa to Commuter Town. Financial Times* 21 Aug 1973.
Charlie Bell, *Speldhurst Sketches – The Heart of the Village*. Dragonfly and Fern Press 1989.
Don Foreman, *Royal Visitors to Tunbridge Wells*. Parapress 1993.

Biographical
   F Boase, *Modern English Biography*. F Cass 1965.
   Arthur Bryant, *Charles II*. Longmans 1932.
   J Busse, *Mrs Montagu, Queen of the Blues*. 1928.
   W Connelly, *Beau Nash*. Werner Laurie 1955.
   Dictionary of National Biography.
   JN Figgis, *The Countess of Huntingdon and her Connexion*. 1941.
   Oliver Goldsmith, *Life of Richard Nash, Esq.* 1762.
   VHH Green, *John Wesley*. Black 1964.
   J Parkes, *The Story of Three David Salomons at Broomhill*. c1930.
   H Townsend, *Edward Hoare*. 1894.
   J Walters, *Splendour and Scandal: the Reign of Beau Nash*. Jarrolds 1968.
T Benge Burr, *The History of Tunbridge Wells*, 1766.
CW Chalklin, *Seventeenth Century Kent*. Longmans 1965; *A Kentish Wealden Parish (Tonbridge)* 1550-1750; Oxford thesis, unpublished: available Tonbridge Reference Library.
R Church, *Kent*. Robert Hale 1948.
G Christian, *Ashdown Forest*. 1967.
Civic Society and Tunbridge Wells Corporation, *Royal Tunbridge Wells Diamond Jubilee* 1969.
HC Darby and EMJ Campbell, *Domesday Geography of SE England*. CU Press 1969.
HS Eeles, *Frant, a Parish History. Courier* 1947.
FW Elers, *Tunbridge Wells General Hospital, 1828ff.* 1910.
AM Everitt, *The Community of Kent and the Great Rebellion*. Leicester University Press 1966.

Geology
   RW Gallois & FH Edmunds, *The Wealden District*. HMSO 1965.
   LD Stamp, *Britain's Structure and Scenery*. Collins, 1940 edn.
   SW Wooldridge & F Goldring, *The Weald*. 1953.
JCM Given, ed, *Royal Tunbridge Wells Past and Present* (with articles on geology, pre-history, flora and fauna, local affairs etc). 1946.

E Hasted, *History of the County of Kent* (Vols 3, 5). 1797 edn.
J Hone, *Tunbridge Wells* (broadcast). Listener, BBC, 23 December 1971.
D Jerrold, *Highways and Byways in Kent*. Macmillan 1908.
FW Jessup, *Kent History Illustrated*. Kent Education Committee 1966.
E Yoxall Jones, *A Prospect of Tunbridge Wells* (pictorial). 1964.
Kent and Sussex Courier, Centenary Edition. 1972; *Souvenir Supplement*, Royal Tunbridge Wells Diamond Jubilee. 1969.
WR Knipe, ed, *Tunbridge Wells and Neighbourhood* (chronicle, papers on geology, natural history, etc) 1916.
EV Lucas, *Highways and Byways in Sussex*. Macmillan 1904.
DD MacKinnon, *History of Speldhurst*; revised D James 1930.
L Melville, *Society at Tunbridge Wells in the Eighteenth Century and After*. Eveleigh Nash 1912.
L Pearce, *Historical Associations of Royal Tunbridge Wells, 1606-1909*. Courier 1912; *Historical Association of the Free Churches of Tunbridge Wells, 1642-1904*. Courier 1904.
EH & ER Pinto, *Tunbridge and Scottish Souvenir Ware*. Bell 1970.

Railways
RH Clark, *The Southern Railway Chronicle and Record*. Oakwood 1964.
JR Kellett, *The Impact of Railways on Victorian Cities*. Routledge & K Paul 1969.
EFD Marshall, *A History of the Southern Railway*; revised RW Kidner. 1938.
M Robbins, *Points and Signals*. Allen and Unwin 1967.
HP White, *A Regional History of the Railways of Great Britain* (Vol 2). Phoenix 1961.

Spas
D Gadd, *Georgian Summer: Bath in the Eighteenth Century*. Adams and Dart 1971.
G Hart, *Cheltenham*. Leicester University Press 1965.
ES Turner, *Taking the Cure*. M Joseph 1967.
E Straker, *Wealden Iron*. Bell 1931.
J Sprange, *The Tunbridge Wells Guide* (including anecdotes) 1780ff.
CH Strange, *The Stranges of Tunbridge Wells*. c1948; *Mount Pleasant Congregational Church 1830-1930; Nonconformity in Tunbridge Wells*. 1948; *The Jubilee of Tunbridge Wells as an Incorporated Borough*. 1939; (ed), *The Future Development of Tunbridge Wells*. 1936.
Tonbridge Historical Sketches; Tonbridge School Series. (Unpublished; available at Tonbridge Library) 1957, 1968 etc.
Victoria County History, Kent, Sussex.
B. Wadmore, *Some Details in the History of the Parish of Tonbridge*. 1906.

Literary, Travel
Mary Berry, *Extracts from Journals and Correspondence of*, 1783-1852; ed Lady T Lewis 1865.
Daniel Defoe, *A Tour through the Whole Island of Great Britain*. 1724.
John Evelyn, Diary and Correspondence of; ed W Bray 1850.
Celia Fiennes, The Journeys of; ed C Morris. Cresset 1947.
Anthony Hamilton, *Memoirs of the Court of Charles II*, by Comte de Grammont. 1741; ed Sir Walter Scott 1811; rev 1930.
JH Jesse, *George Selwyn and his Contemporaries*. 1843.
JJ Jusserand, *A French Ambassador at the Court of Charles II*. 1892.
Narcissus Luttrell, *Travels 1677-80 (No 13)*. 1830.
J Macky, *A Journey through England in Familiar Letters*. 1714.
Mrs Montagu, Letters; ed EJ Climenson, R Blunt 1906, 1923.
Samuel Pepys, Diary. Everyman edn 1906ff. -
Betsy Sheridan, Journal; ed W LeFanu 1960.
Ned Ward, *The London Spy*. 1718.

Architectural
JM Baines, *Burtons's St Leonards, Hastings*. 1956.
J Britton, *Descriptive Sketches of Tunbridge Wells and the Calverley Estate*. 1832.
PA Clarke, *James and Decimus Burton*. RIBA Thesis, unpublished. 1949.
HM Colvin, *Biographical Dictionary of English Architects*. Murray 1954.
W. Craggs, *The Calverley Estate; sketchbook and maps*. TW Museum. 1829.
C Hussey, *Tunbridge Wells*, Country Life 21, 28 Nov, 12 Dec 1968; *Calverley Park, Tunbridge Wells*, Country Life, 18 May 1969; *The Picturesque*. F Cass 1967 edn.
RP Jones, *Life and Works of Decimus Burton*. Architectural Review XVII. 1905.
J Newman, *West Kent and the Weald; Buildings of England*, ed Pevsner. Penguin 1969.
DW Pilcher, *Early 19th Century Architecture in Tunbridge Wells*. AA Journal Sept 1934.

APPENDIX I

A short list of Dates

1606	(1616?) Lord North discovers the chalybeate springs.
1630	Queen Henrietta Maria visits.
1662	King Charles II, Queen Katharine, and the Court on first visit.
1678-99	King Charles Chapel built, Upper Walk rebuilt with colonnade, and paved with pantiles.
1720	Mount Sion Nonconformist Chapel opened.
1735-61	Richard (Beau) Nash of Bath, Master of Ceremonies.
1739	Rusthall Manor Act safeguards Walks and access to springs and Common.
1762	Sir George Kelley becomes first of the resident gentry.
1766	Thomas Benge Burr's *History* published.
1769	Emmanuel Church, Countess of Huntingdon's Connexion, opened.
1801	Population c1,000.
1802-5	Sarah Baker builds theatre and Mrs Shorey the Bath House on Parade (Pantiles). Building begins in Northern area.
1822	Princess Victoria with Duchess of Kent on first visit.
1828-c1840	John Ward and Decimus Burton build New Town and Calverley Park.
1833	Holy Trinity (completed 1829) becomes first parish church of town.
1835	Tunbridge Wells Improvement Act sets up Town Commissioners.
1841-75	William Willicome active as builder.
1845	South Eastern Railway opens station.
1851	Census: population 10,587.
1853-94	Edward Hoare, Vicar of Holy Trinity.
1866	London, Brighton and South Coast Railway opens station.
1889	Charter of Incorporation.
1890	Improvement Act regulates Grove, Common, etc.
1894-5	Mayoralty of Sir David Salomons, Bt. He stages first motor show.
1901	Census: population 33,373.
1902	Opera House opened.
1909	The town becomes Royal Tunbridge Wells.
1934	Kent Review Order: large extension of boundaries. New hospital (Kent and Sussex) opened.
1939	Civic Centre (first part) opened.
1971	Census: population 44,506.
1974	Under local government reorganisation, the newly-created Tunbridge Wells Borough Council became responsible for the town of Royal Tunbridge Wells and surrounding rural areas.
1987	Great hurricane.
1991	Census: population 44,029.
1992	Royal Victoria Place opens.

APPENDIX II

Analysis of Chalybeate Spring Water.
This shows little change from the earliest analysis.

	Parts per million
Ferrous carbonate $FeCo_3$	25.3
Manganous carbonate, $MnCo_3$	4.6
Calcium sulphate, $CaSo_4$	60.9
Magnesium sulphate, $MgSo_4$	13.4
Magnesium chloride, $MgCl_2$	7.8
Sodium chloride, NaCl	57.2
Potassium chloride, KCl	7.3

APPENDIX III

RULES AND REGULATIONS

Humbly recommended by the Master of the Ceremonies to the Company resorting to Tunbridge Wells:

(From John Sprange's Guide, 1786)

I. That there be Two public Balls every Week, on Tuesdays and Fridays. Ladies to pay 2s, Gentlemen 3s6d.

II. To begin with Minuets, and then Country Dances – All restrictions in point of dress to be abolished, except in regard to those Ladies who intend to dance Minuets, who are requested to be properly dressed for that purpose.

III. One Cotillion only, immediately after tea will be danced, and to prevent the time lost in the choice of a particular Cotillion, and in practising it, the Master of the Ceremonies will undertake himself to name it, and its figures shall be previously put up in the Great Rooms, that they may be acquainted with it.

IV. As the custom of dancing, two following dances *only*, with the same Lady, at present prevails pretty generally, the Master of the Ceremonies thinks it proper to establish it as a Rule here.

V. The Master of the Ceremonies thinks it almost needless to observe, that it is deemed a point of good breeding, for those Ladies who have gone down with the dance to continue in their places, till the rest have done the same.

VI. The Master of the Ceremonies desires the company to come early, that the Balls may begin at the usual hour of seven.

VII. The Master of the Ceremonies desires to have the honour of presenting himself to the company on their arrival, that he may not be wanting in the necessary attentions to them.

VIII. The Chapel, being originally built by subscription, is not endowed with any provision for an established Minister. As he depends therefore for his support on the voluntary Contributions of the Company that frequents the place: it is hoped that he may rely with confidence for the reward of his labours, on the benevolence of those who reap the benefits of them.

IX. It is humbly requested of all persons who frequent the Rooms to subscribe, to enable the renters of them to defray the many necessary and heavy expenses attending them.

X. Besides the Two Rooms, the other general places of Subscription are the Circulating Library, the Ladies' Coffee Room, the Gentlemen's Coffee Room, and the Post Office.

XI. The Water-dippers at the Spring, who are appointed by the Lord of the Manor, have no allowance, but depend upon what is given them by those who drink the Waters.

XII. The Master of the Ceremonies hopes it will not be thought improper for him to recommend to families on leaving the place (having been any time here) to consider the Waiters of each of the Rooms. He will not presume to dictate to public generosity: Those only therefore who wish to be directed in this will receive the necessary information, on application to him.

XIII. It has been an old-established custom for every Lady and Gentleman to drop a shilling into the Sweeper's Box, and as the poor man and his family, constantly attend the Walks, and the Rooms morning and evening, and have no other means of subsisting; it is hoped that none will refuse to comply with so small and equitable a bounty.

The following are the PRICES of CARDS.

COMMERCE with one Pack		0. 8. 6	Morning, 7s
LOO, one Pack 6s two		0. 8. 6	
WHIST, two Packs		0. 8. 6	Morning, 7s
PIQUET, or ALL FOURS	First Pack	0. 5. 0	Each Pack after 3s
QUADRILLE		0. 8. 6	Morning, 7s
QUINZE, ad Libitum from		0. 8. 6	
LOTTERY, one Pack 10s two		0.12. 0	

RICHARD TYSON,
Master of the Ceremonies

INDEX
(includes illustrations)

Abbott, Dr G, 144, 185

Abergavenny (f Bergavenny) Lords, Earls, Marquess of, 31, 33, 55, 57, 104, 118, 125, 126, 138, 167, 173

Adam's Well, Rusthall, 14, 54, 84

A Day at the Wells Heritage Centre, 200, 201

Adelaide, Queen, 169

Adie, Charles, property developer, 140, 141, 160

Adult Education Centre, 208

Aeroplane, first, 189

Agricultural interest, shows, and ground, 184

Akers, Aretas, 125, 127, 129

Albert, Prince Consort, 169

Allfree, TR, Romanoff House school, 123

Amelia, Princess, 65

Amsinck, Paul, M/C, *Tunbridge Wells & Neighbourhood*, 84

Anglicans, 122

Anne, Princess and Queen, 37, 49, 51, 60, 67

Assembly rooms, 103, 121, 142, 200

Baden-Powell, Lord, 158, 190

Baker, Sarah, and theatre, 92, 93, 108, 121

Baker, Thomas, *Tunbridge Wells, or the Yeoman of Kent*, 38, 41, 62

Banks, 124, 125, 141

Baptists, Anabaptists, 50, 100, 122

Barfoot, P.C., notebook, 159

Barrow, TT, map, 55, 80

Barton, Margaret, *Tunbridge Wells*, 88

Baston Lodge, Cottage, 116

Bath, Earl of, Wm Pulteney, 85

Bath, houses (T.W.), 108, 109, 142, 143

Baths, cold, 54, 108

Baths, state of, 66

Baths, swimming, 202

Bayes, Thomas, 100

Bayham Abbey and estate, 22, 24, 45

Beale, Cllr, & Sons, property developers, 188

Bede, 21

Bedford Terrace, 109

Beeching, bankers, 124, 141

Benson, Rev Martin, At KCM chapel, 103, 122

Benson, Sir Frank, 170

Berry, Mary, 107

Bishop's Down, 32, 36

Bishop's Down, Grove, 97, 127, 148

Bishop's Down, Park, 138

Bishop's Down, Spa, 146–48

Blake, M/C, 83

Bolton, Duke & Duchess of (Lavinia Fenton, 'Polly Peachum'), 74, 75, 79

Bombs, 192

Bonsor, Sir Cosmo, Chairman, SER, 182

Boone, Mrs, 101, 102

Booth, Charles, 184

Booth, General Wm, 155

Borough of T.W., incorporation campaign, 167, 168, 169

Bowles Rocks, 16, 17

Bowling greens, 17, 44, 46, 139

Bowra, John, survey-map, 55, 56–57, 59, 60–61

Boyle, Lord, letter, 65, 69

Boyne, Viscount, 107

Boyne, House, 127

Bramah, Joseph, and Sons, 113, 137

Bredbury, 148, 154

Brighton, 96

Brighton, Lake, 164

Broadwater Down, 125, 138, 202

Broomhill, 129, 138, 174, 175, 206

Browell, WF, 157

Browne, Dr, *Account of the Wonderful Cures* etc, 54

Buck, Sir Wm, Bt, rapid courtship & marriage of, 40, 48

Buckingham, George Villiers, Duke of, 41

Buckingham, John, styled Earl of, 41

Burges, Sir James Bland, 97

Burney, Fanny, Mme d'Arblay, *Letters*, 81, 88, 96

Burns, Cecil, architect, 188, 193, 204

Burr, Thomas Benge, historian of T.W., 27, 81, 99

Burrow, family, 80

Burrswood, 129

Burton, Decimus, 16, 112, 123, 137, 142, 203, 211
Burton, James, 112
Byng, Hon JMO, 134
Byrom, John, 74
Calverley, estate, area and windmill, 112, 118, 126, 195
Calverley, Grounds and Pavilion, 171, 192, 193, 201
Calverley, Hotel, 113, 114, 115, 119, 169
Calverley, Parade, 114, 137, 140
Calverley, Park, 113, 114, 115, 118, 126, 203
Calverley, Park Crescent (f Promenade), 113, 115, 148, 193, 203
Calverley, Park Gardens, 137
Calverley, Road, 113, 114, 141, 142, 213
Camden, Marquess and family, 118, 137
Camden Hotel, 119
Camden Park, 118, 137, 138
Camden Road and area, 109, 113, 139, 195
Cameron, Julia, photographer, 140
Campbell, Dr, 105
Caroline of Brunswick, Queen, 120
Carter, Elizabeth, 85
Castle Tavern, Hotel, 109, 119
Castlemaine, Lady, 41
Catholics, Roman, 122
Causey, Bell, 67, 68
Chamberlain, Sir John, on T.W., 31
Channel Tunnel, 212, 213
Chancellor House, 97
Charles II, King, 34, 36, 59
Chesterfield, Lord, 88
Christian, Ewan (architect), 139, 154
Chudleigh, Elizabeth, Duchess of Kingston, 89
Churches
   St Augustine, 122, 158, 204
   St Barnabas, 139, 155, 156, 158
   Calverley Road Baptist Tabernacle, 151
   Christ Church, 122, 154, 205
   Christian Science, 204, 205
   Church of Christ, 155
   Emmanuel, 122, 123, 151, 152, 158, 204
   St James, 156, 157
   St John's, 139, 152, 158
   St John's Free Church, later St Andrew, 185
   St Luke, 185
   St Mark, 138
   St Matthew, High Brooms, 185
   Mount Pleasant, 151
   Rehoboth Strict Baptist, 151
   St Peter, 139, 154
   Salem Baptist Church, 154
   Vale Road Wesleyan, 151
   See also Holy Trinity, King Charles the Martyr
Cibber, Colley, 89
Cinemas, 206
Civic Association Report 1945, 193, 198–9
Civic Centre, 114, 201
Civic Society and Association, 193, 195, 201, 206
Civil War, 33
Clanricarde, Earls of, 34
Clifford, *Visitor*, 119
Coaches, 'flies', carriages, 82, 119, 142
Cobbett W, *Rural Rides*, 126
Coffee houses, 44
Coke, Lady Jane, letters, 84
Colbran, J, Guides library, 137, 163
Colbran *Gazette* – see Newspapers, 19
Cold Baths, T.W. and Rusthall, 54, 108
Collett, Caulet, Collette, M/C, 83, 104
Comminges, Duc de, 36
Commissioners, Town Improvement, or Local Board, 126, 165, 167
Common, the, 45, 57, 121, 173, 210
   Diversions on, 17, 91, 107, 121
   See also cricket
Congregationalists, Independents, 122, 155
Congreve, Wm, 41, 74
Conservation Area, 193–4
Corn Exchange, 108, 200
Cowan, CG, *Descriptive Guide to High Rocks*, 17
Cramp's Riding School, 170
Cricket, 91, 121, 149, 178
Crime, 160
Cripps, Charles, property developer, 112
Cripps, WC, Jnr, Town Clerk, 135, 169
Cromwell, Oliver, 33
Cronk, EE, architect, 139, 185

Cronk, HH, architect, cllr, 140
Crown Field, 109, 123, 139, 195
Culverden House, or Great Culverden, 101, 129, 134, 204
Culverden Row, 109
Cumberland, Ernest, Duke of, 104
Cumberland House, 139
Cumberland, Richard, dramatist, 85, 93, 97, 104, 106, 107
Cumberland Walk, 17, 109
Cutts, JE & JP, architects, 139, 157
Cycling, Milk Race, Tour de France, 212
Defoe, Daniel, 41
Delves family, 119, 127, 167
Derrick, Samuel, M/C, 73, 81, 83
Devil, 13
Diana, Princess of Wales, 197
Dippers at well, 28, 58
Dissenters, Chapel, 122
Dodd, C Tattershall (Sr & Jr), 170, 171
Dodd, Joseph J, 170
Dodd, F Lawson, 180
Domesday Book, on Weald, 21, 22
Donkeys, 119
Doogood, Henry, plasterer, 48
Dorrington, Theophilus, *Regulation of Play*, 75
Doughty, CM, traveller, author, 189
Dowton, Wm, player, theatre manager, 93, 121
Dunorlan, 202
EO, Even and Odd, game, 75
Earl's Court, 148, 165, 188, 202, 204
Eccentric characters, 102, 159
Eden House, 129, 169, 170
Edward, Prince of Wales, King Edward VII, 184
Edwards, Thomas, pastor, 154
Egmont, Lord, 97
Elizabeth I, Queen, 25
Elwig, H, architect, cllr, 182
Eridge, 25, 30, 105, 118, 138
Evans, John, *Visit to Tunbridge Wells*, etc, 126
Evelyn, John, 34
Feilding, Robert 'Beau', 41
Fiennes, Celia, 25, 43, 46
Fishmarket, 78, 200
Flowers in Bloom, 212
Font Hill Pavilion, 202

Forum, The, 202
Frant, 22, 25, 32, 118, 122
Frant Road, 138
Frederick, Prince of Wales, 65
Friends, Society of, Quakers, 185
Friendly Societies, Hall, etc, 162
Fry family, lodging housekeepers, 104
Fry, JH, property developer, 112
Garrick, David, 88
Gaming, gambling, 17, 63, 74, 75, 91
Gay, John, playwright, 75
Garden Street, 113
Geology, 15
George Prince of Wales, George II, 65
George III, 84, 96
George IV, 96
Gibraltar Cottage, 47, 80, 165, 166
Given, Dr JCM, 19, 201
Gloucester, Dukes of, 51
Gloucester Tavern, 46, 97, 144
Goldsmith, Oliver, *Life of Richard Nash*, 88
Goulden and Currey, 206
Gower, Sir Robert, MP, mayor, 202
Grammont, Comte de, *Memoirs*, ed Hamilton, 13, 36
Grand, Sarah, novelist & suffragist, 187
Great Hall, 140–141, 206
Grimaldi, 94
Groombridge, 21, 22
Grosvenor family, 109
Grosvenor House, Lodge, 170
Grosvenor Road and Upper, 123, 139, 208
Grove, the, Mount Sion, 54, 82, 98, 139, 173
Grove, the, Queen's, 51, 125, 127, 173
Grove Hill and Road, 118, 139, 187
Guy Fawkes night, 149
Hall, Miss E, diary, 144
Hamilton, Anthony, editor, memoirs of Count Grammont, 36
Hamilton, Elizabeth, 36
Handel, Frederick, 89
Hare, HT, architect, 187
Harrison's Rocks, 16, 17, 21
Hasted, *History of Kent*, 122
Hawkenbury, 154, 204
Haywards, 206
Henrietta Maria, Queen, 32
Heron, Sir Richard, Bt, 97, 104

Hervey family, Earls, Marquesses of Bristol and Herveytown (f Pound Field), 109
High Brooms, 16, 194
High Rocks, 17, 20, 34, 37, 85, 96, 107, 183
High Street (f 'Foot of Mount Sion', qv), 137, 139, 184, 188
Hoare, Canon EW, 151, 155, 156, 160, 178
Hoare, Wm, RA, 69
Hole-in-the-Wall, the, 59
Holland, Col TJ, CB, 175, 187
Holy Trinity, church and parish, 113, 116, 117, 122, 138, 151, 154
Hospitals, Dispensary, Infirmary, 109, 124, 144, 163, 178, 187
Hotels, Inns, 140, 144, 145, 148, 188, 189
  See also Calverley, Kentish, Spa, etc
Hume, David, 88
Humphreys, Mrs, first water-dipper, 28
Hungershall Park, 138
Huntingdon, Selina, Countess of, 100, 101
  See also Emmanuel church
Huntingdon, Wm, 'Sinner Saved', 102
Hurricane, 1987, 200, 210
Industries, manufacturers:
  Bricks, 160
  Luck, porcelain, 142
  Lyle, mineral water, 145, 198
  Motor cars, 189
  Rock Hawkins and Thorpe, 189, 208
  Romary, biscuits, 148, 198
  Smith, G, carriages, 204
  Stevensons, 189
  Tonbridges, 189
  Wealden iron working, 21, 23
Iron Age, 20
James II (f Duke of York), 16, 37
Janson, Sir Thomas, 45
Jay, Thomas, missioner, 159, 160
Jerningham, Lady, 98
Johnson, Dr James, 88
Johnson, Dr Samuel, 83, 88
Johnson, Bishop, and Miss/Mrs, 100
Jones-Gibb, T, 154, 158
Jordan of Jordan's Place cottage and Lane (later Church Road), 47, 49, 80, 126
Katharine of Braganza, Queen, 36
Kean, Charles and Edmund, 121

Kelley, Kelly, Sir George, 97, 104
Kelsey's Brewery, 152
Kendon, Frank, *The Small Years*, 189
Kent, Duchess of, mother of Queen Victoria, 116, 118
Kentish Royal Hotel, 109
King, Dr Wm, 92
King Charles-the-Martyr, chapel, later church, 44, 47, 48, 50, 75, 79, 99, 100, 118, 122, 153
Kip, Kyp, Johannes, engraving of T.W., 17, 46, 48, 52–53, 55
Lambarde, *Perambulation of Kent*, 25
Langridge, GT, property developer, 112
Lander, HC, architect and Fabian, 180
Land Registry, 204
Lansberry, Dr HCF, analysis of 1851 census, 139
Law and Order, 125
Leamington Spa, Royal, 96
Leeds, Duke of, 97, 100
Lew, the (St John's area), 125, 139
Libraries, 105, 119, 121, 201
Linden Park, 138
Liptraps Lane, farm, estate, 19, 188
Lodging houses, 148
Loggon, Loggan, Logan, 76, 86–87, 88, 89
Longfield Road, 198
Lorne, Princess Louise, Marchioness of, 162, 170
Lucas, EV, *Highways and Byways in Sussex*, 16, 172
Lushington House, 114
Lutwidge, JRF, mayor, 180
Lyle, Mineral Waters, 145
Macaulay, Lord, *History*, 40, 121
Macaulay at T.W., 170
Madan, Dr P, *Essay on Waters of Tunbridge*, 35, 100
Madden, H, M/C, 84
Madeira Park, 188
Mansfield, Earl of, 98
Marie Amelie, Queen of France, 169
Margary, ID, Wealden investigations, 20
'Marinus', *Particular Description of T.W.*, etc, 82, 83, 84
Markets, 40
Marlborough, Duke and Duchess of, 65
Marlborough House, 109
Mary of Modena, Queen, 37

Mary Princess of Orange, Queen, 37
Mayfield, St Dunstan at, 13, 21
Mechanics' Institution, 162, 163, 201
Melville, Lewis, *Society at Tunbridge Wells*, 74, 92
Merryweather, Capt, M/C, 84
Metellus, his *Dialogues*, etc, 74
Methodists, 99, 100, 121, 155
Military Camp, 106
Molyneux, Hon FG, 135, 165, 169, 173, 188
Money, JH, excavations by, 20
Monsey, Dr M, 85
Monson Road and Colonnade, 10, 141
Montagu, Mrs Elizabeth, 70, 84, 88, 92
Montagu, Lady Mary Wortley, 85
Motors & traffic, 176, 188, 189, 198
Motors, bus services, 189, 207
Mount Edgecumbe, 171
Mount Ephraim, 34, 46, 97, 104, 148, 188
Mount Ephraim House, 36, 59, 100, 101
Mount Ephraim Hotel (Royal Wells), 119
Mount Pleasant, 112, 122, 131, 189
Mount Pleasant House, later Calverley Hotel, 97, 113, 114
Mount Sion, 34, 54, 93, 97, 98, 104, 109, 153
Mount Sion, Chapel, 101, 122
Mountain, James, 165
Music(k) Gallery, 80, 81, 94, 144
Muskerry, Lord, 40
Muskerry, Lady, later Lady Purbeck, 41
Nash, John, postmaster, etc, 121
Nash, Richard, Beau, 66, 71, 73, 76, 104
Neale, Thomas, developer of Walks, 45
Nevill family (see also Abergavenny), 23
Nevill Ground, 178
Nevill Park, 118, 126, 138
North, Dudley, Lord, 17, 27, 28, 29
North Farm Industrial Estate, 198
North, Lord, Prime Minister, 98
Notables and Celebreties, 203
Okill, Wm, 91, 103
Opera House, 178, 179, 180, 187
Pannuwell, Capt, 104
Pantiles, the, see also Parade, Walks, 17, 51, 64, 90, 144, 193, 199, 200, 210
Parade, the, 104, 122, 144
  See also, Pantiles, Walks

Patty Moon, 129
Pearson, CR and JN, 156, 157
Pelton, Guides, library, 144
Pembury, 166
Pembury Road, 137, 202
Penn's Rocks, 17
Penshurst, 22
Pepys, Samuel, 42
Peto, Sir Morton, 171
Picture House, Poundsbridge, 24
Pinchbeck, C, 55, 83
Pinto, EH & ER, *Tunbridge and Scottish Souvenir Woodwork*, 145
Pitt, Wm, Lord Chatham, 85, 92
Players, leading, at Theatre, Opera House, etc, 92
Pope, WL, 123, 127, 153, 158, 163, 164, 173
Pope, Dr, 88
Population and Censuses, 118, 136, 139, 188, 192
Porter, Sarah, 72–73
Post Offices, 105, 109, 144, 188
Poundsbridge, 24–25
Poverty, hardship, treatment of, 123, 124, 163, 165, 184, 195
Powder Mill Lane, 194
Presbyterians, 49, 99, 100
Priory, the, 113, 117
Pump Room, 143, 144, 148, 183, 199
Purbeck, family, 41, 45, 46, 48
Railways, 130–136, 181, 193, 206–7
Ramslye, 194
Rates and community charge, 167, 169, 181, 212
Rawlins, Thomas, *Tunbridge Wells, or a Day's Courtship*, 38
Richardson, Samuel, 88, 89
Roberts, GT, M/C, 84, 120
Robinson, H Peach, photographer, 140
Rochester, Wilmot, Earl of, 38
Roads, new, 198
Roads, state of, 26, 66, 81, 119, 207–8
Roads, turnpikes, 81, 95
Rodney, 2nd Lord, 105
Romans, in Weald, 21
Rotherfield, 21, 25
Rowzee, Dr Lodwick, *The Queen's Wells*, 32, 33, 35
Royal Chase, 19, 22

Royal Kentish Hotel, 119, 148
Royal Victoria and Sussex, 119
Royal Victoria Place, 196–7, 198
Ruskin, John, *The Two Paths*, 121, 170
Russell, Dr Richard, 95
Rusthall, 14, 16, 21, 22, 35, 40, 44, 120, 121, 124, 194
Rusthall, cold bath, 54
Rusthall Manor, lords and freeholders, 45, 97
Rusthall Manor Acts, 55, 59, 173
Rusthall St Paul's church, 151
Rusthall New Town, 188
St Dunstan, Archbishop of Canterbury, legend of, 13
Salomons, Sir David, Bt, 129, 130, 171
Salomons, Sir David Lionel, Bt, mayor, 138, 174, 176, 178, 189
Salvation Army, 155
Sandown Court and School, 202
Schools: 186, 208
    Art and Craft, 204
    Industrial, etc, 123, 163
    King Charles, 50, 103, 123, 158
    National, 158
    Private, independent, 158, 186, 187, 202, 208
    Ragged School, 162, 165
    Romanoff House Academy, 123
    Royal Victoria National, 118, 123, 127, 204
    Skinners' Company, & Tonbridge controversy, 158, 159, 186
    Modern changes, local authority control, etc, 208
Scoones, Wm, 127
Scott, AT, Archdeacon, 186
Scott, J Oldrid, architect, 178
Scribe, Elizabeth, *letter*, 69, 76
Secker, Archbishop, 100
Services, local authority:
    drainage and public health, 125, 126, 166, 185, 188, 192
    electricity, 175, 193
    gas, 181, 193
    housing, 185, 188, 194, 195
    library and museum, 201
    post and telegraph, 161
    telephone, controversy, 180–81, 204

water supply, 125, 126, 166, 174, 209–10
Seymour, Lady George, and donkey rides, 119
Sharp, Thomas, *Northumberland*, 20
Sherwood Park and Spa, 194, 202–3
Shopping, 142, 144, 150, 198, 204, 206
    Retail Park, Kingstanding, 198
Shorey, Elizabeth, lady of Rusthall Manor, 104, 108
Showfields Estate, 194
Siemens, Sir Wm, 171, 202–3
Sims, George R, on T.W., 142, 173
Sims, Thomas, photographer, 140
Smith, H & J, authors, 171
Somerhill, 25, 36
Societies, voluntary, charitable, cultural, tradesmen's, 139, 144, 150, 159, 163, 164, 171, 178, 181, 183, 188
Southborough, 40, 44
Southfrith, forest and manor, 22, 23, 25
Spa Valley Railway, 207
Speldhurst, 21, 22, 25, 32, 100, 118, 122, 158
Sports, 183
    See also cricket, bowling greens
Sports and 'Y' Centre, 202
Sprange, guides and handbills, 17, 99, 104, 105, 121
Springs, wells, 13, 28, 29, 34, 39, 102–103, 121, 125
Statutes, various, 123, 126, 134, 167, 168, 173, 186
Steele, Sir Richard in *Spectator, Guardian*, 63
Stokes, Dilnot, 167
Stone Age, 20
Stone, now Buss, Stone & Co, solicitors, 112, 125, 127
Stone-Wigg, J, first mayor, 157, 168, 169, 172, 173
Straker, E, Wealden investigations, 20
Strange, family, 91
Strange, CH, architect, artist, writer, cllr, 178, 188, 193
Suffragettes, 187
Sussex Tavern, Hotel, 54, 104, 125, 144, 148
Sussex Arms, 108
Swan Hotel, 119, 144, 145

Taxatio Ecclesiastica, 22
Taylor, Major Stanhope, 130
Technical Institute, 163, 187, 208
Telephone controversy, 180–81, 204
Textus Roffensis, and ancient local
    churches, 21
Thackeray, Wm, *Virginians*, 83, 88
    Tunbridge Toys, 121, 170
Thackeray on Walks, 144, 170
Theatre. See also Baker, Opera House,
    Players, 92, 121, 170, 178, 204–6
Thomson, Rev Sir Henry, Br, 167
Thomson, J Radford, 154
Tillotson, Archbishop, 49
Toad Rock, Rusthall, 16
Tonbridge*, 21, 22, 31, 32, 118, 122,
    124, 208
Tonbridge School, 171
Torrington Project, 198
Touting, 73, 82, 94
Town Hall (f Calverley market hall),
    204
Town Planning, 193
Town Plans, 195
Trackways, ancient, 20
Trinity Theatre and Arts Centre, 204–5
Tunbrigialia, etc, see Water Poets, 73,
    74
Tunbridge Ware, and makers, 46, 47, 80,
    96, 109, 127, 144, 145, 198
Tunbridge Wells and Eridge Railway
    Preservation Society, 207
Turner, Wm, *Nature and Property of Baths
    of England*, 31
Tutty, James, Tutty's Village, 154
Tyson, Richard, M/C, his Rules, 84, 91,
    217
Vauxhall, Southborough, 24
Victoria, Princess and Queen, 114, 116,
    119, 121, 127, 128, 169, 177
Victoria Road, 197
Walks; see also Pantiles, Parade, springs,
    13, 15, 33, 40, 45, 46, 55, 58, 59, 70,
    79, 93, 96, 97, 98, 104, 105, 108, 119,
    120, 126, 142, 144, 200, 210
Walks, Estate, 55, 57

Wallace, Dr, 105
Walmer House, 129
Walpole, Sir Robert, 70, 89
Ward, John, Calverley developer, 112,
    125, 136
Wars: World, I & II, 191–92
Water, Poets, 73
Water, supply, see Services
Watts, Isaac, 99
Waymarks, Drapers, 141, 206
Weald, the, 15, 18, 20, 21, 22, 23, 26
Webber, Dr, and public health riots, 166
Weekes, Dept Store, 140, 206
Weller family, 29, 33, 46, 144
Wellington, Duke and Duchess of, 107
Wellington, Hotel, 148
Wellington, Rocks, 17, 121
Wesley, John, 99, 100, 101
West Kent College, 208
West Station development, 198, 204
Wetherell, John, plasterer, 49
Wheatears, 40
Whiston, Wm, 92, 102
Whitefield, G, 100
Wilde, Oscar, *Importance of Being Earnest*,
    13
Wilds, Amon, architects, 109
Willicombe, Wm, builder and developer,
    137, 142
Wilmott, BS, 167
Windmill Field, 109, 112, 125, 139
Winter garden, projects, 177, 178, 200
Woodbury Park, 139
Workhouse, the, 124, 162, 163, 165
Wybarne, J, damage to wells, 35, 40
York, Dukes and Duchesses of, 93
York and Gloucester, Duke of, 91
Yorke, Martin, 'Major York', 97, 104
Young, Edward, 85
Youth, lack of provision for, 202
YMCA, 197

*Tunbridge was the common form until
the 19c, when Tonbridge became general.
As a rule, I have kept Tunbridge to mean
specifically Tunbridge Wells.